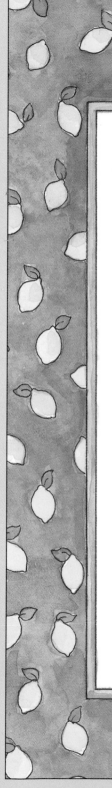

Delicious Fruit Desserts

*More Than 150 Classic and Unique Desserts
for 12 Favorite Fruits*

Dot Vartan

Edited by Elizabeth A. Matlin
Design by Jan Kielp
Cover illustrations by Laura D'Argo

Dorothy Jean's Home Cooking Collection

DJP Dorothy Jean Publishing, Inc.
Evanston, IL

Acknowledgments

It has been almost 10 years since I published the first edition of my first cookbook. The first book is always the easiest because you don't really know what you don't know about the publishing business. Three books later, I am wiser in so many ways. I would not have been able to write any of my books without the love and support of my husband, Gentre. Thanks also to my mother, who assisted me in the kitchen, and to all of my friends and family who provided feedback on the recipes. Special thanks to my editor, Elizabeth Matlin, who was a tremendous help to me in so many ways. And thanks to my designer, Jan Kielp, who created a wonderful page design.

Edited by Elizabeth A. Matlin
Designed by Jan Kielp, jmkdesign, ltd.
Cover illustrations by Laura D'Argo
Proofread by Melissa Stehlik

Dorothy Jean Publishing, Inc.
62 Williamsburg Road
Evanston, IL 60203
SAN #256-0151

ISBN 1-884627-04-8
Library of Congress Catalog Control Number: 2004105101

Library of Congress Cataloging-in-Publication Data
Available from the Library of Congress

Printed in the U.S.A.
10 9 8 7 6 5 4 3 2 1

Other books by Dot Vartan:
Mad About Muffins
Is It Soup Yet?

A Harvest of Delicious Fruit Desserts

Biting into a luscious strawberry, a juicy peach, or a crisp apple makes your taste buds sing and evokes memories of favorite fruit desserts. Maybe it's Grandma's strawberry shortcake, Aunt Betty's peach cobbler, or Mom's apple pie. These fruit reminiscences bring a feeling of comfort and well-being. Even the most sophisticated restaurants will feature fruit crisps and tarts on their menus. Why? There's something heartwarming about fresh apples nestled in flaky pastry and a slice of silky banana cream pie, perhaps because they are familiar, simple, and unpretentious.

Several generations ago, fresh fruit was scarce and expensive in the winter. Now spring and summer fruits, such as strawberries and peaches, are no longer a luxury and available almost year-round. I remember when the long Midwestern winters of my youth seemed even longer due to the lack of fresh fruit. One year, I was thrilled to receive a fruit-of-the-month club gift. First, I had never seen such gorgeous fruit. Second, it amazingly came in the winter! Still, most fruit is best when savored in-season. Peaches may now be a "winter" fruit, but that doesn't mean out-of-season imports are as delectable as freshly picked summer peaches from Georgia, California, or Michigan.

As I gathered information about the various fruits highlighted in this book, I learned of the incredible bounty of fruit grown in the United States. We truly are blessed with beautiful fruited plains! Being from the Midwest, I have always appreciated the blueberries, cherries, peaches, cranberries, and apples grown here. But visiting states where fruit is grown year-round really opened my eyes. I had never seen such large cherries, apricots, and nectarines until I visited California, where the climate is perfectly suited for producing a wide selection of luscious fruits. And now when I enjoy a glass of fresh orange juice, I thank Florida for its abundance of orange groves.

Take notice of the fruit grown in your home state. Visit farmers' markets and fruit stands and buy sun-warmed fruit fresh from the field. Or take family outings to pick apples, peaches, strawberries, or blueberries. Not only will your children learn first-hand where fruit really comes from, but everyone will discover the pleasure of eating

> *Live each season as it passes; breathe the air, drink the drink, taste the fruit, and resign yourself to the influences of each.*
>
> *– Henry David Thoreau*

impeccably fresh fruit. Be sure to try new varieties of fruit, too, that aren't sold in super-markets. There's so much more to apples than Red Delicious and Jonathans.

Naturally sweet and nutritious, fresh fruit requires little or no added sugar yet satisfies everyone's sweet tooth. Capitalize on its health benefits by eating fresh fruit out of hand. Even after a wonderful meal, the question "what's for dessert?" always arises. With the addition of some simple ingredients, fruit can be quickly made into an easy, weeknight dessert or transformed into elaborate creations for special occasions.

Delicious Fruit Desserts is a collection of more than 150 of the best classic—and unique—fruit dessert recipes. The book focuses on twelve of the most popular fruits with a chapter devoted to each one. This should make it easier for you to find recipes that highlight your favorite fruit and to try new ones. From quick and easy to more involved, my recipes are designed to appeal to a variety of personal tastes and all levels of baking experience. Be sure to read the beginning of each chapter to learn about selecting, storing, and preparing fruit, along with a bit of interesting history.

I truly enjoyed learning more about baking with fruit as I developed these recipes. My hope is that you will come home from local markets laden with fruit and also enjoy preparing these recipes for your family and friends!

Have fun baking!

Dot Vartan

Helpful Recipe Tips

- Use "large" eggs for these recipes.
- Use the exact baking dish or pan specified in the recipe. A baking dish refers to glass and a baking pan refers to metal. Since glass conducts and retains heat better than metal, reduce the oven temperature by 25°F when substituting a glass baking dish for a metal baking pan.
- Have more fresh fruit on hand than the recipe calls for in case some of the fruit is overripe or spoiled.
- Store fruit pies at room temperature, covering only the exposed filling so that the crust does not become soggy.
- Use only fresh fruit when specified as the quality of the dessert will be affected if frozen or canned fruit is substituted.
- Always buy the highest quality frozen fruit available for best results.
- When purchasing canned fruits, do not use more than one brand in the same recipe as the size of the fruit can vary from brand to brand.

Table of Contents

Apple

Apricot

Banana

Table of Contents

Blueberry

Cherry

Cranberry

Table of Contents

Lemon

Orange

Peach

Table of Contents

Pear

Pineapple

Strawberry

Apple

Peak Season: U.S. apple crops are harvested from late summer to late fall, depending on the variety. Apples grown in Australia, New Zealand, and South Africa arrive in U.S. markets in spring and early summer when these countries are harvesting their autumn crops and our fresh domestic supplies have been depleted.

Selection: There are three types of apples: eating, cooking, and all-purpose. When buying apples, first decide how they are to be used and select suitable varieties.

- Eating apples are used raw in salads or eaten fresh out of hand.
- Cooking apples are made into applesauce, pies and other fruit desserts.
- All-purpose apples can be used for both eating and cooking.

While most apples fall into the all-purpose category, many varieties are best suited for specific purposes. The recipes in this chapter use Granny Smith or Golden Delicious apples, but feel free to experiment with your favorite all-purpose varieties.

All varieties of apples should be firm with smooth, shiny, well-colored skins that are free of bruises. Brown streaks on the skins (called scald) do not affect quality.

Storage: Since apples continue to ripen at room temperature, they should be refrigerated to maintain freshness. Store them in a ventilated plastic bag in the refrigerator crisper drawer away from foods with strong odors. When eating raw apples, their flavor is best at room temperature.

Preparation: Except when baking whole apples, it's best to remove the skins before baking and cooking. When peeling apples, use a paring knife or vegetable peeler. To remove the cores, quarter the apples lengthwise and use a paring knife to cut out the cores and seeds. Kitchen tools, such as an apple corer or an apple slicer/corer, also make the job easier. Prevent cut apples from turning brown by tossing them with a small amount of lemon juice. One pound apples (2 large, 3 medium, or 4 small) yields 2 to 2 1/2 cups chopped or sliced.

(continued)

A Little History: Apples have been grown for over three thousand years. Varieties now number in the thousands, making this the most important fruit in the temperate world. Lady apples are historically the oldest variety—cultivated by the Etruscans, adored by the Romans, prized by French royalty, and esteemed by early American colonists who brought plantings over from Europe. Newtown Pippin, one of the best-tasting early American varieties, was once considered the best in the world. Thomas Jefferson grew pippins and Benjamin Franklin introduced them to the English royal court. Thanks to John Chapman, better known as Johnny Appleseed, about ten thousand square miles of apple orchards were planted in the U.S. in the nineteenth century, guaranteeing future generations the pleasures of this amazing fruit.

Apple Varieties

Here's a starter list of some popular apple varieties with their characteristics and uses. In the fall, take a trip to the countryside and look for heirloom and other unique varieties at roadside farm stands and orchards. Experiment with different apples and discover new favorites, such as Ginger Gold, Honeycrisp, Macoun, Baldwin, Melrose, Greenings, and Spitzenburg.

Braeburn: A newer all-purpose variety with red to red-gold skin, the Braeburn has a sweet-tart flavor and is very juicy and crisp. Use for eating, salads, applesauce, pies, and baking whole.

Cortland: These crisp, tart, red-skinned apples keep their shape during baking, making them a great choice for a classic high-crusted pie. Slow to brown once cut, all-purpose Cortlands are a superb choice for salads and are also used for eating and applesauce.

Fuji: A newer all-purpose variety with reddish-pink skin, the Fuji has an unusual combination of low-acid sweetness with crisp, juicy flesh. Excellent for eating and salads, it's also a good choice for applesauce and pies.

Gala: With distinctive golden, red-streaked skins, Galas have a mild sweet flavor and are juicy and crisp. Excellent for eating, salads and applesauce, they are also a good choice for pies.

Golden Delicious: These sweet, crisp, pale green to yellow apples hold their shape when baked, are slow to brown when cut and are an excellent all-purpose apple. Use for eating, salads, applesauce, pies, and baking.

Granny Smith: Crisp, juicy and very tart, green-skinned Granny Smiths are excellent all-purpose apples. Use for eating, applesauce, pies, and baking.

Jonagold: A cross between Jonathan and Golden Delicious, Jonagolds have red-streaked yellow skins, a sweet-tart flavor and are juicy and crisp. Use this excellent all-purpose apple for eating, applesauce, pies, and baking.

Jonathan: These crisp, red-skinned, all-purpose apples have a sweet-tart flavor and hold their shape when cooked. Use for eating, applesauce, and pies.

McIntosh: An all-purpose favorite, the red-skinned Mac is medium-crisp with a sweet-tart flavor. It's excellent for eating and applesauce.

Newtown Pippin: Also called pippins, these early American apples have pale green to yellow skin and crisp, slightly tart flesh that browns quickly after cutting. Excellent for pies and tarts, all-purpose pippins are also good for eating, applesauce, and baking whole.

Red Delicious: The most popular fresh-eating apples in the U.S., these red-skinned beauties have a sweet flavor and crisp texture. They are one of the few varieties that are not recommended for cooking or baking.

Rome Beauty: These large, intensely red apples have a mildly tart to sweet flavor and a dry, mealy texture. They are the top choice for whole baked apples since they hold their shape during cooking.

Winesap: This early American variety is juicy with a rusty-red skin. Winesaps keep their mildly tart, spicy flavor after cooking. Use these all-purpose apples for eating, applesauce, pies, and baking.

Baked Apples
Stuffed with Pecans & Raisins

Baked apples can satisfy a sweet tooth quickly and easily.
Feel free to vary the ingredients in the filling to suit your tastes.

Ingredients

- $1/2$ **cup (1 stick) butter, melted**
- $1/4$ **cup dark rum**
- $1/2$ **cup apple juice**
- $1/2$ **cup packed brown sugar**
- $1/4$ **cup ($1/2$ stick) butter, melted**
- 1 **teaspoon cinnamon**
- $1/2$ **cup pecans, finely chopped**
- $1/2$ **cup raisins**
- 4 **large Golden Delicious or Granny Smith apples**

Whipped cream, as a garnish

Preheat the oven to 350°F. Combine $1/2$ cup melted butter, rum, and apple juice in an 8x8x2-inch baking dish; set aside. Combine the brown sugar, $1/4$ cup melted butter, and cinnamon in a small bowl. Stir in the pecans and raisins; set aside.

Peel the skin off the top half of each apple. Scoop out the stems and cores with a melon baller, being careful not to cut through the bottoms. Cut a thin slice from the bottom of each apple to create a stable base. Place the apples upright in the prepared baking dish. Pack the cavities to the top with the pecan mixture. Spoon some of the liquid in the dish over the apples and filling.

Bake for about 45 minutes, until the apples are tender, basting often with the juices. Cover loosely with foil during baking if the filling browns too quickly. Serve warm garnished with whipped cream.

Makes 4 servings

An apple a day keeps the doctor away goes the saying.

Indeed, the apple is very high in fiber, a valuable source of vitamin C and also contains some vitamin A, B vitamins, potassium, iron, and phosphorus. A medium apple is only 80 calories.

Apple Spice Cookies

Enjoy these moist cookies with a cup of tea or glass of milk.

Ingredients

- 2 1/4 cups flour
- 1 teaspoon cinnamon
- 1/2 teaspoon baking soda
- 1/2 teaspoon nutmeg
- 1/2 cup (1 stick) butter, softened
- 1 cup packed brown sugar
- 2 eggs
- 1/4 cup apple juice
- 1 large Granny Smith apple, peeled, cored, and diced
- 1 cup pecans, toasted and chopped

Preheat the oven to 375°F. Grease 2 cookie sheets.

Sift together the flour, cinnamon, baking soda, and nutmeg; set aside. Beat the butter and brown sugar in a large bowl with an electric mixer at high speed until well blended. Beat in the eggs and apple juice. Gradually add the flour to the butter mixture, beating at low speed until well blended. Stir in the apple and pecans.

Drop the dough by teaspoonfuls 2 inches apart onto the prepared cookie sheets. Bake for 13 minutes or until lightly browned. Cool on a wire rack.

Makes 3 1/2 dozen cookies

*Cut an apple in half (across the core)
and you'll see a star shape!*

Apple-Pear Crisp

Pears add a flavorful twist to this classic apple dessert.
If you don't have pears, simply add a few more apples.

Topping

- $^1/_2$ **cup packed brown sugar**
- $^1/_2$ **cup old-fashioned rolled oats**
- $^1/_2$ **cup pecans, chopped and lightly toasted**
- $^1/_4$ **cup flour**
- 1 **teaspoon cinnamon**
- 6 **tablespoons butter, cold and cut into small pieces**

Filling

- $^1/_4$ **cup sugar**
- 1 **tablespoon flour**
- 5 **medium Golden Delicious apples, peeled, cored, and cut into $^1/_2$-inch slices**
- 2 **ripe Bartlett pears, peeled, cored, and cut into $^1/_2$-inch slices**

Preheat the oven to 350°F. Spray a 9x9x2-inch baking dish with cooking spray.

To make the topping: Combine the brown sugar, oats, pecans, flour, and cinnamon in a medium bowl. Cut in the butter with a pastry blender or 2 knives until the mixture resembles coarse crumbs; set aside.

To make the filling: Combine the sugar and flour in a medium bowl. Add the apples and pears; toss to coat. Spoon into the prepared baking dish. Sprinkle the topping evenly over the fruit, lightly pressing it in place. Bake for 45 to 50 minutes, until the filling is bubbling. Serve warm or at room temperature.

Makes 8 servings

Tip: When you need a quick dessert for four, cut the ingredient amounts in half and divide the filling and topping among four 8-ounce ramekins. Reduce the baking time to 25 minutes.

Orchards spread rapidly westward along with the settlers,
far more satisfying their cravings for hard cider
than for apple dumplings.

Apple Crumble Cake

This fresh apple cake is so good that you'll serve it for breakfast, too!

Cake

2¼ cups flour

2 teaspoons baking soda

½ teaspoon nutmeg

½ teaspoon cinnamon

¼ teaspoon salt

¼ teaspoon ground cloves

1 cup granulated sugar

½ cup packed light brown sugar

½ cup shortening

1 cup buttermilk

2 eggs, beaten

4 medium Golden Delicious apples, peeled, cored, and cut into ¼-inch slices

Topping

½ cup coarsely chopped pecans

¼ cup granulated sugar

¼ cup packed light brown sugar

⅛ teaspoon cinnamon

Preheat the oven to 350°F. Grease and flour a 13x9x2-inch baking pan.

To make the cake: Sift together the flour, baking soda, nutmeg, cinnamon, salt, and cloves; set aside. Beat the sugars and shortening in a large bowl with an electric mixer at high speed until blended. Add the buttermilk and eggs; beat until smooth. Add the flour mixture; beat until well combined. Fold in the apples. Pour into the prepared pan, spreading evenly.

To make the topping: Combine the pecans, sugars, and cinnamon in a small bowl. Sprinkle over the batter. Bake for 45 to 50 minutes, until a wooden pick inserted into the center comes out clean. Cool on a wire rack.

Makes 15 servings

In 1998 Americans ate 19.2 pounds per capita of fresh apples a year. Belgians and Italians eat three times that amount. The Dutch eat the most—130 pounds a year.

Apple-Ginger Shortcakes with Caramel Sauce

Hot caramel, apples, and snappy ginger make this a flavorful cold-weather dessert.

Shortcakes

- 2 cups flour
- 1/4 cup sugar
- 1 tablespoon baking powder
- 1 teaspoon ground ginger
- 1/2 teaspoon salt
- 1/2 cup (1 stick) butter, cold and cut into small pieces
- 1/4 cup chopped crystallized ginger
- 1/2 cup milk
- 1 egg
- 2 teaspoons sugar

Filling

- 1 cup sugar
- 1/2 cup water
- 3 tablespoons butter
- 4 large Golden Delicious apples, peeled, cored, and cut into 1/2-inch slices
- 6 tablespoons heavy cream

Whipped cream, as a garnish

Preheat the oven to 425°F. Grease a baking sheet.

To make the shortcakes: Combine the flour, 1/4 cup sugar, baking powder, ground ginger, and salt in a large bowl. Cut in the butter with a pastry blender or 2 knives until the mixture resembles coarse crumbs. Add the crystallized ginger; toss to incorporate. Whisk the milk and egg in a small bowl. Add to the flour mixture; gently toss with a fork until a soft dough forms. Knead the dough in the bowl until all of the flour is incorporated. Shape by hand into six 2-inch rounds. Place the rounds 2 inches apart on the prepared pan. Sprinkle with 2 teaspoons sugar. Bake for 15 minutes or until browned. Cool on a wire rack. *(Shortcakes can be made 1 day ahead.) Reduce the oven temperature to 375°F.*

To make the filling: Bring the sugar and water to a boil over medium heat in a small saucepan. Cook until the sugar caramelizes to a light amber color. Remove the pan from the heat; add the butter and stir until it melts. Pour the caramel into a 13x9x2-inch baking dish. Place the apples over the caramel. Bake at 375°F for 30 minutes, stirring the apples once.

Cut the shortcakes horizontally into halves. Place the bottom halves on 6 individual plates. Spoon the apples evenly over the shortcake bottoms; cover with the shortcake tops.

Pour any remaining caramel into a small saucepan. Whisk the heavy cream into the caramel and simmer briefly over low heat. Drizzle over the shortcakes. Garnish each with a dollop of whipped cream.

Makes 6 servings

Note: Crystallized or candied ginger is fresh gingerroot that has been cooked in a sugar syrup and coated with coarse sugar. Look for it in the spice section of supermarkets or at specialty food stores.

Tip: Lightly coat the knife blade with cooking spray to prevent the crystallized ginger from sticking to the blade during chopping.

Apple-Fig Cobbler

*The Cheddar cheese in the biscuit topping complements
the apples and figs in this warm, comforting dessert.*

Topping

1 1/2 **cups flour**

2 **tablespoons sugar**

2 1/2 **teaspoons baking powder**

1/4 **teaspoon salt**

10 **tablespoons butter, cold and
cut into small pieces**

1 **cup shredded Cheddar cheese**

2/3 **cup milk**

1 **egg**

Filling

6 **tablespoons butter, divided**

10 **medium Golden Delicious
apples, peeled, cored, and
cut into 1/2-inch slices**

1 **cup dried figs**

1/2 **cup sugar**

2 **tablespoons flour**

1 **teaspoon cinnamon**

1/2 **cup apple juice**

1/2 **cup heavy cream**

Whipped cream, as a garnish

Preheat the oven to 375°F. Spray a 13x9x2-inch baking dish with cooking spray.

To make the topping: Whisk the flour, sugar, baking powder, and salt in a medium bowl. Cut in the butter with a pastry blender or 2 knives until the mixture resembles coarse crumbs. Stir in the cheese. Beat the milk and egg in a small bowl. Stir into the flour mixture just until a stiff dough forms; set aside.

To make the filling: Melt 3 tablespoons of the butter in a large skillet over medium heat. Add half the apples. Cook for about 9 minutes, until the fruit is soft, stirring occasionally. Pour into a large bowl; set aside. Repeat with the remaining 3 tablespoons butter, apples, and figs. Combine the sugar, flour, and cinnamon in a small bowl. Pour over the fruit; toss to coat. Stir in the apple juice and heavy cream. Spoon evenly into the prepared baking dish.

Drop the dough topping by heaping tablespoonfuls onto the filling, spacing evenly. Bake for about 45 minutes, until the filling is bubbling and a wooden pick inserted into the topping comes out clean. Serve warm garnished with whipped cream.

Makes 12 servings

Caramel Apples

Everyone loves caramel apples and thanks to this recipe, gooey, homemade caramel is easy to make. Pick out your favorite decorations and have fun!

Ingredients

- 12 wooden chopsticks or wooden pop sticks
- 12 medium Granny Smith apples, washed and dried
- 1 pound dark brown sugar
- 1 cup (2 sticks) butter, softened
- 1 (14-ounce) can sweetened condensed milk
- 2/3 cup dark corn syrup
- 1 1/2 teaspoons vanilla extract
- 1 to 2 tablespoons heavy cream, if needed

Assorted decorations, such as chopped nuts, miniature candies, candy sprinkles, melted chocolate

Line 2 baking sheets with aluminum foil; butter the foil. Push a chopstick into the stem end of each apple; set aside.

Combine the brown sugar, butter, sweetened condensed milk, corn syrup, and vanilla in a large heavy saucepan. Cook over medium-low heat for about 15 minutes, until the sugar dissolves, stirring constantly with a wooden spoon. Increase the heat to medium-high. Bring to a rolling boil, stirring constantly. Cook to 236°F on a candy thermometer, stirring constantly. Pour the caramel into a metal bowl. Do not scrape the pan and do not stir the caramel. Submerge the candy thermometer into the caramel; let it cool for about 20 minutes to 200°F.

Carefully dip each apple completely into the hot caramel. Lift the apple out, letting the excess caramel drip back into the bowl. Spoon additional caramel over the top of the apple to cover completely, if necessary. Place the dipped apple on a prepared baking sheet. Repeat with the remaining apples. (If the caramel becomes too thick to dip into, add 1 to 2 tablespoons heavy cream and whisk briefly in the bowl over low heat to thin it.)

Let the apples stand for about 15 minutes, until the caramel is partially set. Lift each apple; press the caramel pooled around the bottom evenly around the apple. Firmly press the nut and candy decorations into the caramel. Drizzle with melted chocolate. Refrigerate for 1 hour before eating to set the decorations. Store the apples, covered, in the refrigerator for up to 1 week.

Makes 12 servings

Tip: Place the nuts and candies in separate bowls. Hold the dipped apples over the bowls while pressing in the decorations to avoid making a mess.

Apple Upside-Down Cake

*Cornmeal in the cake adds a new twist
to the classic French tarte Tatin.*

Ingredients

- 2 tablespoons butter
- 1/2 cup sugar
- 4 medium Golden Delicious apples, peeled, cored, and each cut into 8 wedges
- 3/4 cup flour
- 2 teaspoons baking powder
- 1/2 teaspoon salt
- 1/2 cup boiling water
- 1/3 cup yellow cornmeal
- 6 tablespoons butter, softened
- 3/4 cup sugar
- 2 eggs
- 1 teaspoon vanilla extract
- 1/3 cup milk

Vanilla ice cream (optional)

Preheat the oven to 350°F. Generously butter a 9x1 1/2-inch round cake pan.

Melt 2 tablespoons butter in a large nonstick skillet over medium heat. Add 1/2 cup sugar; cook about 6 minutes, until the sugar dissolves and the mixture caramelizes to a deep golden brown, stirring occasionally. Add the apples; gently shake the skillet to distribute the caramel evenly. Cover; cook about 5 minutes, until the apples release their juices. Uncover; cook about 13 minutes, until the apples are tender and the caramel thickens and coats them, stirring occasionally. Pour the apples and caramel into the prepared pan, spreading evenly.

Whisk the flour, baking powder, and salt in a small bowl; set aside. Combine the boiling water and cornmeal in a large bowl. Add 6 table-spoons butter and 3/4 cup sugar to the cornmeal. Beat with an electric mixer on medium speed until well blended. Beat in the eggs and vanilla. Add the flour mixture alternately with the milk, beating on medium speed after each addition. Pour batter over the apples, spreading evenly.

Bake for about 40 minutes, until the cake is lightly browned and a wooden pick inserted into the center comes out clean. Cool in the pan for 5 minutes. Run a small knife between the cake and side of the pan. Carefully invert the cake onto an ovenproof or microwav-able platter. Cool for 15 minutes. Serve warm with ice cream, if desired.

Makes 8 servings

Note: The cake can be baked up to 6 hours ahead. Reheat in a 350°F oven for 10 minutes or microwave on Medium for about 2 minutes before serving.

Apple-Raisin Layer Cake
with Maple Frosting

This three-layer spiced apple cake is scrumptious!

Cake

- 3 **medium Granny Smith apples, peeled, cored, and diced**
- 1/4 **cup water**
- 2 1/2 **cups flour**
- 2 **teaspoons baking soda**
- 1 1/2 **teaspoons cinnamon**
- 1/2 **teaspoon salt**
- 1/4 **teaspoon nutmeg**
- 1/4 **teaspoon ground cloves**
- 1 **cup walnuts, toasted and chopped**
- 1 **cup golden raisins**
- 1 **tablespoon flour**
- 2 **cups sugar**
- 1 **cup (2 sticks) butter, softened**
- 2 **tablespoons brandy**
- 1 1/2 **teaspoons vanilla extract**
- 4 **eggs**

Frosting

- 1 **cup (2 sticks) butter, softened**
- 1 **cup packed dark brown sugar**
- 2 **(8-ounce) packages cream cheese, softened**
- 1/2 **cup pure maple syrup**
- 1/4 **teaspoon maple flavoring**
- 2 **cups walnut halves, toasted, as a garnish**

Preheat the oven to 350°F. Spray three 9-inch round cake pans with cooking spray. Line the bottoms with waxed paper; spray the paper with cooking spray. Dust the pans with flour.

To make the cake: Combine the apples and water in a small saucepan. Bring to a simmer over medium-low heat. Simmer, covered, for about 15 minutes, until the apples are tender; set aside. Sift together 2 1/2 cups flour, baking soda, cinnamon, salt, nutmeg, and cloves; set aside. Process the walnuts and raisins with 1 tablespoon flour in a food processor until chopped; set aside.

Beat the sugar, butter, brandy, and vanilla in a large bowl with an electric mixer at high speed until well blended. Add the eggs 1 at a time, beating well after each addition. Gradually add the flour mixture, beating at medium speed until blended. Stir in the apples, raisins, and walnuts. Divide the batter evenly among the prepared pans.

Bake for about 30 minutes, until a wooden pick inserted into the centers comes out clean. Cool in the pans for 10 minutes. Run a small knife between the cakes and the sides of the pans. Remove from the pans to wire racks; cool completely. *(Cake can be made 1 day ahead. Cover tightly and store at room temperature.)*

To make the frosting: Beat the butter and brown sugar in a large bowl with an electric mixer at high speed until well blended and free of any sugar lumps. Add the cream cheese, maple syrup, and maple flavoring; beat until well blended. Refrigerate the frosting for about 20 minutes, until it firms to a spreading consistency.

To assemble: Place 1 cake layer, top side down, on a cake platter. Spread with 3/4 cup of the frosting. Top with the second layer, top side up; spread with 3/4 cup of the frosting. Top with the final layer, top side up. Spread 1 cup of the frosting in a thin layer over the top and side of the cake. Refrigerate for 15 minutes. Spread the remaining frosting over the entire cake. Press the walnuts halfway up the side of the cake to garnish. Refrigerate for at least 30 minutes to set the frosting or until ready to serve. Let stand at room temperature for 1 hour before serving. Refrigerate any leftover cake.

Makes 12 servings

Apple Dumplings

Instead of baking whole apples in dough, these dumplings are made with sliced apples that are rolled up in dough then sliced into spiral rolls and baked in a sweet syrup.

Dough

2 1/2 cups flour

2 tablespoons sugar

2 teaspoons baking powder

1/4 teaspoon baking soda

1/4 teaspoon salt

3/4 cup sour cream

1 egg

Filling

1/4 cup sugar

1/2 teaspoon cinnamon

1/4 teaspoon nutmeg

8 large Golden Delicious apples, peeled, cored, and cut into 1/4-inch slices

Sauce

1 1/2 cups water

1 1/4 cups packed brown sugar

3/4 cup pure maple syrup

2 tablespoons cornstarch

6 tablespoons butter, cut into 12 pieces

Vanilla ice cream (optional)

Preheat the oven to 350°F. Grease a 13x9x2-inch baking pan.

To make the dough: Sift together the flour, sugar, baking powder, baking soda, and salt. Beat the sour cream and egg in a large bowl with an electric mixer at high speed. Add the flour mixture, beating at low speed until a soft dough forms. Roll the dough to a 13x10-inch rectangle on a lightly floured surface so a long side is parallel to the edge of the work surface.

To make the filling: Combine the sugar, cinnamon, and nutmeg in a large bowl. Add the apples; toss to coat. Spoon lengthwise down the center of the dough in a 4-inch-wide strip, leaving a 1-inch border at each short end. Carefully roll up the dough jelly-roll style, starting at the long side nearest you. Cut crosswise into twelve 1-inch-thick slices. Carefully place the dumpling slices, cut sides down, in 3 rows of 4 in the prepared pan, reshaping them if necessary.

To make the sauce: Combine the water, brown sugar, maple syrup, and cornstarch in a medium bowl, stirring until the sugar and cornstarch are completely dissolved. Pour half the sauce over the dumplings. Dot each with 1 piece of butter.

Bake for 30 minutes. Pour the remaining sauce over the dumplings. Bake for 20 to 30 minutes more or until the dumplings are lightly browned. Cool slightly on a wire rack. Spoon the warm dumplings and sauce into individual dessert dishes. Serve with ice cream, if desired.

Makes 12 servings

Note: The dumplings can be baked up to 1 day ahead and reheated in the oven or microwave oven.

Rustic Apple Tart

If pie crusts challenge your baking skills, then this free-form rustic tart is the answer. Assorted nuts, honey, apples, and dates make this dessert a tasty treat.

Crust

- 1¹/₃ cups flour
- 1 teaspoon sugar
- ¹/₂ teaspoon salt
- ¹/₂ cup (1 stick) butter, cold and cut into small pieces
- 3 tablespoons ice water

Filling

- ¹/₄ cup (¹/₂ stick) butter
- 8 small Granny Smith apples, peeled, cored, and each cut into 12 slices
- 7 large dates, pitted and thinly sliced
- 1 teaspoon ground allspice
- ¹/₃ cup honey
- ²/₃ cup chopped assorted nuts (such as pecans, walnuts, pistachios)
- 1 egg yolk
- 2 tablespoons sugar

Whipped cream, as a garnish

To make the crust: Process the flour, sugar, and salt in a food processor until blended. Add the butter. Pulse until the mixture resembles coarse crumbs. Add the water; pulse just until moist clumps form, adding a little more water, if necessary. Do not over-process. Gather the dough into a ball; flatten into a disk. Wrap in plastic wrap; refrigerate for 1 hour.

To make the filling: Melt the butter in a large skillet over medium-high heat. Add the apples and dates. Cook and stir for about 15 minutes, until the fruit is almost tender. (Do not overcook or too much juice will be released.) Reduce the heat to medium. Stir in the allspice and honey; mix well. Cook for 1 minute. Remove from the heat; set aside.

Preheat the oven to 375°F.

Roll out the dough to a 12-inch round between 2 sheets of parchment paper. Remove the top parchment; sprinkle the nuts over the dough. Replace the paper. Roll out to a 13-inch round, embedding the nuts into the dough. Invert the pastry onto a baking sheet, keeping the bottom parchment in place. Remove and discard the top paper. Use a slotted spoon to transfer the fruit to the center of the pastry, spreading to within 2 inches of the edge. Pour half of the fruit juices over the apples. Fold the outer edge of the pastry over the apples using the parchment paper as an aid. Overlap the pastry slightly while folding and press gently to seal (it will only partially cover the apples). If the dough tears, press it back together. Whisk the egg yolk in a small bowl; brush over the crust. Sprinkle the crust and fruit with the sugar.

Bake for about 25 minutes, until the crust is browned. Cool for about 30 minutes on the baking sheet on a wire rack. Serve warm garnished with whipped cream.

Makes 8 servings

Apple Streusel Pie

The buttery cinnamon streusel topping makes this my favorite apple pie.

Crust

1 1/2 cups sifted flour

1/2 teaspoon salt

1/4 cup shortening, cold

1/4 cup (1/2 stick) butter, cold and cut into small pieces

4 to 5 tablespoons ice water, divided

Streusel

1/4 cup sugar

1/4 cup flour

3/4 teaspoon cinnamon

1/2 cup (1 stick) butter, cold and cut into small pieces

Filling

3/4 cup sugar

3 tablespoons flour

2 teaspoons vanilla extract

1 teaspoon cinnamon

1/4 teaspoon salt

1/4 teaspoon nutmeg

7 large Granny Smith apples, peeled, cored, and cut into 1/4-inch slices

Vanilla ice cream (optional)

To make the crust: Combine the flour and salt in a large bowl. Cut in the shortening with a pastry blender or 2 knives until the mixture resembles coarse crumbs. Cut in the butter until the pieces become the size of small peas. Sprinkle 3 tablespoons water over the flour mixture; gently toss with a fork. Add enough of the remaining water, 1 tablespoon at a time, tossing until all the flour is moistened. Gather the dough into a ball; flatten into a disk. Wrap in plastic wrap; refrigerate for at least 1 hour. *(Pastry dough can be refrigerated for up to 3 days. Let the dough stand at room temperature to soften slightly before rolling.)*

Roll out the dough to a 12-inch round on a lightly floured surface. (The dough should be about 1/8 inch thick.) Transfer to a 9-inch pie plate. If the dough does not uniformly cover the side of the pan, cut off some excess dough and press it over the bare spots. Trim any excess dough to within 1 inch from the edge of the pan. Fold the dough under to form a smooth, even edge. Flute the edge by crimping it between your fingers or with the round end of a knife. Cover the pastry crust loosely with plastic wrap. Refrigerate for at least 1 hour or up to 24 hours.

Preheat the oven to 450°F.

To make the streusel: Combine the sugar, flour, and cinnamon in a medium bowl. Cut in the butter with a pastry blender or 2 knives until the mixture resembles coarse crumbs; set aside.

To make the filling: Combine the sugar, flour, vanilla, cinnamon, salt, and nutmeg in a large plastic food-storage bag. Add the apples; close the bag and shake until the apples are coated. Pour the apples into the pie shell, spreading them out and mounding slightly in the center. Sprinkle the streusel evenly over the apples, lightly pressing it in place.

Place the pie on a baking sheet. Bake for 15 minutes. *Reduce the oven temperature to 425°F.* Bake for 40 to 45 minutes more, until the crust is browned. (If the crust browns too quickly, cover the edge with foil.) Serve warm or at room temperature with ice cream, if desired.

Makes 8 servings

Spiced Apple Pie

The inviting aroma of spices will fill your home as
this classic double-crust apple pie bakes in the oven.

Crust

- 2 cups sifted flour
- 1 teaspoon salt
- 1/3 cup shortening, cold
- 1/3 cup butter, cold and cut into small pieces
- 5 to 7 tablespoons ice water, divided

Filling

- 1/2 cup granulated sugar
- 1/4 cup packed light brown sugar
- 3 tablespoons flour
- 2 teaspoons vanilla extract
- 1/2 teaspoon grated lemon zest
- 1 tablespoon fresh lemon juice
- 1 teaspoon cinnamon
- 1/2 teaspoon nutmeg
- 1/2 teaspoon mace
- 1/2 teaspoon ground cloves
- 1/2 teaspoon ground allspice
- 10 medium Granny Smith apples, peeled, cored, and cut into 1/4-inch slices

- 1 egg white, lightly beaten
- 1 tablespoon granulated sugar

Vanilla ice cream (optional)

To make the crust: Combine the flour and salt in a large bowl. Cut in the shortening with a pastry blender or 2 knives until the mixture resembles coarse crumbs. Cut in the butter until the pieces become the size of small peas. Sprinkle 4 tablespoons water over the flour mixture; gently toss with a fork. Add enough of the remaining water, 1 tablespoon at a time, tossing until all the flour is moistened. Gather the dough into 2 balls, one slightly smaller than the other; flatten each into a disk. Wrap in plastic wrap; refrigerate for at least 1 hour. *(Pastry dough can be refrigerated for up to 3 days. Let the dough stand at room temperature to soften slightly before rolling.)*

Roll out the larger dough disk to a 12-inch round on a lightly floured surface. (The dough should be about 1/8 inch thick.) Transfer to a 9-inch pie plate. If the dough does not uniformly cover the side of the pan, cut off some excess dough and press it over the bare spots. Trim any excess dough to within 1/2 inch from the edge of the pan. Cover the pastry crust loosely with plastic wrap. Refrigerate for at least 1 hour or up to 24 hours.

Preheat the oven to 400°F. Position the oven rack on the lowest shelf.

To make the filling: Combine the 1/2 cup granulated sugar, brown sugar, flour, vanilla, lemon zest, lemon juice, cinnamon, nutmeg, mace, cloves, and allspice in a large bowl. Add the apples; toss to coat. Spoon evenly into the prepared pastry crust, mounding the apples slightly in the center.

Roll out the second dough disk to a 10-inch round on a lightly floured surface. Place over the apples. Trim any excess dough to within 1 inch from the edge of the pan. Fold the top crust edge under the bottom edge, pressing together to seal. Flute the edge by crimping it between your fingers or with the round end of a knife. Cut several slits in the top crust to allow steam to escape. Brush the top with the egg white; sprinkle with 1 tablespoon granulated sugar.

Place the pie on a baking sheet. Bake for 1 hour to 1 hour and 10 minutes, until the crust is lightly browned and the juices are bubbling. (If the crust browns too quickly, cover the edge with foil.) Cool on a wire rack for at least 2 hours. Serve warm or at room temperature with ice cream, if desired.

Makes 8 servings

Apple Strudel

Surprise your family with this delicious German specialty.

Ingredients

- 4 **Granny Smith apples, peeled, cored, and cut into** $1/4$-**inch slices**
- $1/2$ **cup granulated sugar**
- 1 **tablespoon cornstarch**
- $1/2$ **teaspoon cinnamon**
- $1/3$ **cup walnuts, toasted and chopped**
- $1/4$ **cup raisins**
- $1/4$ **cup finely crushed vanilla wafers**
- 6 **sheets frozen phyllo dough, thawed**
- $1/2$ **cup (1 stick) butter, melted**
- 1 **tablespoon granulated sugar**
- **Confectioners' sugar**
- **Vanilla ice cream (optional)**

Combine the apples, $1/2$ cup granulated sugar, cornstarch, and cinnamon in a medium saucepan. Cook gently over medium heat for about 30 minutes, until the apples are tender and the juices almost evaporate, stirring occasionally. Stir in the walnuts and raisins; cool completely. Stir in the vanilla wafer crumbs; set aside.

Preheat the oven to 350°F. Lightly butter a baking sheet.

Place 1 phyllo sheet on a dry work surface with a long side parallel to the edge of the surface. (Keep the remaining phyllo covered with plastic wrap and a damp towel as you work.) Brush the phyllo with melted butter. Top with the remaining 5 phyllo sheets, brushing each with melted butter before adding the next sheet. Spoon the apple mixture in a 3-inch-wide strip down the center of the layered phyllo sheets, leaving a 2-inch border around the edges. Carefully roll up the dough jelly-roll style, starting at the long side nearest you and tightly sealing in the apples while rolling. Place the strudel, seam side down, on the prepared baking sheet, folding the ends underneath. Brush melted butter over the surface; sprinkle with 1 tablespoon granulated sugar.

Bake for 30 minutes or until lightly browned. Cool on the baking sheet on a wire rack. Dust with confectioners' sugar and serve warm with ice cream, if desired.

Makes 12 servings

Note: Phyllo dough can be tricky to handle. Be sure to follow the thawing and handling instructions on the package and check the dough in advance to insure that it is not dried out. Specialty stores may carry thicker phyllo sheets. If you buy thicker phyllo, use 4 instead of 6 sheets in this recipe.

Apple-Almond Tart

Almonds get double billing in the crust and the filling
of this scrumptious apple tart.

Crust

- 1 cup flour
- 3 tablespoons sugar
- 1/4 teaspoon salt
- 1/3 cup sliced almonds
- 1/2 cup (1 stick) butter, cold and cut into small pieces
- 3 tablespoons ice water

Filling

- 1 (8-ounce) can almond paste
- 1/4 cup (1/2 stick) butter, softened
- 2 eggs
- 1/3 cup flour
- 2 medium Golden Delicious apples, peeled, cored, and cut into 1/8-inch slices
- 1/3 cup sugar
- 2 tablespoons butter, melted
- 1 tablespoon sugar
- 1/2 teaspoon cinnamon

Whipped cream, as a garnish

To make the crust: Process the flour, sugar, salt, and almonds in a food processor until the almonds are finely chopped. Add the butter. Pulse until the mixture resembles coarse crumbs. Add the water; pulse just until moist clumps form, adding a little more water, if necessary. Do not overprocess. Gather the dough into a ball; flatten into a disk. Wrap in waxed paper; refrigerate for 1 hour. *(Pastry dough can be refrigerated for up to 1 day. Let the dough stand at room temperature to soften slightly before rolling.)*

Spray a 9-inch tart pan with a removable bottom with cooking spray. Unwrap the dough, keeping the waxed paper over the top. Roll out to an 11-inch circle on a lightly floured surface. Remove the waxed paper. (If the waxed paper sticks to the dough, chill it in the refrigerator for a few minutes.)

Gently lift the dough just enough to move the prepared pan underneath it. Press the dough firmly onto the bottom and side of the pan. If the dough does not uniformly cover the side of the pan, cut off some excess dough and press it over the bare spots. The line where the bottom and side of the pastry meet may also be reinforced with excess dough, if necessary. Pierce the bottom of the crust all over with a fork. Cover; freeze for 30 minutes.

Preheat the oven to 375°F. Place the crust on a baking sheet. Bake for 20 minutes or until lightly browned. Cool on a wire rack. Maintain the oven temperature at 375°F.

To make the filling: Process the almond paste, 1/4 cup butter, and eggs in a food processor until smooth. Add the flour; process just until blended. Spread the almond mixture carefully over the bottom of the crust.

Toss the apples with 1/3 cup sugar in a large bowl. Arrange the apples in concentric circles over the almond mixture. Brush with 2 tablespoons butter. Combine the 1 tablespoon sugar and cinnamon in a small bowl. Sprinkle over the apples.

Bake at 375°F for about 40 minutes, until the apples are tender and lightly browned. Cool on a wire rack for 15 minutes. Gently loosen and remove the edge of the pan. Serve warm garnished with whipped cream.

Makes 8 servings

Apple Turnovers

This classic recipe makes a tasty treat for any time of the day!

Pastry

- 2 cups flour
- 1/4 teaspoon salt
- 1/4 teaspoon baking powder
- 5 ounces cream cheese, cold and cut into small pieces
- 3/4 cup (1 1/2 sticks) butter, cold and cut into small pieces
- 3 tablespoons ice water

Filling

- 6 medium Granny Smith apples, peeled, cored, and cut into 1/4-inch slices
- 1 teaspoon grated lemon zest
- 1 teaspoon fresh lemon juice
- 1/3 cup sugar
- 1/2 teaspoon cinnamon
- 1 tablespoon butter
- 1/4 teaspoon vanilla extract
- 2 teaspoons cornstarch

- 1 egg, lightly beaten
  Sugar, for sprinkling

Note: The unbaked turnovers can be made ahead and frozen, tightly wrapped, for up to 6 months. When ready to bake, *do not* thaw them. Follow the baking directions above, brushing with beaten egg, sprinkling with sugar, and cutting steam vents. Increase the baking time by 10 to 15 minutes.

To make the pastry: Process the flour, salt, and baking powder in a food processor until blended. Add the cream cheese; pulse until the mixture resembles coarse crumbs. Add the butter; pulse until the pieces become the size of small peas. Add the water; pulse just until moist clumps form. Transfer to a piece of waxed paper; knead just until the dough holds together. Gather the dough into 2 equal balls; flatten each into a disk. Wrap in plastic wrap; refrigerate for at least 1 hour. (*Pastry dough can be refrigerated for up to 3 days. Let the dough stand at room temperature to soften slightly before rolling.*)

To make the filling: Combine the apples, lemon zest, and juice in a large bowl. Add the sugar and cinnamon; toss to coat. Let stand at room temperature for 30 minutes to 1 hour. Drain the apples over a large bowl, reserving the apples and juices. Melt the butter in a small saucepan over medium heat. Add the apple juices. Cook for 3 to 5 minutes, until thickened. Remove from the heat; cool for 10 minutes. Stir in the vanilla. Toss the apples with the cornstarch. Stir in the cooled apple juice mixture.

Line 2 baking sheets with parchment paper or foil.

Divide each pastry dough disk into 5 equal balls, forming 10 balls total. Working with 1 ball at a time, flatten each into a disk and roll out to a 6-inch round on a lightly floured surface. Spoon 3 tablespoons of the apple filling onto one-half of the dough round, leaving a 1/2-inch border. Fold the other half of the dough over the filling to within 1/4 inch of the bottom edge. Fold the bottom edge over the top edge and press firmly with your fingers to seal. Crimp the edges with a fork. Place the turnovers on the prepared pans. Refrigerate, loosely covered, for 1 hour or freeze for 30 minutes.

Preheat the oven to 400°F.

Brush the turnovers with the egg and sprinkle lightly with sugar. Cut 3 steam vents into the top of each turnover with a paring knife. Bake for 30 to 35 minutes, until the filling is bubbling and the pastry is lightly browned. Cool on a wire rack for 30 minutes. Serve warm.

Makes 10 servings

Delicious Fruit Desserts

Apricot

Peak Season: Early-ripening apricots are the first summer fruit to appear in the market and are available from late May to August. Because fully ripe apricots are very delicate, bruise easily and have a short shelf life, only certain varieties (such as Castlebrite and Katy) can be successfully shipped. Blenheim apricots, considered the best variety grown in the Santa Clara Valley, are rarely available outside of California.

Selection: Fresh apricots are prized for their delicate flavor, velvety skins, and wonderfully sweet aroma. Select plump, fragrant fruit with smooth, golden skins that have no trace of green. Since fully ripe apricots are fragile, they are usually shipped unripe. Avoid overhandling them to prevent bruising.

Dried apricots are imported from Morocco, Australia, and Spain. The drying process is often hastened with sulfur dioxide, which can impart an unpleasant taste. Sun-dried apricots are preferred. Avoid dried fruit that is dark, moldy, or too firm.

Glazed apricots, often from Australia, can be found in specialty stores. They are large dried apricots coated with a honey-sugar glaze.

Storage: Ripen apricots by placing them in a paper bag or warm place for a few days. Once ripe and soft to the touch, refrigerate in a plastic bag for only 1 to 2 days since refrigeration dries them out quickly. Let apricots come to room temperature before eating. Fully ripe fruit is full of juice and should be eaten as soon as possible.

Preparation: Gently wash fresh apricots just before using. Due to their thin skins, they are usually eaten unpeeled. To remove the pit, cut around the seam to the pit and twist gently to separate into halves. Use your fingers to pull out the pit. To prevent cut apricots from turning brown, brush the cut surfaces with lemon juice. One pound apricots yields about 8 to 12 whole, or 2 to 3 cups sliced.

A Little History: Apricots were first cultivated over four thousand years ago in China. From there, this delicate fruit spread throughout central Asia and the Mediterranean where climates provided favorable growing conditions. Eventually apricots made their way to the New World via Spanish explorers. Missionaries planted apricot trees in California and today this state produces over 90% of the U.S. apricot crop. Worldwide, the top apricot growers are Turkey, Italy, Spain, Greece, and France. Apricots are botanically related to peaches but are about the size of small plums with thin, slightly fuzzy skins and smooth, oval pits. Because they bruise easily during shipping, fresh apricots are less widely available than peaches and nectarines. Most of the crop is dried, canned, or made into nectar.

Chocolate-Covered Dried Apricots

*Sweet, honey-glazed apricots coated with rich, dark chocolate are a
quick and easy treat for chocolate lovers.*

Ingredients

- **8 ounces semisweet baking chocolate**
- **1 pound glazed apricots**

Cover the bottom of a baking sheet with waxed paper.

Melt the chocolate in a medium heatproof bowl set over a saucepan of simmering water, stirring constantly until smooth. Remove the bowl from the pan. Dip the apricots 1 at a time about two-thirds into the chocolate; let any excess chocolate drip back into the bowl. Place the apricots on the prepared pan. Refrigerate for 15 minutes to set the chocolate. Remove the apricots from the waxed paper and store in an airtight container in the refrigerator.

Makes about 12 pieces

Note: Glazed apricots can be purchased at specialty stores. They are large dried apricots coated with a honey-sugar glaze.

*Apricots, especially when dried, have one of the highest
levels of vitamin A found in any fruit.
Vitamin A is essential for many functions, including
healthy skin and eyes.*

Mini Apricot Cakes

These little cakes make a great snack for after school or tea time.

Ingredients

- 2 (15-ounce) cans apricot halves, drained and divided
- 1 (8-ounce) can almond paste
- 2 eggs
- 5 tablespoons butter, melted
- 3 tablespoons flour
- $^1/_2$ cup heavy cream, whipped to soft peaks

Preheat the oven to 350°F. Line 8 muffin cups with paper liners.

Process 8 of the apricot halves, almond paste, and eggs in a food processor until smooth. Add the butter and flour. Pulse until blended.

Slice 3 of the remaining apricot halves lengthwise into sixteen $^1/_4$-inch strips. Divide the batter evenly among the prepared muffin cups. Push 2 apricot slices into the batter in each cup.

Bake for 30 to 35 minutes, until lightly browned and a wooden pick inserted into the centers comes out clean. Cool on a wire rack for 15 minutes. Remove from the cups to a wire rack; cool completely.

Process the remaining apricot halves in a food processor until puréed. Transfer to a medium bowl. Fold in $^1/_2$ cup of the whipped cream. Serve the cakes with dollops of apricot cream.

Makes 8 servings

Tips: Use any leftover apricot cream as a topping for waffles and pancakes.

Cakes can be stored in an airtight container for up to 1 week.

A fresh apricot contains about 17 calories and is high in vitamins A and C, potassium, and fiber.

Apricot Oatmeal Cookies

Dried apricots and white chocolate chips add a delicious flavor twist to oatmeal cookies.

Ingredients

- 1 ½ cups flour
- 1 teaspoon baking soda
- ½ teaspoon baking powder
- ½ teaspoon cinnamon
- ¼ teaspoon salt
- ¼ teaspoon nutmeg
- ¾ cup (1 ½ sticks) butter, softened
- ½ cup packed brown sugar
- ½ cup granulated sugar
- 2 eggs
- 2 tablespoons light corn syrup
- 1 teaspoon vanilla extract
- 3 cups old-fashioned oats
- 1 cup chopped dried apricots
- ½ cup white chocolate chips

Preheat the oven to 350°F. Grease 2 cookie sheets.

Sift together the flour, baking soda, baking powder, cinnamon, salt, and nutmeg; set aside. Beat the butter and sugars in a large bowl with an electric mixer at high speed until fluffy. Beat in the eggs, corn syrup, and vanilla. Gradually add the flour mixture, beating at low speed until combined. Stir in the oats, dried apricots, and white chocolate chips by hand.

Drop the dough by rounded teaspoonfuls 2 inches apart onto the prepared cookie sheets. Bake for about 10 minutes, until lightly browned. Cool on the pans for 10 minutes. Remove to wire racks; cool completely.

Makes 4 dozen cookies

Grab some dried apricots for a convenient and nutritious snack when you're on the go.

Apricot Hazelnut Biscotti

*These cardamom-scented biscotti are superb
with a cup of coffee, tea, or hot cocoa.*

Ingredients

- 1 **cup sugar**
- 1/3 **cup butter, softened**
- 2 **teaspoons baking powder**
- 1/2 **teaspoon cardamom**
- 2 **eggs**
- 1 **teaspoon vanilla extract**
- 2 **cups flour**
- 3/4 **cup hazelnuts, chopped**
- 3/4 **cup chopped dried apricots**

Preheat the oven to 375°F. Spray a baking sheet with cooking spray.

Beat the sugar and butter in a large bowl with an electric mixer at high speed until fluffy. Beat in the baking powder and cardamom. Add the eggs and vanilla; beat until well blended. Stir in the flour by hand until completely incorporated. Stir in the hazelnuts and dried apricots. Using flour-coated hands, divide the dough into halves. Shape each half into a 9x3-inch log on the prepared baking sheet. Refrigerate for at least 30 minutes or up to 1 hour.

Bake for 25 to 30 minutes, until a wooden pick inserted into the centers comes out clean. Cool on the pan for 15 minutes. *Reduce the oven temperature to 325°F.*

With a serrated knife, cut each log diagonally into 1/2-inch-thick slices. Place the slices, cut sides down, on the same baking sheet. Bake at 325°F for 8 minutes. Turn the slices over; bake for 8 to 10 minutes more, until dry and crisp. Cool completely on a wire rack. Store in an airtight container at room temperature for up to 2 days or freeze for up to 6 months.

Makes 3 dozen cookies

Tip: For an extra-special touch, dip the biscotti halfway into melted semisweet chocolate. Place on waxed paper. Let stand until the chocolate is set. Store layered between sheets of waxed paper.

*Biscotti originated in Italy in the 1400's. Because of their
capability for long-term storage, they were an ideal food
for sailors, soldiers, and fishermen to take on journeys.*

Simple Apricot Soufflés

These no-fail soufflés make a light and luscious dessert.

Ingredients

- 1 (15-ounce) can apricot halves, drained
- 2 egg yolks, at room temperature
- 2 tablespoons sugar
- 1 tablespoon peach schnapps or apricot liqueur (optional)
- 1 tablespoon fresh lemon juice
- 5 egg whites, at room temperature
- 2 tablespoons sugar
- 1/3 cup raspberry preserves (optional)

Preheat the oven to 350°F. Generously butter six 6- to 8-ounce ramekins or custard cups. Coat them with sugar, tapping out the excess. Place on a baking sheet spaced apart.

Process the apricots in a blender until puréed. Add the egg yolks, 2 tablespoons sugar, peach schnapps, if desired, and lemon juice. Process on medium speed for 2 minutes or until smooth and thickened. Transfer to a large bowl; set aside.

Beat the egg whites in a large bowl with an electric mixer at high speed until soft peaks form. Gradually add 2 tablespoons sugar at low speed, then beat at high speed until stiff peaks form. Fold about 1/4 cup of the egg whites into the apricot mixture. Gently fold in the remaining egg whites until well blended. Divide the batter evenly among the prepared ramekins. Smooth the tops with your finger and run your thumb around the inside edges, wiping off the butter and sugar from the rims.

Bake for 15 to 8 minutes, until puffed and lightly browned. Meanwhile, microwave the preserves in a microwavable dish on High for about 1 minute. Pour through a fine strainer set over a small bowl to remove the seeds.

Drizzle the soufflés with raspberry sauce, if desired, and serve immediately.

Makes 6 servings

Note: Soufflés are best when served immediately after coming out of the oven. They cannot be stored or reheated.

Tip: Assemble all of the ingredients in advance so that after dinner you can quickly prepare the soufflés.

Apricot-Ginger Shortcakes

Caramelized apricots nestled between tasty shortcakes
make a wonderful dessert.

Shortcakes

2 cups flour

$^1/_4$ cup sugar

1 tablespoon baking powder

1 teaspoon ground ginger

$^1/_2$ teaspoon salt

$^1/_2$ cup (1 stick) butter, cold and cut into small pieces

$^1/_4$ cup chopped crystallized ginger

$^1/_2$ cup milk

1 egg

2 teaspoons sugar

Filling

$^2/_3$ cup packed brown sugar

4 tablespoons ($^1/_2$ stick) butter

2 pounds fresh apricots, pitted and sliced

2 tablespoons heavy cream

Whipped cream, as a garnish

Preheat the oven to 425°F. Grease a baking sheet.

To make the shortcakes: Combine the flour, $^1/_4$ cup sugar, baking powder, ground ginger, and salt in a large bowl. Cut in the butter with a pastry blender or 2 knives until the mixture resembles coarse crumbs. Add the crystallized ginger; toss to incorporate. Whisk the milk and egg in a small bowl. Add to the flour mixture; gently toss with a fork until a soft dough forms. Knead the dough in the bowl until all of the flour is incorporated. Shape by hand into six 2-inch rounds. Place the rounds 2 inches apart on the prepared pan. Sprinkle with 2 teaspoons sugar. Bake for 15 minutes or until browned. Cool on a wire rack. *(Shortcakes can be made 1 day ahead.)*

To make the filling: Melt the brown sugar and butter in a large skillet over medium heat. Add the apricots. Cook and stir for about 10 minutes, until the apricots are soft.

Cut 6 of the shortcakes horizontally into halves. Place the bottom halves on 6 individual plates. Spoon the apricots over and around the shortcake bottoms. Cover with the shortcake tops. Whisk the heavy cream into the glaze in the saucepan; simmer briefly over low heat. Drizzle over the shortcakes. Garnish each with a dollop of whipped cream.

Makes 6 servings

Notes: Crystallized or candied ginger is fresh gingerroot that has been cooked in a sugar syrup and coated with coarse sugar. Look for it in the spice section of supermarkets or at specialty food stores.

Tip: Lightly coat the knife blade with cooking spray to prevent the crystallized ginger from sticking to the blade during chopping.

Apricot-Raspberry Cobbler

Warm fresh fruit with a biscuit topping is truly scrumptious!

Topping

- 1 cup flour
- ¼ cup sugar
- 1 teaspoon baking powder
- ¼ teaspoon baking soda
- ¼ teaspoon salt
- ¼ cup (½ stick) butter, cold and cut into small pieces
- ½ teaspoon almond extract
- ½ cup milk

Filling

- ¼ cup sugar
- 1½ tablespoons cornstarch
- 18 fresh apricots, pitted and cut into quarters
- 1 pint fresh raspberries
- 1 teaspoon almond extract

Vanilla ice cream (optional)

Preheat the oven to 375°F. Spray a 9x9x2-inch baking dish with cooking spray.

To make the topping: Whisk the flour, sugar, baking powder, baking soda, and salt in a medium bowl. Cut in the butter with a pastry blender or 2 knives until the mixture resembles coarse crumbs. Add the almond extract and milk. Stir just until a stiff dough forms; set aside.

To make the filling: Combine the sugar and cornstarch in a medium bowl. Add the apricots, raspberries, and almond extract; toss gently to coat. Spoon evenly into the prepared baking dish. Drop the dough topping by heaping tablespoonfuls onto the filling, spacing evenly.

Bake for 35 to 40 minutes, until the filling is bubbling and a wooden pick inserted into the topping comes out clean. Serve warm with ice cream, if desired.

Makes 6 servings

Apricots & Blueberries
in Almond Cream

Fresh apricots and blueberries baked in a sweet, light custard are simply divine!

Ingredients

- 6 fresh apricots, pitted and sliced
- 1 cup fresh blueberries
- 2 tablespoons sugar
- 1 tablespoon cornstarch
- 2 to 3 tablespoons amaretto liqueur (optional)
- 2/3 cup flour
- 1/3 cup whole blanched almonds
- 4 eggs
- 1/2 cup sugar
- 1 cup whole milk
- 1/4 cup (1/2 stick) butter, melted
- 1 teaspoon vanilla extract
- 1/2 teaspoon almond extract

Preheat the oven to 325°F. Generously butter six 1-cup ramekins or custard cups. Place on a baking sheet spaced apart.

Combine the apricots, blueberries, 2 tablespoons sugar, and cornstarch in a large bowl. Divide the fruit mixture equally among the prepared ramekins. Drizzle with amaretto, if desired; set aside.

Process the flour with the almonds in a food processor until the almonds are finely chopped. Beat the eggs and 1/2 cup sugar in a large bowl with an electric mixer at high speed. Add the almond mixture and blend well. Beat in the milk, butter, vanilla, and almond extract. Divide the batter evenly among the ramekins.

Bake for 45 minutes or until lightly browned on top. Serve warm or at room temperature.

Makes 6 servings

Apricot Cake

This delectable cake is crowned with golden apricots.

Ingredients

4 fresh apricots, pitted and cut into halves

OR 1 (15-ounce) can apricot halves, drained

$^1/_3$ cup golden raisins

3 tablespoons rum

1 cup confectioners' sugar

$^1/_2$ cup (1 stick) butter, softened

3 eggs

1 cup flour

$^3/_4$ teaspoon baking powder

$^1/_4$ cup apricot preserves, melted

Preheat the oven to 325°F. Spray a 9x5x2$^1/_2$-inch loaf pan with cooking spray. Lightly dust with flour.

Cut each apricot half into thirds; set aside. Place the raisins in a small bowl; add enough hot water to cover. Soak for 10 minutes or until softened; drain. Return to the bowl and stir in the rum; set aside.

Beat the confectioners' sugar and butter in a large bowl with an electric mixer at high speed until fluffy. Add the eggs 1 at a time, beating well after each addition. Stir in the raisin mixture by hand. Add the flour and baking powder; stir until combined. Pour into the prepared pan, spreading evenly. Press the apricot slices, smooth sides up, in 2 rows down the length of the pan, pushing them down so just a little of their tops are exposed.

Bake for 1 hour, until lightly browned and a wooden pick inserted into the center comes out clean. Cool in the pan for 15 minutes. Run a small knife between the cake and the sides of the pan. Remove from the pan to a wire rack, then invert top side up. Brush the top of the warm cake with the melted preserves to glaze. Cool completely before cutting.

Makes 10 servings

Apricot-Berry Tart

Enjoy summer berries with fresh apricots in this very easy tart.

Crust

- ³/₄ cup flour
- ¹/₂ cup yellow cornmeal
- 3 tablespoons sugar
- ¹/₄ teaspoon salt
- 6 tablespoons butter, cold and cut into small pieces
- 1 egg yolk
- 1 tablespoon milk
- ¹/₂ teaspoon vanilla extract

Filling

- 10 fresh apricots, pitted and cut into quarters
- 2 cups assorted berries (raspberries, blueberries, and blackberries)
- 5 tablespoons sugar

Whipped cream, as a garnish

Preheat the oven to 400°F. Spray a 9-inch tart pan with a removable bottom with cooking spray; place on a baking sheet.

To make the crust: Process the flour, cornmeal, sugar, and salt in a food processor until blended. Add the butter. Pulse until the mixture resembles coarse crumbs. Whisk the egg yolk, milk, and vanilla in a small bowl. With the processor on, slowly add the egg mixture, processing just until the dough begins to come together. Transfer the dough to the prepared pan. Press evenly onto the side and bottom of the pan. Bake for about 15 minutes, until lightly browned. (Gently press the bottom of the crust to flatten if it puffed up during baking.) Cool on a wire rack. *Reduce the oven temperature to 350°F.*

To make the filling: Gently toss the apricots and berries with the sugar in a medium bowl. Let stand at room temperature for 15 minutes.

Spoon the fruit into the prepared crust. Bake at 350°F for 40 to 45 minutes, until the apricots are juicy and tender. Cool completely on a wire rack. Gently loosen and remove the edge of the pan. Serve warm garnished with whipped cream.

Makes 8 servings

Apricot-Gingerbread Cakes
with Caramel Sauce

These mini spice cakes are topped with dried apricots and drenched in caramel sauce.

Cakes

- 1 cup dried apricots, thinly sliced
- 1 ³/₄ cups flour
- 2 teaspoons ground ginger
- 1 teaspoon baking soda
- 1 teaspoon ground allspice
- ³/₄ cup packed brown sugar
- ¹/₂ cup butter (1 stick), softened
- ¹/₂ cup molasses
- 1 egg
- ¹/₃ cup milk

Sauce

- 1 cup packed brown sugar
- 1 cup light corn syrup
- 6 tablespoons butter
- 3 tablespoons chopped crystallized ginger
- ¹/₂ cup heavy cream

Preheat the oven to 350°F. Generously butter 6 jumbo muffin cups.

To make the cakes: Place the dried apricots in a small bowl; add enough hot water to cover. Soak for 10 minutes; drain and set aside.

Sift together the flour, ground ginger, baking soda, and allspice; set aside. Beat the brown sugar and butter in a large bowl with an electric mixer at high speed until fluffy. Add the molasses and egg; beat well. Add the flour mixture alternately with the milk, beating at medium speed after each addition. Stir in ¹/₃ cup of the apricots by hand. Divide the batter evenly among the prepared muffin cups.

Bake for 20 minutes or until a wooden pick inserted into the centers comes out clean. Cool on a wire rack for 10 minutes. Run a small knife between the cakes and the sides of the cups. Remove from the cups to a wire rack; cool completely.

To make the sauce: Combine the brown sugar and corn syrup in a medium saucepan. Cook and stir over low heat until the sugar dissolves. Bring to a boil over high heat. Cook for about 5 minutes or until thickened. Add the butter, remaining apricots, and crystallized ginger. Cook and stir until the butter melts. Add the cream and stir over low heat until smooth.

Place the warm cakes on individual dessert plates. Spoon the sauce over the tops.

Makes 6 servings

Notes: Six mini Bundt cake pans, each with a 1-cup capacity, can be substituted for the jumbo muffin cups.

The cakes can be baked up to 1 day ahead. Reheat in a 350°F oven for 8 minutes or microwave on Medium for about 2 minutes before serving.

The sauce can be made up to 1 day ahead. Refrigerate, covered, until ready to use. Reheat in a saucepan over low heat before serving.

Rustic Apricot Tart

Fresh apricots are nestled in an easy to make free-form almond crust.

Ingredients

- 1 1/3 cups flour
- 1/3 cup sliced almonds
- 3 tablespoons sugar
- 1/4 teaspoon salt
- 1/2 cup (1 stick) butter, cold and cut into small pieces
- 3 tablespoons ice water
- 3 tablespoons sliced almonds
- 1 tablespoon flour
- 2 pounds fresh apricots, pitted and cut into halves
- 3/4 cup sugar
- 1/2 teaspoon pumpkin pie spice
- 2 tablespoons sliced almonds
- 1 egg yolk

Whipped cream, as a garnish

To make the crust: Process 1 1/3 cups flour, 1/3 cup almonds, 3 tablespoons sugar, and salt in a food processor until blended. Add the butter. Pulse until the mixture resembles coarse crumbs. Add the water; pulse just until moist clumps form, adding a little more water, if necessary. Do not overprocess. Gather the dough into a ball; flatten into a disk. Wrap in plastic wrap; refrigerate for 1 hour.

Preheat the oven to 375°F.

Process 3 tablespoons almonds and 1 tablespoon flour in a food processor for 30 seconds or until the almonds are finely chopped; set aside.

Roll out the dough to a 12-inch round between 2 sheets of parchment paper. Remove and discard the top paper. Slide the pastry round onto a baking sheet, keeping the bottom paper in place. Sprinkle the almond mixture over the dough to within 2 inches of the edge. Arrange the apricot halves, cut sides down, over the almonds. Combine the 3/4 cup sugar and pumpkin pie spice in a small bowl. Reserve 1 tablespoon of the sugar mixture; sprinkle the remaining over the apricots. Top with 2 tablespoons almonds. Fold the outer edge of the pastry over the apricots using the parchment paper as an aid. Overlap the pastry slightly while folding and press gently to seal (it will only partially cover the apricots). If the dough tears, press it back together. Whisk the egg yolk in a small bowl; brush over the crust. Sprinkle the reserved sugar mixture over the crust and fruit.

Bake for about 30 minutes, until the crust is browned. Cool for about 30 minutes on the baking sheet on a wire rack. Serve warm garnished with whipped cream.

Makes 8 servings

Apricot-Pumpkin Layer Cake

The marriage of apricots and pumpkin
creates a blissful union in this golden cake.

Cake

- 2 cups cake flour
- 2 teaspoons baking powder
- 2 teaspoons cinnamon
- 1/2 teaspoon baking soda
- 1/2 teaspoon ground allspice
- 1/4 teaspoon salt
- 1 (15-ounce) can apricot halves
- 3/4 cup canned pure pumpkin
- 1/4 cup milk
- 2 teaspoons vanilla extract
- 1 cup sugar
- 1/2 cup (1 stick) butter, softened
- 2 eggs

Filling

- 1 cup dried apricots
- 3 tablespoons water

Frosting

- 1 (8-ounce) package cream cheese, softened
- 1/2 cup (1 stick) butter, softened
- 1/4 cup canned pure pumpkin
- 1 cup confectioners' sugar, sifted

Preheat the oven to 350°F. Grease and flour two 9-inch round cake pans.

To make the cake: Sift together the cake flour, baking powder, cinnamon, baking soda, allspice, and salt; set aside. Drain the apricots, reserving the juice. Process the apricots in a food processor until puréed. Transfer to a small bowl. Stir in the pumpkin, milk, and vanilla; set aside.

Beat the sugar and butter in a large bowl with an electric mixer at high speed until fluffy. Add the eggs 1 at a time, beating well after each addition. Add the flour mixture alternately with the apricot mixture, beating at low speed after each addition. Divide the batter evenly between the prepared pans.

Bake for 25 to 30 minutes, until a wooden pick inserted into the centers comes out clean. Cool in the pans for 10 minutes. Run a small knife between the cakes and the sides of the pans. Remove from the pans to wire racks; cool completely. *(Cake can be made 1 day ahead. Cover tightly and store at room temperature.)*

To make the filling: Combine the dried apricots, water, and reserved apricot juice in a small saucepan. Bring to a boil. Reduce the heat to low. Simmer, covered, for about 15 minutes, until the apricots are very tender. Process the apricot mixture in a food processor until puréed. Cool completely; set aside.

To make the frosting: Beat the cream cheese and butter in a large bowl with an electric mixer at high speed until smooth. Beat in the pumpkin. Gradually add the confectioners' sugar, beating at low speed until blended. Beat on high speed until smooth.

To assemble: Place 1 cake layer, top side down, on a cake platter. Spread with a thin layer of the frosting then the apricot purée. Top with the second layer, top side up; gently press together. Spread a thin layer of frosting over the top and side of the cake. Spread the remaining frosting over the entire cake. Refrigerate, loosely covered, until ready to serve. Let stand at room temperature for 30 minutes before serving.

Makes 12 servings

Delicious Fruit Desserts

Banana

Peak Season: Although grown worldwide in tropical climates, most bananas sold in North America are imported from Central and South America. Unlike most fruit, bananas actually taste better when allowed to ripen off the plant. They are picked and shipped green, then ripen in climate controlled U.S. warehouses. The yellow Cavendish (or Giant Cavendish) banana is the main variety sold and is available year-round. Exotic varieties, such as Manzano, Saba, Brazilian, and the red Makabu, or Morado, are more seasonal.

Selection: Banana ripeness is a matter of taste—the riper the banana the sweeter the taste. Bananas that are yellow with a touch of green at either end are ripe enough to eat, although some people prefer to wait until the peels are flecked with brown spots. In general, select bananas with plump, evenly colored light green to yellow skins. Avoid any with large brown splotches or split skins. Green bananas need several days to ripen.

Storage: To ripen bananas, store them at room temperature since refrigeration halts the ripening process. Placing them in an open paper bag makes them ripen more quickly. Once ripe, refrigerate bananas for several days to prolong their freshness. Refrigeration darkens the peel, but has no effect on the fruit inside. Bananas bruise easily so don't place them in the bottom of a fruit basket. Hanging the fruit from a banana stand prevents bruising and extends the life of the bunch. Mashed bananas can be frozen for up to six months; stir in 1 teaspoon lemon juice for each banana to prevent browning.

Preparation: When a recipe calls for a ripe banana, the peel should be bright yellow with no green tips and few, if any, brown spots. In contrast, the peel of a very ripe banana has many brown spots and the banana's texture should be soft enough to mash easily.

To easily mash bananas, cut them into chunks and mash in a bowl with the back of a fork. Three medium bananas yields 2 cups sliced or $1^1/_3$ cups mashed.

Bananas turn brown when exposed to air or are refrigerated without their peels. If not using peeled bananas immediately, dip them in a mixture of lemon juice and water to prevent discoloration.

A Little History: Native to Asia, bananas have been grown for many thousands of years. Alexander the Great first discovered bananas in 327 B.C. during his conquest of India. Arab traders, and later Spanish and Portuguese explorers, spread them westward. In 1516, a Spanish friar planted the first banana root-stocks in the rich fertile soil of the Caribbean. Bananas were officially introduced to the United States at the 1876 Philadelphia Centennial Exhibition. Each banana was wrapped in foil and sold for ten cents. Today, bananas are America's most popular fruit.

Early bananas had tasteless flesh with bitter black seeds. Thankfully, they have been refined over the years into many delicious varieties that thrive in tropical climates around the world. Contrary to popular belief, bananas don't grow on trees but on very tall plants that produce one long stalk. At the end of the stalk is a large red flower with ten to fourteen hands of bananas. Once harvested, the plant dies and new shoots form another plant.

Banana Oatmeal Cookies

Looking for a new cookie recipe? These soft banana cookies packed with raisins, dates and walnuts are simply delicious!

Ingredients

- 1 1/2 cups flour
- 1 teaspoon cinnamon
- 1/2 teaspoon baking soda
- 1/2 teaspoon salt
- 1/4 teaspoon nutmeg
- 1/4 teaspoon ginger
- 3/4 cup raisins
- 3/4 cup chopped pitted dates
- 1 1/2 cups walnuts, toasted and chopped
- 3/4 cup (1 1/2 sticks) butter, softened
- 1 cup packed brown sugar
- 1 egg
- 2 very ripe bananas, mashed
- 1 3/4 cups old-fashioned oats

Preheat the oven to 375°F. Cover 2 cookie sheets with foil.

Sift together the flour, cinnamon, baking soda, salt, nutmeg, and ginger; set aside. Combine the raisins, dates, and 1 tablespoon of the flour mixture in a medium bowl, tossing until the fruit pieces are separated and coated with flour. Add the walnuts and toss again; set aside.

Beat the butter and brown sugar in a large bowl with an electric mixer at high speed until fluffy. Beat in the egg. Add the bananas and beat until well blended. Gradually add the flour mixture and oats, beating at low speed just until combined. Stir in the walnut mixture by hand.

Drop the dough by heaping tablespoonfuls 2 inches apart onto the prepared cookie sheets, mounding the dough high. Bake for 17 to 18 minutes, until lightly browned. Do not overbake; the cookies should be semisoft. Cool on the pans for 10 minutes. Remove to wire racks; cool completely.

Makes 3 dozen cookies

Bananas pack a nutrient punch. They are a good source of vitamin C, fiber, and potassium.

Banana Chocolate Bars

You might not be able to wait until these bars are cooled before devouring them!

Ingredients

- 2 **cups flour**
- 1 **cup old-fashioned oats**
- 1 **tablespoon baking powder**
- ³/4 **teaspoon salt**
- 1 **cup (2 sticks) butter, softened**
- 1 **cup sugar**
- 1 **cup packed brown sugar**
- 2 **eggs**
- 2 **very ripe bananas, mashed**
- 2 **teaspoons vanilla extract**
- 1 **(11 ¹/2-ounce) package semi-sweet chocolate chunks**
- 1 **cup walnuts, toasted and chopped**

Preheat the oven to 350°F. Spray a 13x9x2-inch baking pan with cooking spray.

Combine the flour, oats, baking powder and salt in a medium bowl; set aside.

Beat the butter and sugars in a large bowl with an electric mixer at high speed until fluffy. Add the eggs 1 at a time, beating well after each addition. Beat in the bananas and vanilla. Gradually add the flour mixture, beating at low speed just until combined. Stir in the chocolate chunks and walnuts by hand. Spread evenly in the prepared pan.

Bake for 45 minutes or until a wooden pick inserted into the center comes out clean. Cool completely in the pan on a wire rack. Cut into 24 bars.

Makes 2 dozen bars

*In India, bananas were called "Fruit of the Wise Men."
According to Indian legend, wise men meditated under
the shady, green leaves of banana plants.*

Bananas Foster

This is a fun dessert to make when you're having a romantic dinner for two. Simply double or triple the ingredients to serve a larger group.

Ingredients

1 1/2 teaspoons sugar

1 1/2 teaspoons cinnamon

3 tablespoons butter

1 cup packed brown sugar

2 large ripe bananas, peeled

3 tablespoons dark rum

4 scoops vanilla ice cream

Combine the sugar and cinnamon in small bowl; set aside. Melt the butter and brown sugar in a large skillet or flambé pan over medium heat. Cook until bubbly. Cut the bananas crosswise into halves, then cut each half lengthwise, forming 4 pieces. Place the bananas, cut sides down, in the pan; spoon the caramelized sugar mixture over them. Cook for 2 minutes.

Remove the pan from the heat. Add the rum. Return the pan to the heat and carefully ignite the rum using a long-stemmed match. Pour the cinnamon-sugar directly into the flame. As the flame dies down, remove the pan from the heat.

For each serving, place 2 scoops ice cream into a dessert bowl. Top with half the bananas and sauce. Serve immediately.

Makes 2 servings

Note: Since the rum is ignited in this recipe, *do not* use a nonstick skillet.

Americans consume about 33 pounds of bananas per person each year!

Banana Toffee Pudding

Everyone will love the bits of toffee candy in this banana pudding.

Pudding

2¹/₂ cups whole milk

6 egg yolks

³/₄ cup sugar

3 tablespoons cornstarch

1 teaspoon vanilla extract

30 vanilla wafers

3 ripe bananas, sliced

1 cup chopped English toffee candy bars

Meringue

4 egg whites, at room temperature

¹/₄ teaspoon cream of tartar

6 tablespoons sugar

To make the pudding: Bring the milk to a simmer in a heavy, medium saucepan over medium heat. Meanwhile, whisk the egg yolks, sugar, and cornstarch in a large bowl about 3 minutes, until the mixture thickens and turns pale yellow. Pour the hot milk into the egg mixture, whisking to combine. Pour the mixture back into the saucepan. Cook, whisking constantly, over medium heat about 3 minutes, until the pudding thickens and comes to a boil. Remove from the heat; stir in the vanilla. Cool slightly.

Arrange 15 of the vanilla wafers in a single layer on the bottom of a 2-quart soufflé or straight-sided baking dish. Layer half the banana slices, half the pudding and 1/2 cup of the toffee on top. Repeat the layers.

Preheat the oven to 400°F.

To make the meringue: Beat the egg whites and cream of tartar in a large bowl with an electric mixer at high speed until soft peaks form. Gradually add the sugar, beating constantly just until the meringue is stiff and shiny; do not overbeat. Spread evenly over the pudding.

Bake for 8 to 10 minutes, until the meringue is lightly browned. Cool on a wire rack for 15 minutes. Refrigerate, uncovered, 4 hours or until the pudding is cold.

Makes 6 to 8 servings

Tropical Banana Upside-Down Cake

This delicious twist on classic upside-down cake is packed with tropical treats.

Ingredients

- 4 tablespoons (¹/2 stick) butter
- ¹/2 cup packed brown sugar
- 2 large ripe bananas, cut diagonally into ¹/4-inch slices
- ¹/2 cup chopped pitted dates
- ¹/2 cup macadamia nuts, chopped
- ¹/2 cup flaked coconut
- 1 ¹/4 cups flour
- 1 ¹/2 teaspoons baking powder
- ¹/2 teaspoon salt
- ¹/3 cup shortening
- ¹/2 cup granulated sugar
- 1 egg
- 1 teaspoon vanilla extract
- ¹/2 cup milk

Vanilla ice cream (optional)

Preheat the oven to 350°F.

Melt the butter in a small saucepan over medium heat. Remove from the heat; stir in the brown sugar. Spread evenly on the bottom of a 9x1¹/2-inch round cake pan. Arrange the banana slices on top. Sprinkle the dates, macadamia nuts and coconut over the bananas; set aside.

Sift together the flour, baking powder and salt; set aside. Beat the shortening and granulated sugar in a large bowl with an electric mixer at high speed until well blended. Add the egg and vanilla; beat until fluffy. Add the flour mixture alternately with the milk, beating at medium speed after each addition. Pour the batter over the fruit, spreading evenly.

Bake for 45 to 50 minutes, until the cake is lightly browned and a wooden pick inserted into the center comes out clean. Cool in the pan for 5 minutes. Run a small knife between the cake and side of the pan. Carefully invert the cake onto an ovenproof or microwavable platter. Cool for 15 minutes. Serve warm with ice cream, if desired.

Makes 8 servings

Note: The cake can be baked up to 6 hours ahead. Reheat in a 350°F oven for 10 minutes or microwave on Medium for 2 minutes before serving.

*Plantains, which look like large green bananas,
are usually cooked and eaten as a vegetable.*

Banana, Raspberry & Chocolate Cakes

Bursting with raspberries, these mini cakes have a chocolate surprise inside!

Ingredients

- 6 ounces semisweet baking chocolate, chopped
- 2 tablespoons butter
- 1 (12-ounce) package frozen raspberries, thawed
- 1/2 cup (1 stick) butter, softened
- 3/4 cup sugar
- 2 eggs
- 1/4 cup milk
- 1 very ripe banana, mashed
- 1 teaspoon vanilla extract
- 1 cup flour
- 1/4 teaspoon salt
- 1 tablespoon sugar

Preheat the oven to 350°F. Grease 10 muffin cups.

Melt the chocolate and 2 tablespoons butter in a small heatproof bowl set over a saucepan of simmering water, stirring constantly until smooth. Remove the bowl from the pan; set aside to cool. Drain the raspberries, reserving the juice; set aside.

Beat 1/2 cup butter and 3/4 cup sugar in a large bowl with an electric mixer at high speed until well blended. Add the eggs, milk, banana, and vanilla; mix well. Stir in the flour and salt by hand. Gently fold in 3/4 cup of the drained raspberries. Spoon 1 heaping teaspoon of the batter into each muffin cup. Top with 1 teaspoon of the melted chocolate and another heaping teaspoon of the batter.

Bake for 20 minutes or until lightly browned around the edges. Cool in the muffin cups for 10 minutes. Run a small knife between the cakes and the sides of the cups. Remove from the cups to wire racks; cool slightly.

Process the remaining raspberries in a blender or food processor until puréed. Pour through a fine strainer set over a bowl to remove the seeds, pressing the purée through the strainer. Discard the seeds in the strainer. Add the reserved raspberry juice and 1 tablespoon sugar to the purée; stir to dissolve the sugar.

Place each warm cake on an individual plate. Pour the raspberry sauce around the cakes. Serve warm.

Makes 10 servings

Note: The cakes can be baked up to 1 day in advance. Reheat in a microwave oven on Medium for 2 minutes before serving.

Banana-Maple Cake

*When your bananas are too ripe to eat, treat your family
to this simply scrumptious cake.*

Cake

2 cups flour

³/₄ teaspoon baking soda

¹/₂ teaspoon baking powder

¹/₄ teaspoon salt

¹/₂ cup (1 stick) butter, softened

1 ¹/₂ cups sugar

2 eggs

³/₄ cup sour cream

1 cup mashed ripe bananas

¹/₃ cup milk

¹/₄ cup pure maple syrup

1 cup pecans, chopped

Frosting

1 (8-ounce) package cream
cheese, softened

²/₃ cup confectioners' sugar, sifted

¹/₂ cup sour cream

Preheat the oven to 350°F. Grease and flour a 13x9x2-inch baking pan.

To make the cake: Sift together the flour, baking soda, baking powder, and salt; set aside. Beat the butter and sugar in a large bowl with an electric mixer at high speed until fluffy. Add the eggs and beat until well blended. Beat in the sour cream, bananas, milk, and maple syrup. Gradually add the flour mixture, beating at low speed just until blended. Stir in the pecans by hand. Pour into the prepared pan, spreading evenly.

Bake for 30 minutes or until a wooden pick inserted into the center comes out clean. Cool completely in the pan on a wire rack.

To make the frosting: Beat the cream cheese, confectioners' sugar and sour cream in a large bowl with an electric mixer at high speed until smooth. Spread the frosting over the cake. Refrigerate, covered, until ready to serve. Refrigerate any leftover cake.

Makes 12 servings

Banana-Rum Cake

*This dense cake is similar to a pound cake but has less butter
and the added flavor of rum.*

Cake

2 1/2 cups flour

2 teaspoons baking powder

1 teaspoon baking soda

1 teaspoon cinnamon

1 3/4 cups packed brown sugar

3/4 cup (1 1/2 sticks) butter, softened

2 eggs

1 cup mashed ripe bananas

1/3 cup milk

1 tablespoon dark rum

Glaze

3/4 cup confectioners' sugar, sifted

2 tablespoons dark rum

1 tablespoon butter, melted

Preheat the oven to 375°F. Spray a 10-inch tube pan with cooking spray.

To make the cake: Sift together the flour, baking powder, baking soda, and cinnamon; set aside. Beat the brown sugar and butter in a large bowl with an electric mixer at high speed until fluffy. Add the eggs and beat well. Combine the bananas, milk, and rum in a small bowl. Add the flour mixture alternately with the banana mixture to the batter, beating at medium speed after each addition. Pour into the prepared pan, spreading evenly.

Bake for 1 hour or until a wooden pick inserted into the center of the cake comes out clean. Cool in the pan for 15 minutes. Remove from the pan to a wire rack; cool completely.

To make the glaze: Combine the confectioners' sugar, rum, and butter in a small bowl, mixing until smooth. Drizzle over the top of the cake.

Makes 16 servings

Banana-Blueberry Tart

This free-form rustic tart is easier to make than a classic pie.
Buttery macadamia nuts complement the fruit in this luscious dessert.

Ingredients

- 1 1/3 cups flour
- 1 teaspoon sugar
- 1/2 teaspoon salt
- 1/2 cup (1 stick) butter, cold and cut into small pieces
- 3 tablespoons ice water
- 1/2 cup macadamia nuts, chopped
- 3 ripe bananas, cut diagonally into 1/4-inch slices
- 1 cup fresh blueberries
- 1/2 cup sugar
- 1/2 teaspoon nutmeg
- 1 teaspoon water
- 1 egg yolk
- Whipped cream, as a garnish

Process the flour, sugar, and salt in a food processor until blended. Add the butter. Pulse until the mixture resembles coarse crumbs. Add the water; pulse just until moist clumps form, adding a little more water, if necessary. Do not overprocess. Gather the dough into a ball; flatten into a disk. Wrap in plastic wrap; refrigerate for 1 hour.

Preheat the oven to 375°F.

Roll out the dough to a 12-inch round between 2 sheets of parchment paper. Invert the pastry onto a baking sheet, keeping the bottom parchment in place. Remove and discard the top paper. Sprinkle half the macadamia nuts over the dough to within 2 inches of the edge. Arrange the banana slices over the nuts. Layer the blueberries and remaining nuts over the bananas. Combine the sugar and nutmeg in a small bowl. Sprinkle all but 1 tablespoon of the sugar mixture over the fruit. Fold the outer edge of the pastry over the fruit using the parchment paper as an aid. Overlap the pastry slightly while folding and press gently to seal (it will only partially cover the fruit). If the dough tears, press it back together. Whisk the egg yolk in a small bowl; brush over the crust. Sprinkle the crust and fruit with the remaining sugar mixture.

Bake for about 25 minutes, until the crust is browned. Cool for about 30 minutes on the baking sheet on a wire rack. Serve warm garnished with whipped cream.

Makes 8 servings

Banana Split Cheesecake

You'll find all your favorite banana-split flavors in this deliciously light cheesecake.

Crust

1 ½ cups graham cracker crumbs

3 tablespoons sugar

4 tablespoons (½ stick) butter, melted

Filling

2 (8-ounce) packages cream cheese, softened

2 (8-ounce) packages neufchâtel cream cheese, softened

1 cup sour cream

4 ripe bananas, mashed

¾ cup sugar

3 tablespoons flour

2 teaspoons vanilla extract

4 eggs

Toppings

1 (8-ounce) can crushed pineapple, drained

⅓ cup strawberry syrup

⅓ cup chocolate syrup

¼ cup pecans, chopped

16 maraschino cherries, drained

Preheat the oven to 325°F. Spray a 9-inch springform pan with cooking spray.

To prepare the crust: Combine the graham cracker crumbs, sugar, and butter in a small bowl. Toss with a fork until the crumbs are moistened. Press onto the bottom and about 1 inch up the side of the prepared pan; set aside.

To prepare the filling: Beat the cheeses and sour cream in a large bowl with an electric mixer at high speed until smooth. Add the bananas, sugar, flour, and vanilla; beat well. Add the eggs 1 at a time, beating well after each addition. Pour into the prepared crust.

Bake for 1 hour and 30 minutes or until the center barely moves when the pan is gently shaken. Cool completely in the pan on a wire rack. (The cake will rise up to the top of the pan during baking but then sinks down as it cools.) Run a knife between the cheesecake and the side of the pan. Release the side of the pan. Refrigerate, covered, for at least 8 hours. *(Cheesecake can be made 1 day ahead.)*

To serve, top each slice with pineapple, strawberry syrup, chocolate syrup, pecans, and a cherry.

Makes 16 servings

Tips: Set out all the toppings and let guests top their own "banana splits."

For best results, do not remove the bottom of the springform pan once the cheesecake is chilled. To prevent it from sliding around, place a rubber jar gripper between the pan bottom and serving plate.

To neatly cut cheesecake, dip a very sharp knife into a glass of hot water before each cut, or thoroughly wipe off the knife blade between each cut.

Black Bottom Banana Cream Pie

Layers of chocolate, banana, custard and whipped cream create a taste sensation.

Crust

1 1/2 **cups sifted flour**

  1/2 **teaspoon salt**

  1/4 **cup shortening, cold**

  1/4 **cup (1/2 stick) butter, cold and cut into small pieces**

   4 **to 5 tablespoons ice water, divided**

Chocolate Filling

  1 **tablespoon cornstarch**

  2 **tablespoons sugar**

  2 **tablespoons unsweetened cocoa**

  1/3 **cup whole milk**

  1/4 **cup semisweet chocolate chips**

(continued)

To make the crust: Combine the flour and salt in a large bowl. Cut in the shortening with a pastry blender or 2 knives until the mixture resembles coarse crumbs. Cut in the butter until the pieces become the size of small peas. Sprinkle 3 tablespoons water over the flour mixture; gently toss with a fork. Add enough of the remaining water, 1 tablespoon at a time, tossing until all the flour is moistened. Gather the dough into a ball; flatten into a disk. Wrap in plastic wrap; refrigerate for at least 1 hour. *(Pastry dough can be refrigerated for up to 3 days. Let the dough stand at room temperature to soften slightly before rolling.)*

Roll out the dough to a 12-inch round on a lightly floured surface. (The dough should be about 1/8 inch thick.) Transfer to a 9-inch pie plate. If the dough does not uniformly cover the side of the pan, cut off some excess dough and press it over the bare spots. Trim any excess dough to within 1 inch from the edge of the pan. Fold the dough under to form a smooth, even edge. Flute the edge by crimping it between your fingers or with the round end of a knife. Cover the pastry crust loosely with plastic wrap. Refrigerate for at least 1 hour or up to 24 hours.

Preheat the oven to 450°F.

Pierce the bottom of the crust all over with a fork to prevent the crust from puffing up. Bake for 15 to 18 minutes, until lightly browned. Cool completely on a wire rack.

To make the chocolate filling: Combine the cornstarch, sugar, and cocoa in a small saucepan. Whisk in the milk. Bring to a boil over medium heat, stirring constantly. Add the chocolate chips. Cook, stirring constantly, until melted. Spread the chocolate mixture on the bottom of the pie crust; set aside.

Black Bottom Banana Cream Pie (cont.)

Custard

- 1 **cup whole milk**
- 2 **egg yolks**
- 1/2 **cup sugar**
- 2 **tablespoons cornstarch**
- 1/2 **teaspoon vanilla extract**

- 3 **large ripe bananas, sliced**
- 1 **cup heavy cream**
- 1/4 **teaspoon vanilla extract**

To make the custard: Bring the milk to a simmer in a heavy, medium saucepan over medium heat. Meanwhile, whisk the egg yolks, sugar, and cornstarch in a large bowl about 3 minutes, until the mixture thickens and turns pale yellow. Pour the hot milk into the egg mixture, whisking to combine. Pour the mixture back into the saucepan. Cook, whisking constantly, over medium heat about 3 minutes, until the pudding thickens and comes to a boil. Remove from the heat; stir in 2 teaspoons vanilla. Cool slightly.

Arrange the banana slices over the chocolate layer. Spread the custard over the bananas. Cover with plastic wrap, gently pressing it directly onto the surface of the custard. Refrigerate for 4 to 8 hours.

Beat the cream in a large bowl with an electric mixer until soft peaks form. Add 1/4 teaspoon vanilla and beat until stiff peaks form; do not overbeat. Spread evenly over the custard. Refrigerate until ready to serve.

Makes 8 servings

*In sixteenth century England, hasty pudding was made
of milk cooked with flour, sugar, and butter. A forerunner
of cornstarch pudding or custard, it could be prepared
more quickly than the traditional boiled pudding.*

Peanut Butter & Banana Pie

Remember peanut butter and banana sandwiches? Now everyone can enjoy this classic combination in an easy, scrumptious pie.

Crust

1 1/2 cups graham cracker crumbs

1/2 cup peanuts

3 tablespoons sugar

3 tablespoons butter, melted

Filling

1 1/2 cups whole milk

6 egg yolks

1/3 cup sugar

2 tablespoons cornstarch

1/4 cup smooth peanut butter

1 teaspoon vanilla extract

2 ripe bananas, sliced

1 cup heavy cream

1/4 teaspoon vanilla extract

Preheat the oven to 350°F. Spray a 9-inch pie plate with cooking spray.

To make the crust: Place the graham cracker crumbs in a large bowl. Process the peanuts until finely ground; do not overprocess. Stir the ground peanuts and sugar into the graham cracker crumbs. Add the butter and toss with a fork until the crumbs are moistened. Press onto the bottom and side of the prepared pie plate. Bake for 10 minutes; cool on a wire rack.

To make the filling: Bring the milk to a simmer in a heavy, medium saucepan over medium heat. Meanwhile, whisk the egg yolks, sugar, and cornstarch in a large bowl about 3 minutes, until the mixture thickens and turns pale yellow. Pour the hot milk into the egg mixture, whisking to combine. Pour the mixture back into the saucepan. Cook, whisking constantly, over medium heat about 3 minutes, until the pudding thickens and comes to a boil. Remove from the heat; stir in the peanut butter and 1 teaspoon vanilla. Cool slightly.

Arrange the banana slices on the bottom of the prepared crust. Spread the pudding evenly over the bananas. Cover with plastic wrap, gently pressing it directly onto the surface of the pudding. Refrigerate for 4 to 8 hours.

Beat the cream in a large bowl with an electric mixer until soft peaks form. Add 1/4 teaspoon vanilla and beat until stiff peaks form; do not overbeat. Spread over the top of the pie, making decorative peaks. Refrigerate until ready to serve.

Makes 8 servings

Delicious Fruit Desserts

Blueberry

Peak Season: Michigan and Indiana harvest 40% of all the cultivated blueberries in America. New Jersey, Florida, Georgia, Louisiana, Mississippi, North Carolina, Oregon, and Washington grow the remainder. The North American harvest, which includes berries from British Columbia, runs from mid-April through early October with the peak harvest in July. In the winter, fresh blueberries are imported from South America, Australia, and New Zealand.

There are two types of blueberries: cultivated and wild. Bluecrop is the major cultivated blueberry variety found in most grocery stores. Jersey, Tifblue, Blueray, Bluetta, Duke, and Elliott are other cultivated varieties that can be found at fruit stands and farmers' markets. Wild blueberries are smaller and grow on more compact bushes than cultivated berries. They also have a brighter blue color and often a more tart flavor.

Because blueberries grow on bushes, they are either carefully hand picked to sell fresh or mechanically harvested for freezing. This accounts for the higher cost of fresh berries. Many blueberry farms now allow you to pick your own at bargain prices.

Selection: Whether you pick your own blueberries or buy them at the store, look for firm, plump berries with a deep-blue color. A powdery white film on the surface is a sign of freshness. Avoid any that are tinged with green or red as this indicates underripe berries. If packaged in a carton, check the bottom to make sure it is free of any juice stains.

Storage: Remove the blueberries from their container and sort through them to remove any that are overripe, crushed, or moldy. Discard any tiny stems as well. Refrigerate the berries, unwashed, in an airtight container for up to one week. As blueberries dry out, they will begin to wrinkle and shrink.

Freeze washed and dried blueberries in a single layer on a baking sheet. Once frozen, transfer the berries to freezer bags and freeze for up to nine months.

Preparation: Gently rinse blueberries under cold water just before using. Spread them out on paper towels to dry. To bake with frozen berries, use them straight from the freezer. Do not thaw them before adding to batters to prevent them from leaving blue streaks of juice.

A Little History: Wild blueberries are a Native American fruit, growing throughout America and gathered for centuries by both Native Americans and colonists. In the Northeast, blueberries were revered and much folklore developed around them. Parts of the blueberry plant were used as medicine—a tea made from the leaves of the plant was thought to benefit the blood and blueberry juice was used to treat coughs. The juice also made an excellent dye for baskets and cloth. Early settlers relied on the berries as a staple food, eating them fresh off the bush and adding them to soups, stews, and many other dishes. During the Civil War, soldiers ate canned wild blueberries from Maine to prevent scurvy and drank a blueberry beverage to conserve food supplies. By the late 1800's, the commercial blueberry industry had begun in the Northeast.

Blueberries in Irish Cream

Blueberries and Irish cream liqueur make a simple but elegant dessert.

Ingredients

- 2 cups fresh blueberries
- 1 (6-ounce) container low-fat vanilla yogurt
- $^1/_4$ cup Irish cream liqueur

Divide the blueberries evenly among 4 dessert dishes. Combine the yogurt and liqueur in a small bowl. Divide evenly over the berries in each dish. Serve immediately or refrigerate, covered, for up to 8 hours.

Makes 4 servings

Blueberry Sauce

Serve this delicious sauce over ice cream, pudding, and pound cake or as a crêpe filling.

Ingredients

- $^1/_2$ cup crème de cassis liqueur
- 1 tablespoon cornstarch
- 1 tablespoon fresh lemon juice
- 1 tablespoon butter
- 2 cups fresh blueberries

Combine the liqueur, cornstarch, and lemon juice in a small bowl. Melt the butter in a heavy, medium saucepan over low heat. Gradually stir in the liqueur mixture. Cook for 5 minutes, until the mixture thickens, stirring constantly. Add the blueberries. Cook for 8 minutes, until the berries begin to pop, stirring constantly. Remove from the heat; cool to room temperature. Store, covered, in the refrigerator for up to 5 days. Reheat before serving.

Makes 2 cups

Tip: To make crepes, see recipe on page 118.

Blueberry Bars

These easy bars satisfy blueberry cravings in the summer or winter.

Crust

  2 cups old-fashioned oats

  1 cup flour

  ¹/₃ cup packed light brown sugar

  ¹/₃ cup walnuts, chopped

  ¹/₂ teaspoon baking soda

  ¹/₂ teaspoon salt

  ³/₄ cup (1 ¹/₂ sticks) butter, melted

Filling

  ¹/₃ cup sugar

  2 tablespoons flour

  1 teaspoon grated lemon zest

  3 cups fresh or frozen blueberries

  2 tablespoons fresh lemon juice

Preheat the oven to 350°F. Spray a 13x9x2-inch baking dish with cooking spray.

To make the crust: Combine the oats, flour, brown sugar, walnuts, baking soda, and salt in a medium bowl. Add the butter and stir until crumbly. Reserve ³/₄ cup of the crust mixture. Press the remaining crust mixture evenly onto the bottom of the prepared dish. Bake for 10 minutes or until puffed and lightly browned. Press down the higher outside edges of the crust; cool completely on a wire rack. Maintain the oven temperature at 350°F.

To make the filling: Combine the sugar, flour, and lemon zest in a small bowl; set aside. Combine the blueberries and lemon juice in a medium saucepan. Cook over medium heat for about 10 minutes, until the berries begin to pop, stirring often. Add the sugar mixture; cook for about 10 minutes, until the filling thickens, stirring often. Spread the hot filling evenly over the entire crust. Sprinkle the reserved crust mixture over the filling. Bake for 15 to 20 minutes, until the topping is lightly browned. Cool on a wire rack for 1 hour before cutting into 36 bars.

Makes 3 dozen bars

One cup of fresh blueberries provides over 20% of the recommended daily value of vitamin C and is only about 80 calories.

Blueberry-Raspberry Tart

This delectable tart is so easy and requires no baking!

Crust

2 cups vanilla wafer crumbs

6 tablespoons butter, melted

Filling

1 (8-ounce) package cream cheese, softened

1/2 cup sugar

1 (6-ounce) container raspberry yogurt

3 cups fresh blueberries

Spray a 9-inch tart pan with a removable bottom with cooking spray.

To make the crust: Combine the vanilla wafer crumbs and butter in a large bowl. Toss with a fork until the crumbs are moistened. Press onto the bottom and side of the prepared pan; set aside.

To make the filling: Beat the cream cheese and sugar in a medium bowl with an electric mixer at high speed until smooth. Add the yogurt and beat at low speed until well blended. Pour into the crust, spreading evenly. Refrigerate, loosely covered, for 4 hours or until set.

To serve, gently loosen and remove the edge of the pan. Top with the blueberries.

Makes 8 servings

Tip: Substitute a 9-inch pie plate for the tart pan, if desired.

Fresh blueberries are considered a good source of fiber.
Just one cup provides three grams of dietary fiber.

Blueberry & Dried Apricot Crisp

Fresh blueberries, warm from the oven with a brown sugar topping,
are truly scrumptious!

Topping

- ¹/₂ cup old-fashioned oats
- ¹/₂ cup flour
- ¹/₂ cup packed light brown sugar
- ¹/₂ cup walnuts, chopped
- 2 teaspoons cinnamon
- 1 teaspoon nutmeg
- 6 tablespoons butter, cold and cut into small pieces

Filling

- 5 cups fresh blueberries
- 1 cup dried apricots, chopped
- ¹/₄ cup sugar
- Grated zest of 1 lemon
- Juice of 1 lemon

Preheat the oven to 325°F. Spray a 9x9x2-inch baking dish with cooking spray.

To make the topping: Combine the oats, flour, brown sugar, walnuts, cinnamon, and nutmeg in a medium bowl. Cut in the butter with a pastry blender or 2 knives until the mixture resembles coarse crumbs; set aside.

To make the filling: Combine the blueberries and dried apricots in a medium bowl. Add the sugar, lemon zest, and juice; toss to coat. Spoon into the prepared baking dish. Sprinkle the topping evenly over the fruit, lightly pressing it in place. Bake for 45 minutes or until the filling is bubbling. Serve warm or at room temperature.

Makes 8 servings

Tip: When you need a quick dessert for four, cut the ingredient amounts in half and divide the filling and topping among four 8-ounce ramekins. Reduce the baking time to 25 minutes.

While huckleberries and blueberries often are used
interchangeably there are some differences.
Huckleberries have a more tart flavor than blueberries
and only grow wild, so they are not widely available fresh.

Blueberry Cobbler

Nothing says summer like this juicy blueberry cobbler.

Topping

- 1 cup flour
- 1 teaspoon baking powder
- 1/2 teaspoon cinnamon
- 1/8 teaspoon nutmeg
- 1/2 cup sugar
- 4 tablespoons (1/2 stick) butter, softened
- 1 egg
- 1/2 teaspoon vanilla extract

Filling

- 4 cups fresh blueberries
- 1/2 cup sugar
- 1 teaspoon fresh lemon juice

- 1 tablespoon sugar
- Vanilla ice cream (optional)

Preheat the oven to 350°F. Spray an 8x8x2-inch baking dish with cooking spray.

To make the topping: Combine the flour, baking powder, cinnamon, and nutmeg in a bowl; set aside. Beat the sugar and butter in a large bowl with an electric mixer at high speed until smooth. Beat in the egg and vanilla. Stir in the flour mixture by hand just until a soft dough forms; set aside.

To make the filling: Combine the blueberries, sugar, and lemon juice in a large bowl. Spoon evenly into the prepared baking dish.

Drop the dough topping by heaping tablespoonfuls onto the filling, spacing evenly. Sprinkle the topping with 1 tablespoon sugar. Bake for about 50 minutes, until the filling is bubbling and a wooden pick inserted into the topping comes out clean. Serve warm with ice cream, if desired.

Makes 6 servings

*The National Blueberry Festival
is held every August in South Haven, Michigan.
See www.blueberryfestival.com for more information.*

Blueberry-Lemon Pizza Tart

This pizza-style tart is a fun and easy way to enjoy fresh blueberries.

Crust

- 1 1/2 cups flour
- 1/2 cup sugar
- 1 tablespoon baking powder
- 1 tablespoon grated lemon zest
  Pinch salt
- 2 tablespoons butter, cold and cut into small pieces
- 1 egg yolk
- 2 teaspoons water
- 1 teaspoon vanilla extract
- 2/3 cup ricotta cheese

Filling

- 1 1/2 cups (12 ounces) cream cheese, softened
- 1/4 cup sugar
- 1 (6-ounce) container lemon yogurt
- 3 cups fresh blueberries

To make the crust: Combine the flour, sugar, baking powder, lemon zest, and salt in a large bowl. Cut in the butter with a pastry blender or 2 knives until the mixture resembles coarse crumbs. Whisk the egg yolk, water, and vanilla in a medium bowl. Add the ricotta cheese and stir until blended. Add to the flour mixture. Mix with your hands for about 3 minutes, until a soft dough forms. Gather the dough into a ball; flatten into a disk. Wrap in plastic wrap; refrigerate for at least 2 hours. *(Pastry dough can be refrigerated for up to 3 days.)*

Preheat the oven to 350°F. Spray a 12-inch pizza pan with cooking spray.

Unwrap the dough, keeping the plastic wrap over the top. Roll out to a 13-inch circle on a lightly floured surface. Remove the plastic wrap. Transfer to the prepared pan. Fold in the edge of the dough to make a 1-inch rim. Bake for 25 minutes or until lightly browned. Cool completely on a wire rack.

To make the filling: Beat the cream cheese and sugar in a medium bowl with an electric mixer at high speed until smooth. Add the yogurt and beat at low speed until well blended. Spread evenly over the crust. Top with the blueberries. Refrigerate, loosely covered, for 1 hour or until ready to serve.

Makes 8 servings

Note: Substitute an equal amount of mixed fresh berries (blueberries, strawberries, raspberries, blackberries) for the blueberries, if desired.

Blueberry Crumble Cake

This simple, crumb-topped cake is bursting with blueberries.

Topping

- 1 cup flour
- 1/4 cup packed light brown sugar
- 1 teaspoon cinnamon
- 6 tablespoons butter, cold and cut into small pieces
- 1/2 cup walnuts, chopped

Cake

- 2 cups flour
- 1 1/2 teaspoons baking powder
- 1/4 teaspoon salt
- 3/4 cup sugar
- 1/2 cup (1 stick) butter, softened
- 1 teaspoon vanilla extract
- 1 egg
- 1/2 cup milk
- 4 cups fresh blueberries

Preheat the oven to 350°F. Grease and flour a 10-inch springform pan.

To make the topping: Combine the flour, brown sugar, and cinnamon in a medium bowl. Cut in the butter with a pastry blender or 2 knives until the mixture resembles coarse crumbs. Stir in the walnuts; set aside.

To make the cake: Sift together the flour, baking powder, and salt; set aside. Beat the sugar, butter, and vanilla in a large bowl with an electric mixer at high speed until well blended. Beat in the egg. Add the flour mixture alternately with the milk, beating at medium speed after each addition. Gently fold in the blueberries by hand. Pour into the prepared pan, spreading evenly. Sprinkle the topping evenly over the batter.

Bake for 1 hour to 1 hour and 10 minutes, until a wooden pick inserted into the center comes out clean. Cool in the pan for 10 minutes. Run a small knife between the cake and side of the pan. Release the side of the pan. Cool on a wire rack for at least 30 minutes before serving. Serve warm or at room temperature.

Makes 10 servings

Blueberry-Lemon Pound Cake
with Lemon Sauce

This luscious pound cake tastes great with or without the lemon sauce.

Cake

- 2 cups flour
- 1 teaspoon baking powder
- $1/2$ teaspoon baking soda
-   Pinch salt
- 1 cup (2 sticks) butter, softened
- 1 cup sugar
- 1 teaspoon vanilla extract
- 4 eggs, separated
- 1 (6-ounce) container low-fat lemon yogurt
- 1 tablespoon grated lemon zest
- 2 cups fresh blueberries

Lemon Sauce

- $1/2$ cup sugar
- 1 tablespoon cornstarch
- 1 cup water
- 1 tablespoon butter
- $1/2$ teaspoon grated lemon zest
- 2 tablespoons fresh lemon juice

Preheat the oven to 350°F. Grease and flour a 9x5x3-inch loaf pan with cooking spray.

To make the cake: Sift together the flour, baking powder, baking soda, and salt; set aside. Beat the butter, sugar, and vanilla in a large bowl with an electric mixer at high speed until well blended. Add the egg yolks 1 at a time, beating well after each addition. Add the yogurt and lemon zest; beat at medium speed until combined. Gradually add the flour mixture, stirring with a spatula until blended.

Beat the egg whites in a large bowl with an electric mixer at high speed until soft peaks form. Fold into the batter with a spatula until just combined. Gently fold in the blueberries until just combined. Pour into the prepared pan, spreading evenly.

Bake for 1 hour and 10 minutes or until lightly browned and a wooden pick inserted into the center comes out clean. Cool in the pan for 1 hour. Run a small knife between the cake and the sides of the pan. Remove from the pan to a wire rack, then invert top side up; cool completely.

To make the lemon sauce: Combine the sugar and cornstarch in a small bowl. Bring the water to a boil in a small saucepan. Gradually whisk in the sugar mixture. Cook over medium-high heat, whisking constantly, until the sauce thickens and turns clear. Remove from the heat and whisk in the butter, lemon zest and juice; cool slightly.

Serve cake slices topped with the warm lemon sauce.

Makes 10 servings

Note: The sauce can be made up to 6 hours ahead. Refrigerate, covered, until ready to serve. Reheat in a microwave oven on HIGH for about 1 minute before serving.

Blueberry Crumble Pie

A graham cracker crust and topping replace the usual
pastry and streusel in this enticing blueberry pie.

Crust

   2 **cups graham cracker crumbs**

   4 **tablespoons sugar**

   5 **tablespoons butter, melted**

Filling

   5 **cups fresh blueberries**

   1 **cup sour cream**

   3/4 **cup packed light brown sugar**

   3 **tablespoons flour**

1 1/2 **teaspoons vanilla extract**

   1/4 **teaspoon grated lemon zest**

Preheat the oven to 375°F. Spray a 9-inch pie plate with cooking spray.

To make the crust: Combine the graham cracker crumbs and sugar in a large bowl. Add the butter and toss with a fork until the crumbs are moistened. Reserve 1/2 cup of the crust mixture. Press the remaining crust mixture onto the bottom and side of the prepared pie plate.

To make the filling: Pour the blueberries into the crust, spreading them out evenly. Combine the sour cream, brown sugar, flour, vanilla, and lemon zest in a medium bowl. Spread evenly over the blueberries. Sprinkle the reserved crust mixture over the top of the pie.

Bake for 40 minutes or until the filling is set and the topping is lightly browned. Cool completely on a wire rack. Serve at room temperature. Refrigerate any leftover pie.

Makes 8 servings

Blueberry Cheesecake

Blueberries adorn the top and filling of this creamy cheesecake.

Crust

1 ½ **cups shortbread cookie crumbs**

1 **cup blanched whole almonds**

2 **tablespoons sugar**

¼ **cup (½ stick) butter, melted**

Filling

2 **cups fresh blueberries**

4 **(8-ounce) packages cream cheese, softened**

¾ **cup sugar**

4 **eggs**

½ **cup sour cream**

1 **teaspoon vanilla extract**

Topping

2 **cups fresh blueberries**

⅔ **cup blueberry jam**

1 **cup heavy cream**

1 **tablespoon sugar**

Preheat the oven to 350°F. Spray a 10-inch springform pan with cooking spray.

To make the crust: Place the cookie crumbs in a large bowl. Process the almonds in a food processor until finely ground; do not overprocess. Stir the ground almonds and sugar into the cookie crumbs. Add the butter and toss with a fork until the crumbs are moistened. Press onto the bottom and three-fourths of the way up the side of the prepared pan. Bake for 15 minutes; cool on a wire rack. Maintain the oven temperature at 350°F.

To make the filling: Process the blueberries in a food processor until coarsely chopped; set aside. Beat the cream cheese and sugar in the large bowl of an electric mixer at high speed until smooth. Add the eggs 1 at a time, beating well after each addition. Add the sour cream and vanilla; beat until well blended. Stir in the blueberries by hand. Pour the filling evenly over the crust.

Bake for 1 hour and 20 minutes or until the center barely moves when the pan is gently shaken. Cool completely in the pan on a wire rack. Run a knife between the cheesecake and the side of the pan. Release the side of the pan. Refrigerate, covered, for at least 8 hours.

To make the topping: Place the blueberries in a medium bowl. Heat the jam in a small saucepan over low heat until melted. Pour over the berries and toss to coat; cool completely. Beat the cream in a large bowl with an electric mixer until soft peaks form. Add the sugar and beat until stiff peaks form; do not overbeat. Spread the whipped cream evenly over the top of the cheesecake. Mound the blueberry mixture in the center of the cheesecake. Refrigerate for 1 hour before serving.

Makes 12 servings

Tip: For best results, do not remove the bottom of the springform pan once the cheesecake is chilled. To prevent it from sliding around, place a rubber jar gripper between the pan bottom and serving plate.

Buttermilk Layer Cake
with Blueberry Filling

Even a small bite of this cake is a taste sensation.

Filling

3 cups fresh blueberries

$^1/_4$ cup sugar

1 $^1/_2$ teaspoons fresh lemon juice

Cake

2 cups cake flour

1 tablespoon baking powder

$^1/_4$ teaspoon salt

1 cup sugar

$^1/_2$ cup (1 stick) butter, softened

1 $^1/_2$ teaspoons vanilla extract

4 egg yolks

$^2/_3$ cup buttermilk

Frosting

$^1/_2$ cup (4 ounces) cream cheese, softened

$^1/_2$ cup (1 stick) butter, softened

3 cups confectioners' sugar, sifted

2 tablespoons frozen orange juice concentrate, thawed

$^1/_2$ teaspoon vanilla extract

To make the filling: Combine the blueberries, sugar, and lemon juice in a large saucepan. Bring to a boil over high heat, stirring until the sugar dissolves. Cook for about 8 minutes, stirring constantly, until the mixture thickens. Remove the pan from the heat. Mash the berries coarsely with a fork. Refrigerate for at least 1 hour. *(Filling can be made 1 day ahead.)*

Preheat the oven to 350°F. Spray two 9-inch round cake pans with cooking spray. Line the bottoms with waxed paper; spray the paper with cooking spray. Dust the pans with flour.

To make the cake: Sift together the cake flour, baking powder, and salt; set aside. Beat the sugar, butter, and vanilla in a large bowl with an electric mixer at medium speed for about 5 minutes, until well blended. Add the egg yolks 1 at a time, beating well after each addition. Add the flour mixture alternately with the buttermilk, beating at medium speed after each addition. Divide the batter evenly between the prepared pans.

Bake for 30 minutes or until a wooden pick inserted into the centers comes out clean. Cool in the pans for 10 minutes. Run a small knife between the cakes and sides of the pans. Remove from the pans to wire racks. Remove the waxed paper, then invert the layers top sides up; cool completely. *(Cake can be made 1 day ahead. Cover tightly and store at room temperature.)*

To make the frosting: Beat the cream cheese and butter in a large bowl with an electric mixer at high speed until smooth. Gradually add the confectioners' sugar at low speed until well blended. Add the orange juice concentrate and vanilla. Beat at high speed until smooth.

To assemble: Place 1 cake layer, top side down, on a cake platter. Spread with the blueberry filling to within $^1/_2$ inch of the edge. Top with the second layer, top side up; gently press together. Spread a thin layer of frosting over the top and side of the cake. Spread the remaining frosting over the entire cake. Refrigerate, loosely covered, until ready to serve. Let stand at room temperature for 30 minutes before serving.

Makes 12 servings

Delicious Fruit Desserts

Blueberry Pie

Keep this classic double-crust pie recipe handy when blueberry season arrives.

Crust

- 2 cups sifted flour
- 1 teaspoon salt
- 1/3 cup shortening, cold
- 1/3 cup butter, cold and cut into small pieces
- 5 to 7 tablespoons ice water, divided

Filling

- 3/4 cup sugar
- 3 tablespoons quick-cooking tapioca
- 2 teaspoons grated lemon zest
- 2 tablespoons fresh lemon juice
- 5 cups fresh blueberries
- 2 tablespoons butter, cut into small pieces

- 1 egg white, lightly beaten
- 1 tablespoon sugar

Vanilla ice cream (optional)

To make the crust: Combine the flour and salt in a large bowl. Cut in the shortening with a pastry blender or 2 knives until the mixture resembles coarse crumbs. Cut in the butter until the pieces become the size of small peas. Sprinkle 4 tablespoons water over the flour mixture; gently toss with a fork. Add enough of the remaining water, 1 tablespoon at a time, tossing until all the flour is moistened. Gather the dough into 2 balls, one slightly smaller than the other; flatten each into a disk. Wrap in plastic wrap; refrigerate for at least 1 hour. *(Pastry dough can be refrigerated for up to 3 days. Let the dough stand at room temperature to soften slightly before rolling.)*

Roll out the larger dough disk to a 12-inch round on a lightly floured surface. (The dough should be about 1/8 inch thick.) Transfer to a 9-inch pie plate. If the dough does not uniformly cover the side of the pan, cut off some excess dough and press it over the bare spots. Trim any excess dough to within 1/2 inch from the edge of the pan. Cover the pastry crust loosely with plastic wrap. Refrigerate for at least 1 hour or up to 24 hours.

Preheat the oven to 400°F.

To make the filling: Combine the sugar, tapioca, lemon zest, and juice in a large bowl. Add the blueberries and toss to coat. Let stand for 15 minutes. Spoon evenly into the prepared pastry crust; dot with the butter.

Roll out the second dough disk to a 10-inch round on a lightly floured surface. Place over the blueberries. Trim any excess dough to within 1 inch from the edge of the pan. Fold the top crust edge under the bottom edge, pressing together to seal. Flute the edge by crimping it between your fingers or with the round end of a knife. Cut several slits in the top crust to allow steam to escape. Brush the top with the egg white; sprinkle with 1 tablespoon sugar.

Place the pie on a baking sheet. Bake on the lower oven rack for 50 to 60 minutes, until the crust is lightly browned and the juices are bubbling. (If the crust browns too quickly, cover the edge with foil.) Cool on a wire rack for at least 2 hours. Serve warm or at room temperature with ice cream, if desired.

Makes 8 servings

Blueberry, Blackberry & Tart Cherry Pie

Fresh summer fruit peeks out of the lattice crust on this scrumptious pie.

Crust

- 2 cups sifted flour
- 1 teaspoon salt
- 1/3 cup shortening, cold
- 1/3 cup butter, cold and cut into small pieces
- 5 to 7 tablespoons ice water, divided

Filling

- 1 cup sugar
- 1/4 cup cornstarch
- 2 tablespoons orange marmalade, melted
- 1 tablespoon grated orange zest
- 1/4 teaspoon ground allspice
- 2 cups fresh blueberries
- 1 1/2 cups fresh blackberries
- 1 1/2 cups fresh tart cherries, pitted

- 1 egg white, lightly beaten
- 1 teaspoon sugar

Vanilla ice cream (optional)

To make the crust: Combine the flour and salt in a large bowl. Cut in the shortening with a pastry blender or 2 knives until the mixture resembles coarse crumbs. Cut in the butter until the pieces become the size of small peas. Sprinkle 4 tablespoons water over the flour mixture; gently toss with a fork. Add enough of the remaining water, 1 tablespoon at a time, tossing until all the flour is moistened. Gather the dough into 2 balls, one slightly smaller than the other; flatten each into a disk. Wrap in plastic wrap; refrigerate for at least 1 hour. *(Pastry dough can be refrigerated for up to 3 days. Let the dough stand at room temperature to soften slightly before rolling.)*

Roll out the larger dough disk to a 12-inch round on a lightly floured surface. (The dough should be about 1/8 inch thick.) Transfer to a 9-inch pie plate. If the dough does not uniformly cover the side of the pan, cut off some excess dough and press it over the bare spots. Trim any excess dough to within 1/2 inch from the edge of the pan. Cover the pastry crust loosely with plastic wrap. Refrigerate for at least 1 hour or up to 24 hours.

Preheat the oven to 400°F.

To make the filling: Combine the sugar, cornstarch, marmalade, orange zest, and allspice in a large bowl. Add the berries and cherries; toss gently to coat. Spoon evenly into the prepared pastry crust.

Roll out the second dough disk to a 10-inch round on a lightly floured surface. Cut into ten 1/2-inch-wide strips. Place 5 strips over the filling, spacing evenly. Place the remaining 5 strips diagonally over the top, forming a lattice. Trim any excess dough even with the edge of the bottom crust. Fold the lattice ends under the bottom edge, pressing together to seal. Flute the edge by crimping it between your fingers or with the round end of a knife. Brush the lattice top with the egg white; sprinkle with 1 teaspoon sugar.

Place the pie on a baking sheet. Bake on the lower oven rack for 1 hour and 15 minutes or until the crust is lightly browned and the juices are bubbling. (If the crust browns too quickly, cover the edge with foil.) Cool on a wire rack for at least 2 hours. Serve warm or at room temperature with ice cream, if desired.

Makes 8 servings

Cherry

Peak Season: Cherry growing in the U.S. is divided into two regions: the west/northwest and the east. Washington, California, and Oregon are the largest producers of sweet cherries. Tart cherries are primarily produced in the Grand Traverse Bay area of Michigan and Door County in Wisconsin. They are also grown commercially in New York, Pennsylvania, and Utah. Most fresh cherries are available from May through August, though tart cherries have a shorter season than sweet varieties. Frozen cherries and dried sweet and tart cherries are sold year-round in grocery and gourmet food stores.

Selection:
There are two types of cherries: sweet and tart. When buying cherries, first decide how they are to be used and select suitable varieties.
- **Sweet cherries** are larger and firmer than tart cherries and can be eaten out of hand as well as cooked.
- **Tart cherries** are smaller and softer than sweet cherries. They are too tart to be eaten raw and are used for preserves, pies, cobblers, and other desserts. Since most canned pie fillings are made with tart cherries, they are also called pie cherries.

Cherries are usually sold loose, so take the time to sort through them. Choose firm, plump cherries with smooth, shiny skins and green stems (cherries with stems attached are fresher). Because cherries don't ripen further after picking, avoid those that are small, hard, or poorly colored, as well as any that are soft or sticky with brown spots. Leaves of cherry trees are poisonous and should not be used even as a garnish.

Storage:
Refrigerate cherries, unwashed, in a bowl loosely covered with plastic wrap for up to 3 days. Avoid placing cherries in the sun or warm areas, as they may quickly become limp.

Fresh cherries can also be stored in the freezer for up to 10 months. Remove the stems, wash, pat dry and remove the pits. Place the cherries on a baking sheet in a single layer, spacing them apart so they don't touch. Once frozen, place the cherries in a plastic freezer bag. There's no need to thaw the cherries before cooking or baking.

(continued)

A Little History: Cherries, a favorite summer fruit, have pleased palates around the world for centuries. In fact, archeologists have found cherry pits dating back to the Stone Age in many caves in Europe. Sweet cherries were named after the town Cerasus in Turkey, where they were first cultivated. Brought to America in the 1600's, cherry trees were planted in the gardens of French settlers in the upper Midwest. Modern day U.S. cherry production began in the mid 1800's in Michigan and Oregon. Ornamental cherry trees remain a favorite for home gardens. In 1912, Japan presented President Taft with a gift of ornamental cherry trees. The cherry blossoms are so beautiful that each spring tourists travel to Washington, D.C. just to see the trees—now numbering well over three thousand.

More about Cherries

Preparation: Other than a quick rinse under cold water, fresh cherries can be eaten out of hand with no preparation at all. To use them in cooking or baking, remove the pits with a cherry pitter or by hand with a paring knife. Work over a bowl to collect the juices. To remove the pits by hand, make a slit top to bottom around the circumference of each cherry. Pull it apart and pop out the pit with the tip of a paring knife. This method results in the cherries being both pitted and halved, which is the way many recipes call for them. Don't squeeze the pit out as this smashes the fruit and causes the juice to splatter. It's a good idea to protect clothing while pitting cherries as the juice can stain. Squeeze fresh lemon juice over your hands to remove any cherry stains from them.

1 pound fresh sweet cherries, pitted and stemmed = about $1^3/4$ cups
1 pound fresh tart cherries, pitted and stemmed = about $2^1/4$ cups
1 (15-ounce) can tart cherries, drained = $1^1/2$ cups
1 (10-ounce) package frozen cherries = 1 cup

Varieties

Sweet cherries: Bing cherries are the most common and popular of the sweet cherries. They are large and plump with a firm texture and shiny mahogany-red skins. The pits are relatively small and the flesh has a rich, sweet flavor. Other sweet dark-colored cherry varieties include Lambert, Van, Black Tartarian, and Windsor. Two light-colored sweet cherry varieties are Royal Ann and Ranier. Royal Anns are mainly used to produce maraschino cherries. They are pitted, macerated in a sugar syrup, and dyed bright red or green.

Tart cherries: Montmorency cherries, which originated in the Montmorency Valley of France, are the most common of the tart cherries and are primarily sold fresh rather than canned. They have medium-red skins and very juicy beige-colored flesh. Other tart cherries varieties include Early Richmond and Morello. Since most tart cherry varieties are used for canning, they are usually available fresh only at farmers' markets and fruit stands.

Brandied Cherries

This is a great way to preserve fresh summer cherries for a treat in the winter.

Ingredients

- 1 **pound fresh sweet or tart cherries**
- **Sugar**
- 2 **cups kirsch or brandy**

Stem and pit the cherries, if desired. (If the pits are left in, cut the stems short.) Layer the cherries and sugar (use $1/2$ cup sugar for sweet cherries; $3/4$ cup sugar for tart cherries) in a 1-quart jar with a tight-fitting lid. Pour the brandy over the cherries and sugar. Cover the jar, twisting the lid to seal tightly. Gently shake the jar several times to dissolve the sugar. Store in a cool place for 1 month before serving, turning the jar upside down daily during the first week to distribute the liquid. Refrigerate the cherries after 1 month. They will keep, in the refrigerator, for 3 more months. Serve over ice cream, cheesecake, pound cake, waffles, and pancakes. They are also delicious served with roasted meats and poultry.

Makes 4 cups (cherries with liquid)

Notes: Kirsch, the German word for cherry, also refers to cherry brandy. It is often called kirschwasser.

Double or triple this recipe if you have more cherries on hand.

Tip: The sweetened, cherry-flavored brandy improves with time and can be enjoyed on its own as a liqueur.

Cherries are low in calories (about 75 per cup), fat free and a good source of potassium, vitamin C, and fiber.

Cherry Chocolate Cookies

Cherry and chocolate are a classic flavor combination.
Watch out, these cookies disappear fast!

Ingredients

- 1 (12-ounce) package semisweet chocolate chips, divided
- 1 1/2 cups flour
- 1/4 cup unsweetened cocoa
- 1 teaspoon baking powder
- 1/4 teaspoon salt
- 3/4 cup sugar
- 2/3 cup butter, softened
- 2 eggs
- 1 teaspoon vanilla extract
- 1 3/4 cups old-fashioned oats
- 48 maraschino cherries, drained and patted dry

Preheat the oven to 350°F.

Melt 1 cup of the chocolate chips in a small heatproof bowl set over a small saucepan of simmering water, stirring constantly until smooth. Remove the bowl from the pan; set aside to cool.

Sift together the flour, cocoa, baking powder, and salt; set aside. Beat the sugar and butter in a large bowl with an electric mixer at high speed until well blended. Beat in the eggs, vanilla, and melted chocolate. Stir in the flour mixture and oats by hand. Cover the bowl with plastic wrap. Refrigerate the dough for 1 hour.

Shape the dough into forty-eight 1-inch balls. Place 2 inches apart on ungreased cookie sheets. Press the center of each ball with your thumb. Place 1 maraschino cherry into each indentation. Bake for 10 to 12 minutes, until set. Cool on the pans for 5 minutes. Remove to wire racks; cool completely.

Melt the remaining 1 cup chocolate chips in a small heatproof bowl set over a small saucepan of simmering water, stirring constantly until smooth. Drizzle over the cookies.

Makes 4 dozen cookies

Maraschino cherries are made from light-colored
Royal Anns that are pitted, macerated in a sugar syrup
and dyed bright green or red.

Cherry Pecan Bars

Pecan pie lovers will enjoy these bars, too!

Crust

1 3/4 **cups flour**

2/3 **cup confectioners' sugar**

1/4 **cup cornstarch**

1/2 **teaspoon salt**

3/4 **cup (1 1/2 sticks) butter, cold and cut into small pieces**

Topping

1/4 **cup (1/2 stick) butter**

1 1/4 **cups packed light brown sugar**

1/2 **cup light corn syrup**

4 **cups pecans, coarsely chopped**

2 **cups dried cherries**

3/4 **cup heavy cream**

2 **teaspoons vanilla extract**

Preheat the oven to 350°F. Line a 13x9x2-inch baking pan with foil, leaving a 1-inch overhang on all sides. Butter the foil.

To make the crust: Process the flour, confectioners' sugar, cornstarch, and salt in a food processor until blended. Add the butter. Pulse until moist clumps form. Press onto the bottom of the prepared pan. Bake for 25 to 30 minutes, until lightly browned. Cool completely on a wire rack. *Reduce the oven temperature to 325°F.*

To make the topping: Melt the butter in a large saucepan over low heat. Add the brown sugar and corn syrup. Cook over medium heat, stirring constantly, until the sugar dissolves and the mixture comes to a boil. Boil for 1 minute. Stir in the pecans, dried cherries, and cream. Return to a boil. Cook for 3 minutes, stirring constantly, until the mixture thickens. Remove from the heat. Stir in the vanilla. Spread evenly over the crust. Bake at 325°F for 20 to 25 minutes, until the topping darkens and is bubbling. Cool completely in the pan on a wire rack. Using the foil, lift from the pan to a cutting board. Cut into 2x1-inch bars with a sharp knife.

Makes 4 dozen bars

Tip: Store bars layered between sheets of waxed paper in an airtight container at room temperature.

Medical research is revealing that the deep red pigments that give cherries their beautiful color may also help ease the pain of arthritis, gout, and even headaches.

Cherries Jubilee

Use fresh or canned cherries to prepare this simple, classic dessert.

Ingredients

- ¹/₄ **cup water**
- 2 **teaspoons cornstarch**
  Juice of 1 lemon
- ³/₄ **cup water**
- ¹/₄ **cup sugar**
- 1 **pound fresh Bing cherries, pitted**
- ¹/₄ **cup kirsch or brandy**
- 1 **quart vanilla ice cream**

Pour ¹/₄ cup water into a small bowl. Whisk in the cornstarch until smooth; set aside. Pour the lemon juice into a large skillet or flambé pan. Add the ³/₄ cup water and sugar. Bring to a boil over medium heat, stirring to dissolve the sugar. Stir in the cornstarch mixture and cook for 2 to 3 minutes, until thickened. Add the cherries. Reduce the heat to low. Cook for 5 to 7 minutes, until just tender; do not overcook. Remove the pan from the heat. Add the kirsch. Return the pan to the heat and carefully ignite the kirsch using a long-stemmed match. Shake the pan to turn the cherries. (The flame will die quickly.) As the flame dies down, remove the pan from the heat.

To serve, place 2 scoops ice cream in each of 6 dessert bowls. Top with the cherries and sauce. Serve immediately.

Makes 6 servings

Note: Since the kirsch is ignited in this recipe, *do not* use a nonstick skillet.

Canned Cherry Variation: Substitute 2 (15-ounce) cans Bing cherries for the fresh cherries. Drain the cherries, reserving the syrup. Proceed as directed above, substituting the reserved cherry syrup for the water, omitting the ¹/₄ cup sugar, and reducing the cherry cooking time to 2 minutes.

Cherries were Queen Victoria's favorite fruit.
This dish was created in 1887 for her Golden Jubilee—
a celebration of her fiftieth year on the throne.

Cherry-Almond Crisp

Crunchy almonds complement this scrumptious cherry crisp.

Topping

- ³/₄ **cup flour**
- ¹/₂ **cup packed brown sugar**
- ¹/₄ **teaspoon cinnamon**
- ¹/₄ **teaspoon ground allspice**
- 6 **tablespoons butter, cold and cut into small pieces**
- ²/₃ **cup slivered almonds**

Filling

- 2 **tablespoons sugar**
- 1 **tablespoon cornstarch**
- 1 ¹/₂ **pounds fresh sweet cherries, pitted**
- OR 2 **(15-ounce) cans Bing cherries, drained**
- ¹/₄ **teaspoon almond extract**
- 3 **tablespoons currant jelly, melted**

Preheat the oven to 375°F. Spray a 9x9x2-inch baking dish with cooking spray.

To make the topping: Combine the flour, brown sugar, cinnamon, and allspice in a medium bowl. Cut in the butter with a pastry blender or 2 knives until the mixture resembles coarse crumbs. Stir in the almonds; set aside.

To make the filling: Combine the sugar and cornstarch in a medium bowl. Add the cherries; toss to coat. Let stand for 10 minutes. Stir in the almond extract and currant jelly. Spoon the cherries with their juices into the prepared baking dish. Sprinkle the topping evenly over the fruit, lightly pressing it in place. Bake for 45 to 50 minutes, until the filling is bubbling. Serve warm or at room temperature.

Makes 6 servings

*The National Cherry Festival is held every
July in Traverse City, Michigan,
the cherry-producing capital of the world.
See www.cherryfestival.org for more information.*

Cherry & Blueberry Cobbler

Two favorite fruits pair up for this delicious treat.

Topping

- ³/₄ cup flour
- ¹/₃ cup sugar
- ¹/₄ cup cornmeal
- 1 ¹/₂ teaspoons baking powder
- ¹/₈ teaspoon salt
- 3 tablespoons butter, cold and cut into small pieces
- ¹/₃ cup milk
- 1 egg

Filling

- 3 tablespoons sugar
- 2 tablespoons quick-cooking tapioca
- 1 ¹/₂ pounds fresh tart cherries, pitted
- OR 3 (14 ¹/₂-ounce) cans red tart cherries, drained
- 3 cups fresh or frozen blueberries

Whipped cream or vanilla ice cream (optional)

Preheat the oven to 375°F. Spray a 9x9x2-inch baking dish with cooking spray.

To make the topping: Combine the flour, sugar, cornmeal, baking powder, and salt in a medium bowl. Cut in the butter with a pastry blender or 2 knives until the mixture resembles coarse crumbs. Beat the milk and egg in a small bowl. Stir into the flour mixture just until a stiff dough forms; set aside.

To make the filling: Combine the sugar and tapioca in a large bowl. Stir in the cherries and blueberries. Spoon evenly into the prepared baking dish.

Drop the dough topping by heaping tablespoonfuls onto the filling, spacing evenly. Bake for 35 to 40 minutes, until the filling is bubbling and a wooden pick inserted into the topping comes out clean. Serve warm or at room temperature with whipped cream or ice cream.

Makes 6 servings

Cherry Clafouti

Fresh cherries baked in a light custard are an easy and delicious dessert.

Ingredients

- 1 **pound fresh sweet cherries, pitted**

OR 1 **(16-ounce) package frozen pitted sweet cherries, thawed and drained**

- 2 **tablespoons sugar**
- 1 **tablespoon cornstarch**
- 2 to 3 **tablespoons brandy (optional)**
- $^1/_3$ **cup slivered almonds**
- 4 **eggs**
- $^1/_2$ **cup sugar**
- $^2/_3$ **cup flour**
- 1 **cup whole milk**
- $^1/_4$ **cup ($^1/_2$ stick) butter, melted**
- 1 **teaspoon vanilla extract**
- $^1/_2$ **teaspoon almond extract**

Preheat the oven to 325°F. Generously butter six 8-ounce ramekins or custard cups. Place on a baking sheet spaced apart.

Combine the cherries, 2 tablespoons sugar and cornstarch in a large bowl. Divide the cherries evenly among the prepared ramekins. Drizzle with the brandy, if desired.

Process the almonds in a food processor until finely chopped; set aside. Beat the eggs and $^1/_2$ cup sugar in a large bowl with an electric mixer at high speed until well blended. Add the almonds and flour; beat until combined. Beat in the milk, butter, vanilla, and almond extract. Divide the batter evenly over the cherries.

Bake for 40 minutes or until set in the centers and lightly browned. Serve warm or at room temperature.

Makes 6 servings

*This is a classic peasant pudding from the
Limousin region in central France.
It is traditionally made with unpitted black cherries
and served during the grape harvest.*

Molten Chocolate Cakes
with Cherry Sauce

Luscious chocolate lava pours out of the centers of these individual cakes.

Ingredients

- 6 ounces bittersweet baking chocolate, chopped
- ½ cup (1 stick) butter, cut into small pieces
- 3 eggs
- 3 egg yolks
- 2 teaspoons vanilla extract
- 1½ cups confectioners' sugar, sifted
- ½ cup flour, sifted
- 1 (15-ounce) can Bing cherries, undrained
- ¼ cup sugar
- 2 tablespoons kirsch or brandy
- ¼ teaspoon almond extract

Preheat the oven to 425°F. Butter four 8-ounce ramekins or custard cups. Place on a baking sheet spaced apart.

Melt the chocolate and butter in a small heavy saucepan over low heat, stirring constantly until smooth. Remove from the heat; cool slightly.

Beat the eggs, egg yolks, and vanilla in a large bowl with an electric mixer at high speed for 1 minute. Add the confectioners' sugar and beat for about 5 minutes, until the mixture thickens. Stir in the chocolate mixture. Gently fold the flour in by hand. Divide the batter evenly among the prepared ramekins.

Bake for 15 to 18 minutes, until the tops are set but move slightly when the ramekins are gently shaken. Let stand for 5 minutes.

Meanwhile, combine the cherries with their juice, sugar, kirsch, and almond extract in a medium saucepan. Cook over medium heat until the sugar dissolves.

To serve, carefully invert each ramekin onto an individual plate. Serve immediately topped with the cherry sauce.

Makes 4 servings

Delicious Fruit Desserts

Cherry Cake

The flavors of almond paste and dried cherries create
a delightful cake for afternoon tea.

Ingredients

- 2 **cups flour**
- 2 **teaspoons baking powder**
- 3 **eggs**
- 2/3 **cup sugar**
- 1 **(8-ounce) can almond paste**
- 1/2 **cup vegetable oil**
- 1/2 **cup milk**
- 1 **cup dried cherries**

Preheat the oven to 350°F. Grease and flour a 9-inch springform pan.

Sift together the flour and baking powder; set aside. Beat the eggs and sugar in a large bowl with an electric mixer at medium speed until well blended. Add the almond paste and beat until smooth. Beat in the oil and milk. Add the flour mixture and beat at low speed until well blended. Stir in the dried cherries by hand. Pour into the prepared pan, spreading evenly.

Bake for 55 minutes or until a wooden pick inserted into the center comes out clean. Cool in the pan on a wire rack for 15 minutes. Run a knife between the cake and the side of the pan. Release the side of the pan. Cool completely. Remove the bottom of the pan from the cake before serving.

Makes 12 servings

Elegant tea parties became fashionable in the mid 1800's.
At that time lunch was eaten quite early in the day and
dinner wasn't served until 8 or 9 o'clock at night.
Refreshments served with tea in the late afternoon
provided sustenance until dinnertime.

Cherry Cheesecake

A chocolate crust and cherries in the filling make this cheesecake a dream!

Crust

- 2 **cups chocolate graham cracker crumbs**
- 6 **tablespoons butter, melted**

Filling

- 1 **(15-ounce) can Bing cherries, drained**
- 4 **(8-ounce) packages cream cheese, softened**
- 1 **cup sugar**
- 4 **eggs**
- 1 **cup sour cream**
- 2 **teaspoons vanilla extract**

Preheat the oven to 350°F. Spray a 10-inch springform pan with cooking spray. Wrap the outside of the pan with 2 layers of foil; place on a baking sheet.

To make the crust: Combine the graham cracker crumbs and butter in a medium bowl. Toss with a fork until the crumbs are moistened. Press onto the bottom and three-fourths of the way up the side of the prepared pan. Bake for 8 minutes; cool on a wire rack. Maintain the oven temperature at 350°F.

To make the filling: Process the cherries in a food processor until coarsely chopped; set aside. Beat the cream cheese and sugar in a large bowl with an electric mixer at high speed until smooth. Add the eggs 1 at a time, beating well after each addition. Beat in the sour cream, vanilla, and cherries. Pour into the prepared crust.

Bake for about 1 hour and 20 minutes, until the center barely moves when the pan is gently shaken. Remove the foil from the pan. Cool completely in the pan on a wire rack. Run a knife between the cheesecake and the side of the pan. Release the side of the pan. Refrigerate, covered, for at least 8 hours. Let stand at room temperature for 30 minutes before serving.

Makes 12 servings

Tips: For best results, do not remove the bottom of the spring-form pan once the cheesecake is chilled. To prevent it from sliding around, place a rubber jar gripper between the pan bottom and serving plate.

To neatly cut cheesecake, dip a very sharp knife into a glass of hot water before each cut, or thoroughly wipe off the knife blade between each cut.

Rustic Cherry Tart

A free-form cornmeal crust is the perfect setting for luscious cherries.

Ingredients

- 1 1/3 **cups flour**
- 1/3 **cup cornmeal**
- 3 **tablespoons sugar**
- 1/4 **teaspoon salt**
- 1/2 **cup (1 stick) butter, cold and cut into small pieces**
- 4 **to 5 tablespoons ice water, divided**
- 3 **(15-ounce) cans Bing cherries, drained**
- 1 **teaspoon almond extract**
- 2 **tablespoons sugar**
- 1 **egg, beaten**
- 1 **teaspoon sugar**
- **Vanilla ice cream (optional)**

Combine the flour, cornmeal, 3 tablespoons sugar, and salt in a medium bowl. Cut in the butter with a pastry blender or 2 knives until the mixture resembles coarse crumbs. Sprinkle 4 tablespoons water over the flour mixture; gently toss with a fork. Add enough of the remaining water until the flour is moistened. Knead the dough in the bowl 4 or 5 times, until all the flour is incorporated. Gather the dough into a ball; flatten into a disk. Wrap in plastic wrap; refrigerate for 1 hour.

Preheat the oven to 425°F.

Combine the cherries and almond extract in a large bowl. Sprinkle with 2 tablespoons sugar and toss to coat; set aside.

Roll out the dough to a 13-inch round between 2 sheets of parchment paper. Remove and discard the top paper. Slide the pastry round onto a baking sheet, keeping the bottom paper in place. Using a slotted spoon, transfer the cherry mixture to the center of the pastry, spreading to within 2 inches of the edge; reserve the cherry juices. Fold the outer edge of the pastry over the cherries using the parchment paper as an aid. Overlap the pastry slightly while folding and press gently to seal (it will only partially cover the cherries). If the dough tears, press it back together. Whisk the egg in a small bowl; brush over the crust. Sprinkle 1 teaspoon sugar over the crust and fruit. Pour the reserved juices over the cherries.

Bake for 35 to 45 minutes, until the crust is browned and the cherries are bubbling. Cool for about 30 minutes on the baking sheet on a wire rack. Serve warm with ice cream, if desired.

Makes 8 servings

Black Forest Cake

This delicious traditional German cake makes a beautiful presentation.

Cake

2 1/4 **cups cake flour**

  1/2 **cup unsweetened cocoa**

   1 **tablespoon baking powder**

   1 **cup (2 sticks) butter, softened**

   1 **cup granulated sugar**

   2 **teaspoons vanilla extract**

   3 **eggs**

   1 **cup milk**

Filling

   1 **pound fresh Bing cherries, pitted**

OR 1 **(15-ounce) can Bing cherries, well drained**

  3/4 **cup kirsch or brandy, divided**

   3 **tablespoons granulated sugar**

   1 **cup heavy cream**

   3 **tablespoons confectioners' sugar, sifted**

(continued)

Preheat the oven to 350°F. Grease and flour two 9-inch round cake pans.

To make the cake: Sift together the cake flour, cocoa, and baking powder; set aside. Beat the butter, granulated sugar, and vanilla in a large bowl with an electric mixer at high speed until well blended. Add the eggs 1 at a time, beating well after each addition. Add the flour mixture alternately with the milk, beating at medium speed after each addition. Divide the batter evenly between the prepared pans.

Bake for about 30 minutes, until a wooden pick inserted into the centers comes out clean. Cool in the pans for 10 minutes. Run a small knife between the cakes and the sides of the pans. Remove from the pans to wire racks; cool completely. *(Cake can be made 1 day ahead. Cover tightly and store at room temperature.)*

To make the filling: Place the cherries in a medium bowl. Pour 1/2 cup of the kirsch over the cherries. Let stand at room temperature for at least 1 hour or up to 24 hours.

Combine the remaining 1/4 cup kirsch and granulated sugar in a small saucepan. Bring to a boil. Cook for about 5 minutes, until the sugar is dissolved and the mixture is syrupy. Remove from the heat; cool the syrup completely.

Beat the cream in a large bowl with an electric mixer until soft peaks form. Add the confectioners' sugar and beat until stiff peaks form; do not overbeat. Refrigerate, covered, until ready to use.

To assemble: Place 1 cake layer, top side down, on a cake platter. Brush with half of the kirsch syrup; spread with half of the whipped cream. Drain the cherries well and place them over the whipped cream. Top with the second layer, top side up. Refrigerate the cake and remaining whipped cream, covered, while preparing the icing and chocolate curls.

Black Forest Cake (cont.)

Icing & Chocolate Curls

¹/₂ **cup heavy cream**

8 **ounces bittersweet baking chocolate, chopped and divided**

To make the icing and chocolate curls: Bring the cream to a boil in a heavy, small saucepan. Place 4 ounces of the chocolate in a large heatproof bowl. Pour the hot cream over the chocolate and stir gently with a spatula until the chocolate is completely melted and shiny. Quickly spread the warm icing over the top of the cake, allowing some to drip down the sides. Refrigerate for about 20 minutes, until the chocolate is set.

Melt the remaining 4 ounces chocolate in a small heatproof bowl set over a small saucepan of simmering water, stirring constantly until smooth. Remove the bowl from the pan; wipe any moisture from the bottom of the bowl. Pour the chocolate onto a baking pan and spread into a thin layer. Let the chocolate cool slightly at room temperature until barely set; do not refrigerate. Holding a metal spatula upside down, slip the edge under the chocolate and push firmly along the pan to create chocolate curls. If the chocolate gets too firm to curl, soften it by heating the bottom of the pan briefly with a blow dryer. Refrigerate chocolate curls for 15 minutes or until firm.

To finish: Spread the remaining whipped cream around the side of the cake, making decorative peaks in between the icing. (Or use a pastry bag fitted with a large star tip to pipe the whipped cream onto the cake.) Carefully press the chocolate curls into the whipped cream around the side of the cake.

Makes 12 servings

Note: Grated chocolate may be substituted for the chocolate curls. Grate the chocolate pieces on a box grater and press into the whipped cream with your hands.

Tip: To easily cut 12 equal slices, first cut the cake in half, then cut each half into 6 slices.

Cherry-Almond Trifle

Layers of cake, custard, and cherries make this summertime treat irresistible.

Cake

- 1 (8-ounce) can almond paste
- 1 cup sugar
- 1 cup (2 sticks) butter, softened and cut into pieces
- 2 teaspoons vanilla extract
- 4 eggs
- 1/4 cup milk
- 1 cup flour
- 1 1/2 teaspoons baking powder
- 1/4 teaspoon salt

Cherries

- 2 cups fresh Bing cherries, pitted and halved
- 1/2 cup orange juice
- 1/4 cup sugar
- 1 tablespoon cornstarch
- 1/4 teaspoon cinnamon
- 1 1/4 teaspoons amaretto liqueur
- 1/4 teaspoon vanilla extract

(continued)

For best results, prepare the cherries, cake, and custard a day ahead and assemble the trifle the afternoon it's served.

Preheat the oven to 325°F. Spray two 9-inch round cake pans with cooking spray. Line the bottoms with waxed paper; spray the paper with cooking spray. Dust the pans with flour.

To make the cake: Process the almond paste and sugar in a food processor until the mixture resembles fine crumbs. Add the butter and vanilla; process until well blended. Add the eggs 1 at a time, processing after each addition. Add the milk; process until well blended. Add the flour, baking powder, and salt. Pulse just until combined; do not overprocess. Divide the batter evenly between the prepared pans.

Bake for about 1 hour, until lightly browned and a wooden pick inserted into the centers comes out clean. (This cake is dense and does not rise very high.) Cool in the pans for 10 minutes. Run a small knife between the cakes and the sides of the pans. Remove from the pans to wire racks; cool completely. Cover and store at room temperature overnight.

To make the cherries: Combine the cherries, orange juice, sugar, cornstarch, and cinnamon in a medium saucepan. Cook over medium heat until the sugar dissolves and the mixture comes to a boil, stirring constantly. Reduce the heat to low; simmer for about 20 minutes, until thickened, stirring frequently. Remove from the heat. Stir in the amaretto and vanilla; cool completely. Refrigerate, covered, until ready to use. *(Cherries can be made 3 days ahead.)*

Delicious Fruit Desserts

Cherry-Almond Trifle (cont.)

Custard

1 1/2 cups whole milk

6 egg yolks

1/3 cup sugar

2 tablespoons cornstarch

1 teaspoon vanilla extract

3 cups chopped fresh Bing cherries, divided

1 cup heavy cream, whipped to stiff peaks

10 fresh Bing cherries with stems, as a garnish

To make the custard: Bring the milk to a simmer in a heavy, medium saucepan over medium heat. Meanwhile, whisk the egg yolks, sugar, and cornstarch in a large bowl about 3 minutes, until the mixture thickens and turns pale yellow. Pour the hot milk into the egg mixture, whisking to combine. Pour the mixture back into the saucepan. Cook, whisking constantly, over medium heat about 3 minutes, until the pudding thickens and comes to a boil. Remove from the heat; stir in the vanilla. Cool slightly. Pour the custard into a medium bowl; cover with plastic wrap, gently pressing it directly onto the surface of the pudding. Refrigerate 4 hours or overnight.

To assemble: Cut each cake layer horizontally into halves. (Only 3 of the 4 halves will be used.) Cover the bottom of a 3-quart trifle dish or straight-sided glass bowl with 1 cake layer, cutting it to fit if necessary. Spread 1/2 cup of the cooked cherries over the cake to the side of the bowl. Spread a generous cup of custard over the cherries. Top with 1 cup of the chopped cherries. Repeat layering 2 times, reserving 1/2 cup of the cooked cherries. Spread the whipped cream over the top, mounding it slightly around the edge. Spoon the remaining cooked cherries in the center of the whipped cream. Refrigerate, covered, for 4 to 8 hours before serving. Just before serving, garnish the top with the stemmed cherries.

Makes 16 servings

Tips: To easily cut a cake layer horizontally, wrap a long piece of unflavored dental floss tightly around the perimeter of the cake where it should be split. Cross the ends of the floss and slowly but firmly pull on each end. The floss will cut cleanly and evenly through the cake.

Cut the leftover cake into wedges and serve with Blueberry Sauce (page 48).

Cherry Crumble Pie

Fresh sweet cherries, flaky pastry, and a crunchy streusel topping—
this is pie heaven!

Crust

- 1 1/2 cups sifted flour
- 1/2 teaspoon salt
- 1/4 cup shortening, cold
- 1/4 cup (1/2 stick) butter, cold and cut into small pieces
- 4 to 5 tablespoons ice water, divided

Filling

- 3 pounds fresh sweet cherries, pitted
- 2/3 cup sugar
- 3 tablespoons quick-cooking tapioca
- 1 tablespoon kirsch or brandy

Topping

- 1/2 cup flour
- 1/2 cup packed light brown sugar
- 1/2 teaspoon cinnamon
- 1/2 cup (1 stick) butter, cold and cut into small pieces
- 3/4 cup old-fashioned oats
- 1/2 cup sliced almonds

Vanilla ice cream (optional)

To make the crust: Combine the flour and salt in a large bowl. Cut in the shortening with a pastry blender or 2 knives until the mixture resembles coarse crumbs. Cut in the butter until the pieces become the size of small peas. Sprinkle 3 tablespoons water over the flour mixture; gently toss with a fork. Add enough of the remaining water, 1 tablespoon at a time, tossing until all the flour is moistened. Gather the dough into a ball; flatten into a disk. Wrap in plastic wrap; refrigerate for at least 1 hour. *(Pastry dough can be refrigerated for up to 3 days. Let the dough stand at room temperature to soften slightly before rolling.)*

Roll out the dough to a 12-inch round on a lightly floured surface. (The dough should be about 1/8 inch thick.) Transfer to a 9-inch pie plate. If the dough does not uniformly cover the side of the pan, cut off some excess dough and press it over the bare spots. Trim any excess dough to within 1 inch from the edge of the pan. Fold the dough under to form a smooth, even edge. Flute the edge by crimping it between your fingers or with the round end of a knife. Cover the pastry crust loosely with plastic wrap. Refrigerate for at least 1 hour or up to 24 hours.

To make the filling: Combine the cherries with their juice, sugar, tapioca, and kirsch in a large bowl. Let stand for about 30 minutes, until the tapioca looks translucent, stirring occasionally.

Preheat the oven to 425°F.

To make the topping: Combine the flour, brown sugar, and cinnamon in a large bowl. Cut in the butter with a pastry blender or 2 knives until the mixture resembles coarse crumbs. Stir in the oats and almonds.

Pour the cherries into the crust. Sprinkle the topping evenly over the cherries, lightly pressing it in place.

Place the pie on a baking sheet. Bake for 15 minutes. *Reduce the oven temperature to 375°F.* Bake for 40 to 45 minutes more, until the crust is browned. (If the crust browns too quickly, cover the edge with foil.) Serve warm or at room temperature with ice cream, if desired.

Makes 8 servings

Cranberry

Peak Season: Harvested in late September and early October, fresh cranberries are in grocery stores through December. Since their fresh season is so short, many cooks buy extra bags to freeze and use throughout the year.

Selection: Cranberries are usually sold in 12-ounce plastic bags, making it impossible to select individual berries. Purchase bags that contain mostly firm, plump, and dark red berries.

Storage: Refrigerate fresh cranberries in their unopened plastic bag for up to one month. Once opened, wrap any remaining berries tightly in plastic wrap. Fresh cranberries can also be frozen for up to one year. Freeze them, unwashed, in the original bag or an airtight freezer container.

Preparation: Rinse fresh or frozen cranberries under cold water just before using them. Discard any that are soft, shriveled, or discolored. It's not necessary to thaw frozen berries before adding them to most recipes. To easily chop fresh or frozen cranberries, pulse them in a food processor to the desired texture. One 12-ounce bag yields about 3 cups whole berries or 2 1/2 cups chopped.

A Little History: Cranberries are a Native American fruit grown in bogs on trailing vines that thrive in the special soil and water of wetlands. At harvest time, cranberry bogs are flooded with water and the berries float to the surface where they are gently beaten off the vines by machines. Native Americans first used these tart, red, wild berries for food, fabric dye, and as a healing agent. American settlers adopted these uses and this versatile berry also became a valuable bartering tool. Originally named craneberries by the Pilgrims because their small, pink blossoms resembled the heads of sandhill cranes, cranberries are also called bounceberries due to their unique ability to bounce when fresh. Rich in vitamin C, cranberries were carried by American whalers and mariners on their voyages to prevent scurvy. In 1810, Captain Henry Hall of Massachusetts became the first person to successfully cultivate cranberries. By 1871 the first U.S. cranberry growers association was formed, and farmers now harvest about 43,000 acres of cranberries each year. Cranberries are commercially grown in Massachusetts, New Jersey, Wisconsin, Oregon, and Washington and are available fresh, dried, and processed into juice and sauces.

Chocolate-Covered Dried Cranberries

Dried cranberries drenched in chocolate
are a delicious flavor duo and an easy treat to prepare.

Ingredients

- **8 ounces semisweet or white baking chocolate**
- **1 (6-ounce) package dried cranberries**

Cover the bottom of a baking sheet with waxed paper.

Melt the chocolate in a medium heatproof bowl set over a saucepan of simmering water, stirring constantly until smooth. Remove the bowl from the pan. Add the dried cranberries and stir until coated with chocolate. Drop the chocolate-covered cranberries by heaping teaspoonfuls 1 inch apart onto the prepared pan, forming mounds. Scrape any remaining chocolate from the bowl with a spatula and pour it over the cranberries.

Refrigerate for 15 minutes to set the chocolate. Remove the mounds from the waxed paper and store in an airtight container in the refrigerator.

Makes about 16 pieces

Dried cranberries can be substituted for raisins
in most baking recipes.

Cranberry & White Chocolate Chunk Cookies

Try these irresistible cookies as a change of pace from ordinary chocolate chip cookies.

Ingredients

- 1 1/2 **cups flour**
- 1 **teaspoon baking soda**
- 1/2 **teaspoon salt**
- 2/3 **cup butter, softened**
- 2/3 **cup packed brown sugar**
- 2 **eggs**
- 1 1/2 **cups old-fashioned oats**
- 1 **cup dried cranberries**
- 1 **cup white chocolate chips**
- 1/2 **cup walnuts, chopped**

Preheat the oven to 375°F.

Sift together the flour, baking soda, and salt; set aside. Beat the butter and brown sugar in a large bowl with an electric mixer at high speed until well blended. Add the eggs and beat well. Gradually add the flour mixture, beating at low speed just until combined. Stir in the oats, dried cranberries, white chocolate chips, and walnuts by hand.

Drop the dough by rounded teaspoonfuls onto ungreased cookie sheets. Bake for 10 to 12 minutes, until lightly browned. Cool on a wire rack.

Makes 2 dozen cookies

Fresh cranberries are a good source of vitamins A and C. With only 47 calories per cup, they contain antioxidants that may help protect against cancer and reduce the risk of heart disease and stroke. They also contain lots of fiber, which aids in digestion and helps lower cholesterol.

Cranberry Blondies

If you like blondies, you'll love them with dried cranberries!

Ingredients

- 1 ¼ cups flour
- ½ teaspoon baking powder
- ⅛ teaspoon salt
- 1 cup packed brown sugar
- 6 tablespoons butter, softened
- 1 egg
- 2 teaspoons vanilla extract
- 1 cup dried cranberries

Preheat the oven to 350°F. Spray an 8x8x2-inch baking pan with cooking spray.

Sift together the flour, baking powder, and salt; set aside. Beat the brown sugar and butter in a large bowl with an electric mixer at high speed until well blended. Add the egg and vanilla; beat well. Gradually add the flour mixture, beating at low speed just until combined. Stir in the dried cranberries by hand. Spread evenly in the prepared pan.

Bake for 30 to 35 minutes, until a wooden pick inserted into the center comes out clean. Cool completely in the pan on a wire rack. Cut into 16 squares.

Makes 16 blondies

Every September the largest cranberry festival in the world is held in Warrens, Wisconsin. See www.cranfest.com, for more information.

Cranberry-Coconut Bars

*These moist bars are bursting with crunchy macadamia nuts,
sweet coconut, and tart cranberries.*

Ingredients

3 cups flour

1 teaspoon baking powder

1/4 teaspoon baking soda

1/4 teaspoon salt

1/2 cup (1 stick) butter, softened

1 cup sugar

3/4 cup packed brown sugar

1/4 cup milk

1 egg

1 cup flaked coconut

1 cup chopped macadamia nuts

3 cups fresh cranberries,
chopped

Preheat the oven to 350°F. Spray a 13x9x2-inch baking pan with cooking spray.

Sift together the flour, baking powder, baking soda, and salt; set aside. Beat the butter and sugars in a large bowl with an electric mixer at high speed until well blended. Add the milk and egg; beat well. Gradually add the flour mixture, beating at low speed just until combined. (The dough will be stiff.) Stir in the coconut, macadamia nuts, and cranberries by hand. Spread evenly in the prepared pan.

Bake on the lower oven rack for 40 to 45 minutes, until a wooden pick inserted in the center comes out clean. Cool completely in the pan on a wire rack. Cut into 48 bars.

Makes 4 dozen bars

*About 70% of the cranberries harvested each year are
processed into juice, juice blends, or juice concentrates.
Cranberry juice is great on its own or mixed with
other fruit juices.*

Cranberry-Apple Crisp

Two fall favorites meet in this terrific treat that is so easy to make.

Topping

- ¹/₂ **cup packed brown sugar**
- ¹/₃ **cup old-fashioned oats**
- ¹/₄ **cup flour**
- 2 **teaspoons cinnamon**
- ¹/₂ **teaspoon nutmeg**
- 3 **tablespoons butter, cold and cut into small pieces**

Filling

- 5 **medium Granny Smith apples, peeled, cored, and cut into ¹/₄-inch slices**
- 2 **cups fresh cranberries, chopped**
- ¹/₄ **cup sugar**
- 1 **teaspoon cinnamon**
- ¹/₂ **teaspoon nutmeg**
- ¹/₂ **cup pecans, chopped**

Preheat the oven to 375°F. Spray a 9x9x2-inch baking dish with cooking spray.

To make the topping: Pulse the brown sugar, oats, flour, cinnamon, and nutmeg in a food processor until well blended. Add the butter. Pulse until the mixture resembles coarse crumbs; set aside.

To make the filling: Toss the apples, cranberries, sugar, cinnamon, and nutmeg in a large bowl. Spoon half the fruit mixture into the prepared baking dish. Top with the pecans and remaining fruit mixture. Sprinkle evenly with the topping, lightly pressing it in place.

Bake for 45 to 50 minutes, until the filling is bubbling. Serve warm or at room temperature.

Makes 8 servings

Cranberry Chocolate Pie

This amazing chocolate, walnut, and cranberry pie is perfect for holiday entertaining.

Crust

- 1 1/2 cups sifted flour
- 1/2 teaspoon salt
- 1/4 cup shortening, cold
- 1/4 cup (1/2 stick) butter, cold and cut into small pieces
- 4 to 5 tablespoons ice water, divided

Filling

- 4 ounces semisweet baking chocolate
- 3/4 cup (1 1/2 sticks) butter
- 3 eggs
- 1 cup flour
- 3/4 cup sugar
- 1/8 teaspoon salt
- 3 cups fresh cranberries, chopped
- 1 1/2 cups walnuts, chopped
- 2 tablespoons brandy

Whipped cream, as a garnish

To make the crust: Combine the flour and salt in a large bowl. Cut in the shortening with a pastry blender or 2 knives until the mixture resembles coarse crumbs. Cut in the butter until the pieces become the size of small peas. Sprinkle 3 tablespoons water over the flour mixture; gently toss with a fork. Add enough of the remaining water, 1 tablespoon at a time, tossing until all the flour is moistened. Gather the dough into a ball; flatten into a disk. Wrap in plastic wrap; refrigerate for at least 1 hour. *(Pastry dough can be refrigerated for up to 3 days. Let the dough stand at room temperature to soften slightly before rolling.)*

Roll out the dough to a 12-inch round on a lightly floured surface. (The dough should be about 1/8 inch thick.) Transfer to a 9-inch pie plate. If the dough does not uniformly cover the side of the pan, cut off some excess dough and press it over the bare spots. Trim any excess dough to within 1 inch from the edge of the pan. Fold the dough under to form a smooth, even edge. Flute the edge by crimping it between your fingers or with the round end of a knife. Cover the pastry crust loosely with plastic wrap. Refrigerate for at least 1 hour or up to 24 hours.

Preheat the oven to 350°F.

To make the filling: Melt the chocolate and butter in a small saucepan over low heat, stirring constantly. Remove from the heat; set aside to cool slightly. Meanwhile, beat the eggs in a large bowl with an electric mixer at high speed. Gradually beat in the flour, sugar, and salt. Add the chocolate mixture and blend well.

Spoon the cranberries evenly into the prepared pastry crust. Sprinkle with half of the walnuts; drizzle with the brandy. Pour the chocolate mixture evenly over the top. Sprinkle with the remaining walnuts.

Bake on the lower oven rack for 40 to 45 minutes, until the filling is set in the center. Cool on a wire rack. Serve warm garnished with whipped cream.

Makes 8 servings

Cranberry Sour Cream Cake

This delectable cake is crowned with luscious cranberries.

Topping

- ½ cup (1 stick) butter
- 1 cup sugar
- 2 tablespoons water
- 1 teaspoon cinnamon
- 4 cups fresh cranberries
- 2 tablespoons Grand Marnier liqueur (optional)

Cake

- 1½ cups flour
- ½ teaspoon baking soda
- ½ teaspoon salt
- 6 tablespoons butter, softened
- ½ cup sugar
- ½ cup packed brown sugar
- 2 eggs
- 1 teaspoon vanilla extract
- ¾ cup sour cream

Preheat the oven to 350°F. Spray a 9-inch springform pan with cooking spray. Wrap the outside of the pan with foil; place on a baking sheet.

To make the topping: Melt the butter in a medium saucepan over low heat. Add the sugar, water, and cinnamon. Cook until the sugar dissolves, stirring frequently. Stir in the cranberries and liqueur, if desired. Spread evenly on the bottom of the prepared pan; set aside.

To make the cake: Sift together the flour, baking soda, and salt; set aside. Beat the butter and sugars in a large bowl with an electric mixer at high speed until fluffy. Add the eggs 1 at a time, beating well after each addition. Beat in the vanilla. Add the flour mixture alternately with the sour cream, beating at low speed after each addition. Pour evenly over the topping in the pan.

Bake for 50 minutes or until a wooden pick inserted into the center comes out clean. Cool in the pan for 10 minutes. Run a knife between the cake and side of the pan. Carefully invert the cake onto a cake plate. Remove the foil and the side and bottom of the pan. Cool completely.

Makes 12 servings

Delicious Fruit Desserts

Cranberry-Hazelnut Tart

Dried cranberries, dried apricots, and hazelnuts create a flavorful tart.

Crust

- ¹/₄ cup hazelnuts, toasted and skins removed
- 4 teaspoons sugar
- ¹/₈ teaspoon salt
- 1¹/₄ cups plus 2 tablespoons flour
- ¹/₂ cup (1 stick) butter, cold and cut into small pieces
- 3 to 4 tablespoons cold water, divided

Filling

- 1 cup dried cranberries
- 1 cup dried apricots, finely chopped
- 3 eggs
- ³/₄ cup light corn syrup
- 6 tablespoons butter, melted
- ¹/₃ cup sugar
- 2 tablespoons grated orange zest
- 2 tablespoons Grand Marnier liqueur
- 1 tablespoon flour
- 1 tablespoon fresh orange juice
- 1 teaspoon vanilla extract
- 1 cup hazelnuts, toasted, skins removed, and chopped

Chocolate Sauce (page 145), as a garnish

To make the crust: Process the hazelnuts with the sugar and salt in a food processor until finely ground. Add the flour and pulse to blend. Add the butter. Pulse until the mixture resembles coarse crumbs. Add 2 tablespoons water and pulse 6 times. Pinch a small amount of the dough between your fingers. If it does not hold together, add 1 tablespoon water and pulse 3 times. Repeat this procedure until the dough is the proper consistency. Gather the dough into a ball; flatten into a disk. Wrap in plastic wrap; refrigerate for at least 1 hour. *(Pastry dough can be refrigerated for up to 3 days. Let the dough stand at room temperature to soften slightly before rolling.)*

Spray a 9-inch tart pan with a removable bottom with cooking spray. Roll out the dough to an 11-inch circle on a lightly floured surface. Gently lift the dough just enough to move the prepared pan underneath it. Press the dough firmly onto the bottom and side of the pan. If there are places where the dough doesn't reach to the top of the pan, break off any excess dough and press it into place. Reinforce the seam where the bottom and side meet with excess dough. Pierce the bottom of the crust all over with a fork. Cover; freeze for 30 minutes.

Preheat the oven to 350°F. Place the crust on a baking sheet. Bake for 20 minutes or until lightly browned. Cool on the baking sheet on a wire rack. Maintain the oven temperature at 350°F.

To make the filling: Place the dried cranberries and apricots in a small bowl; add enough hot water to cover the fruit. Soak for 20 minutes; drain and set aside.

Beat the eggs, corn syrup, butter, sugar, orange zest, liqueur, flour, orange juice, and vanilla in a large bowl with an electric mixer at high speed until well blended. Stir in the soaked fruit and hazelnuts by hand. Pour into the crust.

Bake at 350°F for about 50 minutes, until the filling is set and lightly browned. Cool on a wire rack. Gently loosen and remove the edge of the pan. Serve with chocolate sauce drizzled over the top and pooled on the sides of the dessert plates.

Makes 10 servings

Cranberry-Glazed Layer Cake

This impressive cake tastes as spectacular as it looks!

Glaze

- 1 (12-ounce) package fresh cranberries
- 1 cup sugar
- 1 cup water
- Grated zest of 1 orange

Cake

- 3 cups cake flour
- 1 tablespoon plus 1 teaspoon baking powder
- 3/4 teaspoon salt
- 3/4 cup (1 1/2 sticks) butter, softened
- 1 1/2 cups sugar
- 6 egg yolks
- Grated zest of 1 orange
- 1 1/2 teaspoons orange extract
- 1 1/2 teaspoons vanilla extract
- 1 cup whole milk

(continued)

To make the glaze: Pulse the cranberries with the sugar in a food processor until coarsely chopped. Transfer to a medium saucepan. Add the water and orange zest. Bring to a boil, stirring occasionally. Reduce the heat to low; simmer for about 10 minutes, until the mixture thickens, stirring occasionally. Cool to room temperature. Refrigerate, covered, 8 hours or overnight.

Preheat the oven to 350°F. Spray two 9-inch round cake pans with cooking spray. Line the bottoms with waxed paper; spray the paper with cooking spray. Dust the pans with flour.

To make the cake: Sift together the cake flour, baking powder and salt; set aside. Beat the butter and sugar in a large bowl with an electric mixer at high speed until fluffy. Add the egg yolks, orange zest, orange extract, and vanilla; beat well. Add the flour mixture alternately with the milk, beating at medium speed after each addition. Divide the batter evenly between the prepared pans.

Bake for 25 to 35 minutes, until a wooden pick inserted into the centers comes out clean. Cool in the pans for 10 minutes. Run a small knife between the cakes and the sides of the pans. Remove from the pans to wire racks. Remove the waxed paper, then invert the layers top sides up; cool completely.

Cranberry-Glazed Layer Cake (cont.)

Frosting

1 1/2 cups (12 ounces) cream cheese, softened

3/4 cup (1 1/2 sticks) butter, softened

2 tablespoons frozen orange juice concentrate, thawed

1 1/2 teaspoons vanilla extract

3 1/2 cups confectioners' sugar, sifted

To make the frosting: Beat the cream cheese, butter, orange juice concentrate, and vanilla in a large bowl with an electric mixer at high speed until smooth. Add the confectioners' sugar 1 cup at a time, beating at low speed until well blended. Beat at high speed until smooth.

To assemble: Place 1 cake layer, top side down, on a cake platter. Spread with 2/3 cup of the frosting and 1 cup of the glaze, leaving a 1/2-inch border around the edge. Top with the second layer, top side up; gently press together. Spread a thin layer of frosting over the top and side of the cake. Reserve 1/2 cup of the frosting. Spread the remaining frosting over the entire cake. Spoon the reserved frosting into a pastry bag fitted with a medium star tip. Pipe a decorative border around the top edge of the cake. Refrigerate for about 1 hour, until the frosting is firm. Spread 1 cup of the remaining glaze over the top of the cake. Refrigerate, loosely covered, until ready to serve.

Makes 12 servings

Note: Store any leftover cranberry glaze in the refrigerator for up to 4 days. Use as a topping for waffles, toast, or ice cream.

Tips: To avoid getting cake crumbs in the frosting bowl, use separate spatulas for removing the frosting from the bowl and spreading.

To easily cut 12 equal slices, first cut the cake in half, then cut each half into 6 slices.

Cranberry, Chocolate & Grand Marnier Trifle

This dessert is quite stunning for a large dinner party.

Cake

- 5 eggs
- 1/2 cup plus 2 tablespoons sugar
- 2 teaspoons vanilla extract
- 1/2 teaspoon salt
- 1/2 cup plus 2 tablespoons flour, sifted
- 2 tablespoons unsalted butter, melted and warm

Cranberries

- 2 (12-ounce) packages fresh cranberries
- 1 1/2 cups sugar
- Grated zest of 1 orange
- 1 cup fresh orange juice
- 1 teaspoon ground ginger
- 1/2 cup chopped crystallized ginger (optional)

Pudding

- 1 1/2 cups whole milk
- 6 egg yolks
- 1/3 cup sugar
- 2 tablespoons cornstarch
- 4 ounces semisweet or bitter-sweet baking chocolate, chopped
- 2 tablespoons Grand Marnier liqueur

(continued)

For best results, prepare the cake, cranberries, and pudding a day ahead and assemble the trifle the morning it's served.

Preheat the oven to 350°F. Lightly spray a 15 1/2x10 1/2x1-inch baking pan with cooking spray. Line the bottom with waxed paper, extending it slightly over the short sides of the pan; spray the paper with cooking spray.

To make the cake: Beat the eggs, sugar, vanilla, and salt in a large bowl with an electric mixer at high speed for about 12 minutes, until the batter thickens and falls in a heavy ribbon when the beaters are lifted. Add half the flour at a time, gently folding it in by hand. Drizzle the butter over the batter and fold in gently. Do not overmix or the batter will deflate. Pour into the prepared pan, spreading evenly.

Bake for about 15 minutes, until lightly browned and the surface springs back when lightly touched. Cool completely in the pan on a wire rack. Cover with foil and store at room temperature overnight.

To make the cranberries: Combine the cranberries, sugar, orange zest, orange juice, and ground ginger in a large heavy saucepan. Bring to a boil; cook for about 5 minutes, stirring until the sugar dissolves and the cranberries pop. Stir in the crystallized ginger, if desired. Cool slightly. Refrigerate, covered, overnight.

To make the pudding: Bring the milk to a simmer in a heavy, medium saucepan over medium heat. Meanwhile, whisk the egg yolks, sugar, and cornstarch in a large bowl about 3 minutes, until the mixture thickens and turns pale yellow. Pour the hot milk into the egg mixture, whisking to combine. Pour the mixture back into the saucepan. Cook, whisking constantly, over medium heat about 3 minutes, until the pudding thickens and comes to a boil. Remove from the heat; whisk in the chocolate until completely melted and the pudding is smooth. Stir in the liqueur. Cool slightly. Pour the pudding into a medium bowl; cover with plastic wrap, gently pressing it directly onto the surface of the pudding. Refrigerate 4 hours or overnight.

Delicious Fruit Desserts

Cranberry, Chocolate & Grand Marnier Trifle (cont.)

Ingredients

- **6 tablespoons Grand Marnier liqueur, divided**
- **1 cup heavy cream, whipped to stiff peaks**

To assemble: Cut the cake into 3 equal sections. Remove 1 section at a time to a cutting board and cut into 3x1-inch pieces. Cover the bottom of a 3-quart trifle dish or straight-sided glass bowl with 2 layers of cake pieces. Sprinkle with 2 tablespoons liqueur. Spread a generous cup of cranberries over the cake to the side of the bowl. Spread a generous cup of pudding over the cranberries. Repeat layering 2 times, reserving $1/2$ cup cranberries. Spread whipped cream over the top, mounding it slightly around the edge. Spoon the remaining cranberries in the center of the whipped cream. Refrigerate, covered, for 4 to 8 hours before serving.

Makes 16 servings

Note: Substitute a store-bought (16-ounce) pound cake for the homemade cake, if desired.

The word trifle *comes from the old French term* trufle, *which means something whimsical or of little consequence. Early trifles were simply cooked cream flavored with spices. Later, stale cake or biscuits and alcohol were combined with the cream. By the end of the 1800's, the proper English trifle had arrived—egg custard layered with fruit, sherry-soaked sponge cake, and whipped cream. And no trifle was truly successful without the perfect trifle bowl. Many of these dishes are now considered heirloom-quality glass.*

Cranberry Swirl Cheesecake

A ruby swirl of tart cranberries runs through this creamy cheesecake creating a taste sensation.

Cranberries

2 cups fresh cranberries

3/4 cup fresh orange juice

2/3 cup sugar

1/2 teaspoon cinnamon

1/4 teaspoon nutmeg

Crust

1 1/2 cups vanilla wafer crumbs

3 tablespoons sugar

1/4 cup (1/2 stick) butter, melted

Filling

4 (8-ounce) packages cream cheese, softened

1 cup sugar

4 eggs

1 cup sour cream

1 tablespoon vanilla extract

To make the cranberries: Combine the cranberries, orange juice, sugar, cinnamon, and nutmeg in a large saucepan. Cook over medium heat for about 5 minutes, until the cranberries pop, stirring constantly. Remove from the heat; cool slightly. Process the cranberry mixture in a food processor until coarsely chopped. Pour through a fine strainer set over a small bowl, pressing the cranberries to remove the excess liquid. Discard the liquid. Refrigerate the cranberries, covered, for at least 4 hours.

Preheat the oven to 350°F. Spray a 10-inch springform pan with cooking spray. Wrap the outside of the pan with 2 layers of foil; place on a baking sheet.

To make the crust: Combine the vanilla wafer crumbs, sugar, and butter in a small bowl. Toss with a fork until the crumbs are moistened. Press onto the bottom and three-fourths of the way up the side of the prepared pan. Bake for 8 minutes; cool on a wire rack. Maintain the oven temperature at 350°F.

To make the filling: Beat the cream cheese and sugar in a large bowl with an electric mixer at high speed until smooth. Add the eggs 1 at a time, beating well after each addition. Beat in the sour cream and vanilla. Pour one-third of the filling evenly over the crust. Drop one-third of the cranberries by teaspoonfuls over the filling. Repeat layering 2 times with the remaining filling and cranberries. Use a knife to swirl the cranberries through the filling, being careful not to touch the crust on the bottom and side.

Bake for about 1 hour and 30 minutes, until the center barely moves when the pan is gently shaken. Remove the foil from the pan. Cool completely in the pan on a wire rack. Run a knife between the cheesecake and the side of the pan. Release the side of the pan. Refrigerate, covered, for at least 8 hours before serving. Let stand at room temperature for 30 minutes before serving.

Makes 12 servings

Tip: For best results, do not remove the bottom of the springform pan once the cheesecake is chilled. To prevent it from sliding around, place a rubber jar gripper between the pan bottom and serving plate.

Lemon

Peak Season: Lemons grow on tall evergreen trees that bloom year-round and produce blossoms, buds, and fruit all at once. Because they can grow up to 17 inches in diameter, lemons are usually hand picked when they are smaller in size and still relatively green. The top lemon-producing countries are the United States, Mexico, Italy, Spain, and India. California produces 30% of the world market and the majority of domestic lemons. The main lemon varieties sold in the U.S. are Eureka and Lisbon. The Meyer lemon, a cross between a lemon and orange, is a sweeter variety that is not yet widely available.

Selection: The juiciest lemons are firm, plump, and heavy for their size. The skins should be glossy and bright yellow with no hint of green, which indicates that they are unripe. Choose thin-skinned lemons for juicing and thick-skinned lemons for zesting. Avoid lemons that are very hard, or spongy and soft.

Storage: Refrigerate lemons in a plastic bag for up to 3 weeks, checking them occasionally for signs of mold. Since lemons yield more juice when they are not cold, they can be stored at room temperature for 7 to 10 days. Once cut, wrap lemons tightly in plastic wrap and refrigerate for up to 3 days. If the zest has been removed from a lemon, store the zested lemon in the refrigerator and juice it within 1 week.

(continued)

A Little History: Citrus fruits are native to southern China and Southeast Asia, where they have been cultivated for thousands of years. Through the centuries many cultures have adapted lemons and other citrus fruits for many beneficial uses. In the eighth and ninth centuries, Arab traders brought them to the Middle East from India and they eventually spread throughout the Mediterranean. Lemons became popular in Europe when they were brought back from the Crusades. They were used to offset the spiciness of food, to redden ladies' lips in King Louis XIV's court, and to combat scurvy on sailing voyages. From Europe, lemons traveled to the New World with Christopher Columbus. The U.S. commercial lemon industry got its start in 1849 during the California gold rush. The lack of vitamin C in the miners' diets caused scurvy. As a result, lemons were in high demand and lemon trees were planted in abundance to meet this need.

More about Lemons

Preparation: Both the lemon juice and zest play important roles in dessert making. The tart juice is a complement to sugar while the aromatic peel adds flavor and fragrance. Lemon juice also slows down the browning of cut apples, bananas, and pears, and helps remove stains on hands from cherry, raspberry, pomegranate, or other bright fruit juices.

Scrub lemons thoroughly in warm, soapy water to remove surface wax and traces of insecticides. This is especially important if the zest is to be used. One medium lemon yields about 3 tablespoons juice and 2 teaspoons grated zest.

The use of the word lemon to signify "dud" is totally without merit. Its use for medicinal and household purposes, as well as its versatility to flavor dishes, makes the lemon an invaluable fruit.

Zesting: The outermost, colored part of lemon skin is called the zest. (The white part underneath the zest is the pith and has a bitter taste.) Cut lemon zest into wide strips to use in poaching liquids and julienne strips for garnishing, or finely grate it for baking. Several types of kitchen tools are used to remove the zest. For grated zest, use the fine holes on a box-shaped grater or a rasp grater. Use a vegetable peeler or sharp paring knife to remove the zest in wide strips and a zester to create thin strips. Avoid removing the white pith to prevent a bitter taste. Since it's easier to remove zest from a whole lemon, zest it before cutting.

Juicing: To extract the most juice from a lemon, bring it to room temperature. Roll the lemon on the counter a few times using firm pressure to release the juice inside. While electric juicers make extracting large quantities of juice easier, there are good low-tech juicing options. One is to simply squeeze the juice into an upturned palm with fingers split just enough to let the juice, but not the seeds, through. Another is to press and rotate the lemon half over a hand-held reamer (a grooved, cone-shaped tool) or a citrus juicer with a bowl to catch the juices. Add the squeezed lemon hulls to poaching liquids or sprinkle them with coarse salt and rub over copper pots as polish. Refrigerate any leftover squeezed juice, tightly covered, for 1 week. Or, freeze the juice in ice cube trays then transfer the cubes to freezer bags for long-term storage. The flavor of fresh-squeezed lemon juice is far superior to bottled lemon juice.

Candied Lemon Zest

Candied lemon zest is a pretty garnish for any fruit dessert.

Ingredients

- 3 lemons
- 1 cup sugar
- 1 cup water
- 3 tablespoons fresh lemon juice
- 1 tablespoon light corn syrup

Wash the lemons thoroughly. Cut off and discard the ends. Stand the lemons upright and cut downward with a sharp paring knife to remove the zest in wide strips, leaving the white pith on the lemons. Cut each piece of zest lengthwise into 1/4-inch-wide strips.

Fill a medium saucepan with water; bring to a boil. Add the lemon zest; return the water to a boil. Cook for 5 minutes. Drain and rinse under cold water; set aside.

Bring the sugar, water, lemon juice, and corn syrup to a boil in the same saucepan over high heat, stirring until the sugar dissolves. Boil for 2 minutes; reduce the heat to medium-low. Add the lemon zest. Simmer, covered, for 1 hour or until the zest is translucent.

Remove from the heat; cool the zest in the syrup for 1 hour at room temperature. Pour the syrup and candied zest into a glass jar. Refrigerate, tightly covered, for up to 1 month. Drain and discard the syrup from the zest before using.

Uses: Stir candied lemon zest into quick bread, fruitcake, and muffin batters. Or, cut it into thin ribbons and use as a garnish for poached fruits, pies, tarts, and cakes. Dipped into melted chocolate, it makes a wonderful candy.

Crystallized Lemon Zest:

To make crystallized lemon zest, drain off the syrup and toss the candied zest in granulated sugar to coat. Place in a single layer on a wire rack and let stand 8 to 12 hours at room temperature until completely dry. (Or place the wire rack on a baking sheet and dry in a 175°F oven.) Store the crystallized zest in an airtight container for up to 1 week. Dip into melted chocolate for the ultimate treat.

Lemon Granita

*Serve this icy dessert to refresh palates between courses
or as a cool treat on a hot summer day.*

Ingredients

2 ½ **cups water**

1 **cup sugar**

2 **tablespoons grated lemon zest**

1 **cup fresh lemon juice**

**Fresh cherries or strawberries,
as a garnish**

Chill a 13x9-inch baking pan in the freezer.

Bring the water and sugar to a boil in a large saucepan over medium-high heat, stirring until the sugar dissolves. Remove from the heat; stir in the lemon zest and juice. Let stand, covered, for 10 minutes to infuse the syrup with lemon flavor. Pour through a strainer into the cold baking pan. Cool to room temperature. Cover the pan with foil. Freeze for 1 hour or until ice crystals form around the edges. Stir with a fork to incorporate the ice crystals. Freeze, stirring every 30 minutes, for about 2 hours, until the mixture is slushy with ice crystals throughout it.

When ready to serve, run the tines of a fork over the top of the granita to fluff up the ice crystals. Spoon it into small dessert dishes. Garnish with cherries or strawberries.

Makes about 1 quart

Note: The granita can be frozen for up to 1 month, though is best when served slightly slushy. If completely frozen, let stand at room temperature for 10 to 20 minutes before serving.

Delicious Fruit Desserts

Lemon Bars

This is a favorite recipe that my mother use to bake for us.

Crust

  1 **cup flour**
 $^1/_4$ **cup confectioners' sugar**
 $^1/_2$ **cup (1 stick) butter, softened**

Filling

  2 **eggs**
  1 **cup sugar**
  2 **tablespoons flour**
  2 **tablespoons fresh lemon juice**

Frosting

 1 $^1/_2$ **cups confectioners' sugar, sifted**
  2 **tablespoons butter, softened**
  1 **tablespoon milk**
  1 **teaspoon vanilla extract**

Preheat the oven to 350°F.

To make the crust: Blend the flour and confectioners' sugar in a large bowl. Add the butter. Beat with an electric mixer at high speed until combined. Press onto the bottom and $^1/_2$ inch up the sides of an 8x8x2-inch baking pan. Bake for 20 minutes or until lightly browned; set aside.

To make the filling: Beat the eggs in a large bowl with an electric mixer at high speed until frothy. Add the sugar, flour, and lemon juice. Beat at low speed just until combined. Spread evenly over the warm crust. Bake for 20 minutes or until set. Cool on a wire rack for at least 30 minutes.

To make the frosting: Beat the confectioners' sugar, butter, milk, and vanilla in a large bowl with an electric mixer at medium speed until smooth. Spread evenly over the cooled bars. Refrigerate for at least 1 hour before serving. Cut into 16 squares.

Makes 16 bars

Lemons were said to symbolize faithful love.
The Victorians used lemon blossoms
as an emblem of fidelity.

Lemon Shortbread

Lemon adds a nice twist to buttery shortbread cookies.

Ingredients

- 2 cups (4 sticks) butter, softened
- 1 cup sugar
- 2 tablespoons grated lemon zest
- 1 tablespoon fresh lemon juice
- 1 teaspoon lemon extract
- 5 cups flour
- 2 tablespoons sugar

Preheat the oven to 325°F.

Beat the butter and 1 cup sugar in a large bowl with an electric mixer at high speed until fluffy. Add the lemon zest, juice, and lemon extract; beat until blended. Gradually add the flour, beating at low speed just until blended (the dough will be crumbly). Knead the dough in the bowl by hand for about 5 minutes, until a small bit pinched between your fingers starts to hold together. Press the dough evenly into a 17x11-inch baking pan. Smooth the top with the back of a large spoon. Cut into $2^1/_2$x1-inch rectangles. (Cut 17 horizontal rows 1 inch apart and 4 vertical rows $2^3/_4$ inches apart.) Bake for 45 minutes, until crisp and lightly browned. Cool for 10 minutes then recut the pieces. Sprinkle with 2 tablespoons sugar. Cool completely. Store in an airtight container for up to 1 week.

Makes 68 cookies

One whole lemon contains over 100% of the recommended daily value of vitamin C and only about 20 calories.

Lemon Sugar Cookies

How can sugar cookies get any better? Add the zest of lemon!

Ingredients

- 3 ¼ **cups flour**
- 2 ½ **teaspoons baking powder**
- ½ **teaspoon salt**
- 1 ½ **cups sugar**
- ¾ **cup (1 ½ sticks) butter, softened**
- 2 **eggs**
- 3 **tablespoons grated lemon zest**
- 2 **tablespoons fresh lemon juice**
- ⅓ **cup sugar**

Preheat the oven to 400°F. Grease 2 cookie sheets.

Sift together the flour, baking powder, and salt; set aside. Beat the 1 ½ cups sugar and butter in a large bowl with an electric mixer at high speed until fluffy. Add the eggs, lemon zest, and juice; beat until blended. Gradually add the flour mixture, beating at low speed just until combined.

Pour ⅓ cup sugar into a small bowl. Shape the dough by table-spoonfuls into balls; roll them in the sugar. Place 3 inches apart on the prepared cookie sheets. Flatten each ball with the bottom of a glass to a 2-inch diameter.

Bake about 10 to 12 minutes, until the edges are lightly browned. Cool on the pans for 5 minutes. Remove to wire racks; cool completely.

Makes 3 dozen cookies

Note: Rinse the sugar off the cookie sheets and regrease them between batches of cookies.

*Lemon trees bloom and produce fruit year-round.
An average tree produces 500 to 600 pounds
of lemons each year.*

Iced Lemon Cookies

Honey paired with lemon creates a delicious flavor duo in these easy drop cookies.

Cookies

2 1/4 **cups flour**

1 **teaspoon baking powder**

1/2 **teaspoon salt**

1/2 **cup (1 stick) butter, softened**

1/2 **cup sugar**

1/3 **cup honey**

1 **egg**

2 **teaspoons grated lemon zest**

1 **teaspoon lemon extract**

1/4 **cup milk**

Icing

1 **cup confectioners' sugar, sifted**

2 **teaspoons grated lemon zest**

2 **tablespoons fresh lemon juice**

Preheat the oven to 350°F. Grease 2 cookie sheets.

To make the cookies: Sift together the flour, baking powder, and salt; set aside. Beat the butter and sugar in a large bowl with an electric mixer at high speed until fluffy. Add the honey, egg, lemon zest, and lemon extract; beat until blended. Add the flour mixture alternately with the milk, beating at medium speed after each addition.

Drop the dough by tablespoonfuls 2 inches apart onto the prepared cookie sheets. Bake for about 12 minutes, until lightly browned. Meanwhile, make the icing.

To make the icing: Whisk the confectioners' sugar, lemon zest, and juice in a small bowl until combined. Brush over the hot cookies while they are still on the cookie sheets. Remove cookies to wire racks and cool completely.

Makes 3 dozen

Note: Rinse the icing off the cookie sheets and regrease them between batches of cookies.

Lemon juice is believed to alleviate the symptoms of colds and sore throats. The vitamin C may help boost the immune system while its astringent and antiseptic qualities may nurture the body's healing capabilities.

Lemon Poppy Seed Cake

This easy cake makes a great treat any time of the day.

Cake

- 2 cups flour
- 1 teaspoon baking powder
- 1 teaspoon salt
- 1 1/2 cups sugar
- 3/4 cup (1 1/2 sticks) butter, softened
- 4 eggs
- 1 cup milk
- Grated zest of 1 lemon
- 3 tablespoons fresh lemon juice
- 6 tablespoons poppy seeds

Syrup

- 3 tablespoons fresh lemon juice
- 3 tablespoons sugar

Preheat the oven to 350°F. Spray a 10-inch fluted tube pan with cooking spray.

To make the cake: Sift together the flour, baking powder, and salt; set aside. Beat the sugar and butter in a large bowl with an electric mixer at high speed until fluffy. Add the eggs 1 at a time, beating well after each addition. Add the flour mixture alternately with the milk, beating at medium speed after each addition. Beat in the lemon zest, juice, and poppy seeds at low speed. Pour into the prepared pan, spreading evenly.

Bake for 45 minutes or until a wooden pick inserted into the center of the cake comes out clean. Cool in the pan for 10 minutes. Meanwhile, make the syrup.

To make the syrup: Heat the lemon juice and sugar in a small saucepan over medium heat until the sugar dissolves, stirring constantly.

Carefully invert the cake onto a heatproof cake plate. Poke small holes over the top and side of the cake with a wooden pick. Brush the syrup over the hot cake. Let the cake stand for at least 1 hour before serving or cool completely.

Makes 16 servings

Drinking tea or plain hot water with lemon and honey relaxes and soothes the throat and may help relieve a cough.

Lemon-Glazed Cake

A lemony icing spread over this luscious cake melts into a pretty glaze.

Cake

     3 cups flour, sifted
 $1/2$ teaspoon baking soda
 $1/2$ teaspoon salt
     2 cups sugar
     1 cup (2 sticks) butter, softened
     3 eggs
     1 cup milk
       Grated zest of 3 lemons
     2 tablespoons fresh lemon juice

Glaze

     2 cups confectioners' sugar, sifted
 $1/2$ cup (1 stick) butter, softened
       Grated zest of 3 lemons
 $1/2$ cup fresh lemon juice

Preheat the oven to 325°F. Spray a 10-inch tube pan with cooking spray.

To make the cake: Sift together the flour, baking soda, and salt; set aside. Beat the sugar and butter in a large bowl with an electric mixer at high speed until fluffy. Add the eggs 1 at a time, beating well after each addition. Add the flour mixture alternately with the milk, beating at medium speed after each addition. Beat in the lemon zest and juice at low speed. Pour into the prepared pan, spreading evenly.

Bake for 1 hour or until a wooden pick inserted into the center of the cake comes out clean. Cool in the pan for 10 minutes. Meanwhile, make the glaze.

To make the glaze: Beat the confectioners' sugar and butter in a large bowl with an electric mixer at high speed until smooth. Beat in the lemon zest and juice.

Remove the cake from the pan to a wire rack. Carefully invert the cake onto a heatproof cake plate, so the top side is up. Spread the glaze over the hot cake. Cool completely.

Makes 16 servings

Lemon Mousse
with Fresh Berries

Summer berries topped with lemon mousse is an easy, refreshing dessert.

Ingredients

- 4 tablespoons (1/2 stick) butter
- 1 cup sugar
- 1 tablespoon grated lemon zest
- 3/4 cup fresh lemon juice
- 6 egg yolks
- 2 cups heavy cream, whipped to soft peaks
- 1 pint strawberries, cut into halves
- 1/2 pint fresh blueberries
- 1/2 pint fresh raspberries
- 1/2 pint fresh blackberries

Melt the butter in a heavy, medium saucepan over medium-low heat. Remove from the heat; whisk in the sugar, lemon zest, and juice. Add the egg yolks and whisk until smooth. Cook over medium-low heat, stirring constantly, about 10 minutes, until the mixture thickens and coats the back of a wooden spoon. Do not bring to a boil or the eggs will cook. Pour through a fine strainer set over a bowl. Cool to room temperature, whisking occasionally. Refrigerate, covered, for at least 2 hours. *(Lemon curd can be made up to 1 month ahead. Store, covered, in the refrigerator.)*

Beat the lemon curd in a large bowl with an electric mixer at high speed until smooth. Reserve 3/4 cup of the whipped cream. Gently fold the remaining whipped cream into the lemon curd just until combined. Do not overmix; a few white streaks of cream may be visible. *(Lemon mousse can be made up to 3 days ahead. Store, covered, in the refrigerator.)*

Reserve 8 strawberry halves. Divide the remaining berries among 8 dessert bowls or parfait glasses. Spoon the lemon mousse over the berries. Top each with a dollop of the reserved whipped cream. Garnish with the reserved strawberry halves.

Makes 8 servings

Simple Lemon Soufflés

Impress your friends and family with these delicious no-fail soufflés.

Ingredients

- $1/4$ **cup sugar**
- 3 **egg yolks, at room temperature**
  Grated zest of 1 lemon
- $1/4$ **cup fresh lemon juice**
- 4 **egg whites, at room temperature**

Preheat the oven to 350°F. Generously butter six 6- to 8-ounce ramekins or custard cups. Coat them with sugar, tapping out the excess. Place on a baking sheet spaced apart.

Whisk $1/4$ cup sugar and egg yolks in a large bowl about 3 minutes, until the mixture thickens and turns pale yellow. Stir in the lemon zest and juice. Beat the egg whites in a large bowl with an electric mixer at high speed until stiff peaks form. Gently fold the egg whites into the egg yolk mixture until well blended. Divide the mixture evenly among the prepared ramekins. Smooth the tops with your finger and run your thumb around the inside edges, wiping off the butter and sugar from the rims.

Bake for 15 minutes or until puffed and lightly browned. Serve immediately.

Makes 6 servings

Note: Soufflés are best when served immediately after coming out of the oven. They cannot be stored or reheated.

Tip: Assemble all of the ingredients in advance so that after dinner you can quickly prepare the soufflés.

Lemon-Raspberry Pudding Cake

While this dessert bakes, a spongy cake forms over a layer of custard,
creating two desserts in one!

Ingredients

- ²/₃ cup sugar
- ¹/₄ cup flour
- 1 tablespoon grated lemon zest
- ¹/₈ teaspoon salt
- 1 cup buttermilk
- 3 egg yolks
- ¹/₄ cup fresh lemon juice
- 2 tablespoons butter, melted
- 3 egg whites, at room temperature
- 1 (12-ounce) package frozen raspberries, thawed and drained
- Boiling water

Preheat the oven to 350°F. Butter an 8-inch round or 8x8x2-inch baking dish.

Combine the sugar, flour, lemon zest, and salt in a medium bowl. Whisk the buttermilk, egg yolks, lemon juice, and butter in another medium bowl until well blended. Pour into the sugar mixture; whisk until smooth.

Beat the egg whites in a large bowl with an electric mixer at high speed until soft peaks form. Fold into the batter. Gently fold in the raspberries. Pour into the prepared baking dish. Place the dish in a roasting pan. Pull out the oven rack and place the roasting pan on the rack. Pour enough boiling water into the pan to come one-third up the side of the baking dish.

Bake for 35 minutes or until the surface springs back when lightly touched in the center. Cool for 10 minutes on a wire rack. Serve warm. Refrigerate any leftover cake.

Makes 6 servings

Lemon Cream Tart

Luscious, silky lemon cream makes this simple tart glorious.

Crust

1 ½ **cups flour**

¼ **cup sugar**

½ **cup (1 stick) butter, cold and cut into small pieces**

3 **tablespoons milk**

1 **egg yolk**

Lemon Cream

1 **cup sugar**

Grated zest of 3 lemons

4 **eggs**

¾ **cup fresh lemon juice**

1 **cup (2 sticks) butter, softened and cut into small pieces**

Fresh strawberries, raspberries, or other fresh fruit, as a garnish

To make the crust: Process the flour and sugar in a food processor until blended. Add the butter. Pulse until the mixture resembles coarse crumbs. Whisk the milk and egg yolk in a small bowl. With the processor on, slowly add the egg mixture, processing just until moist clumps form. Do not overprocess. Gather the dough into a ball; flatten into a disk. Wrap in plastic wrap; refrigerate for 1 hour. *(Pastry dough can be refrigerated for up to 3 days. Let the dough stand at room temperature to soften slightly before rolling.)*

Spray a 9-inch tart pan with a removable bottom with cooking spray. Roll out the dough to an 11-inch round between 2 sheets of parchment paper. Remove the top paper and invert the pastry into the tart pan. Remove the second paper. Press the dough firmly onto the bottom and side of the pan. If there are places where the dough doesn't reach to the top of the pan, break off any excess dough and press it into place. Reinforce the seam where the bottom and side meet with excess dough. Pierce the bottom of the crust all over with a fork. Cover; freeze for 30 minutes.

Preheat the oven to 350°F. Place the crust on a baking sheet. Bake for 20 minutes or until lightly browned. Cool completely on a wire rack. Gently loosen and remove the edge of the pan.

To make the lemon cream: Place the sugar and lemon zest in a heavy, medium saucepan; rub together with your fingers until the sugar is moist and very aromatic. Whisk in the eggs and lemon juice. Cook over medium-low heat, whisking constantly, for 15 minutes. Do not bring to a boil or the eggs will cook. (The mixture will begin to thicken after about 10 minutes, but continue cooking and whisking constantly for another 5 minutes.) Pour through a fine strainer set over a blender container. Add the butter. Blend until the butter is completely incorporated. Pour into the prepared crust. Refrigerate, covered, for at least 4 hours. Serve garnished with fresh fruit.

Makes 8 servings

Note: The lemon cream can be made up to 4 days ahead. Store, covered, in the refrigerator.

Lemon Cheesecake

This delectable cheesecake is infused with lemon flavor, from the topping to the filling.

Lemon Curd

- 4 tablespoons (½ stick) butter
- ¾ cup sugar
- 1 tablespoon grated lemon zest
- 6 tablespoons fresh lemon juice
- 4 egg yolks

Crust

- ⅔ cup flour
- 2 tablespoons sugar
- 2 tablespoons butter, cold
- 1 tablespoon ice water

Filling

- 3 (8-ounce) packages cream cheese, softened
- 1 cup sugar
- 3 eggs
- 1 tablespoon grated lemon zest
- 2 tablespoons fresh lemon juice
- 1 teaspoon lemon extract
- 1 cup sour cream

To make the lemon curd: Melt the butter in a heavy, medium saucepan over medium-low heat. Remove from the heat; whisk in the sugar, lemon zest, and juice. Add the egg yolks and whisk until smooth. Cook over medium-low heat, stirring constantly, about 10 minutes, until the mixture thickens and coats the back of a wooden spoon. Do not bring to a boil or the eggs will cook. Pour through a fine strainer set over a bowl. Cool to room temperature, whisking occasionally. Refrigerate, covered, for at least 2 hours. *(Lemon curd can be made up to 5 days ahead. Store, covered, in the refrigerator.)*

Preheat the oven to 400°F. Spray a 9-inch springform pan with cooking spray. Bring 5 teaspoons of the lemon curd to room temperature.

To make the crust: Process the flour and sugar in a food processor until blended. Add the butter. Pulse until the mixture resembles fine crumbs. With the processor on, slowly add the water, processing just until moist clumps form. (Do not let the dough form a ball.) Press evenly onto the bottom only of the prepared pan. Bake for 10 minutes. Cool on a wire rack. Reduce the oven temperature to 325°F.

To make the filling: Beat the cream cheese and sugar in a large bowl with an electric mixer until smooth. Add the eggs 1 at a time, beating well after each addition. Beat in the lemon zest, juice, lemon extract, and sour cream. Pour over the prepared crust. Drop the 5 teaspoons room temperature lemon curd by teaspoonfuls around the edge of the filling. Use a knife to swirl the lemon curd through the filling, being careful not to touch the crust.

Bake at 325°F for 1 hour and 40 minutes or until the center barely moves when the pan is gently shaken. Cool completely in the pan on a wire rack. Run a knife between the cheesecake and the side of the pan. Release the side of the pan. Whisk the remaining lemon curd until smooth. Spread evenly over the top of the cheesecake. Refrigerate, covered, for at least 8 hours.

Makes 12 servings

Lemon Meringue Pie

This scrumptious lemon pie is a true American classic.

Crust

1 ¹/₂ **cups sifted flour**

¹/₂ **teaspoon salt**

¹/₄ **cup shortening, cold**

¹/₄ **cup (¹/₂ stick) butter, cold and cut into small pieces**

4 **to 5 tablespoons ice water, divided**

(continued)

To make the crust: Combine the flour and salt in a large bowl. Cut in the shortening with a pastry blender or 2 knives until the mixture resembles coarse crumbs. Cut in the butter until the pieces become the size of small peas. Sprinkle 3 tablespoons water over the flour mixture; gently toss with a fork. Add enough of the remaining water, 1 tablespoon at a time, tossing until all the flour is moistened. Gather the dough into a ball; flatten into a disk. Wrap in plastic wrap; refrigerate for at least 1 hour. *(Pastry dough can be refrigerated for up to 3 days. Let the dough stand at room temperature to soften slightly before rolling.)*

Roll out the dough to a 12-inch round on a lightly floured surface (The dough should be about ¹/₈ inch thick.) Transfer to a 9-inch pie plate. If the dough does not uniformly cover the side of the pan, cut off some excess dough and press it over the bare spots. Trim any excess dough to within 1 inch from the edge of the pan. Fold the dough under to form a smooth, even edge. Flute the edge by crimping it between your fingers or with the round end of a knife. Cover the pastry crust loosely with plastic wrap. Refrigerate for at least 1 hour or up to 24 hours.

Preheat the oven to 400°F. Place the pie plate on a baking sheet. Line the pastry crust with foil; fill with dried beans or pie weights. Bake for 15 minutes or until lightly browned around the edge. Remove the foil and beans. Bake for 20 minutes more or until barely browned. *Reduce the oven temperature to 300°F.*

Lemon Meringue Pie (cont.)

Filling

1 **cup sugar**

5 **tablespoons cornstarch**

1 1/2 **cups water**

1/2 **cup fresh lemon juice**

6 **egg yolks**

2 **tablespoons grated lemon zest**

2 **tablespoons butter, softened**

Meringue

6 **egg whites**

1/2 **teaspoon cream of tartar**

1/3 **cup sugar**

To make the filling: Whisk the sugar and cornstarch in a heavy, medium saucepan until blended. Gradually add the water and lemon juice, whisking until the cornstarch dissolves and the mixture is smooth. Whisk in the egg yolks and lemon zest. Cook over medium-high heat, whisking constantly, for about 10 minutes, until the filling thickens and boils. Remove from the heat; whisk in the butter. Pour into the prepared crust.

To make the meringue: Beat the egg whites and cream of tartar in a large bowl with an electric mixer until soft peaks form. Gradually add the sugar, beating constantly just until the meringue is stiff and shiny; do not overbeat. Mound the meringue over the filling, spreading all the way to the edge of the crust to seal completely. Using the back of a spoon, swirl the meringue decoratively, forming peaks. Bake at 300°F for about 20 minutes, until the meringue is lightly browned. Cool on a wire rack for 1 hour. Refrigerate for at least 2 hours, until cold. Refrigerate any leftover pie.

Makes 8 servings

Note: The pie can be made up to 1 day ahead. Store, uncovered, in the refrigerator.

Lemon Layer Cake

Your taste buds will be singing with the lemon flavor found in every layer of this cake.

Cake

- 3 cups flour
- 1 tablespoon baking powder
- 1 teaspoon baking soda
- 1/2 teaspoon salt
- 2 cups sugar
- 1 cup (2 sticks) butter, softened
- 2 teaspoons fresh lemon juice
- 4 eggs
- 1 1/4 cups milk

Lemon Curd

- 4 tablespoons (1/2 stick) butter
- 3/4 cup sugar
- 1 tablespoon grated lemon zest
- 6 tablespoons fresh lemon juice
- 4 egg yolks

Frosting

- 1 (8-ounce) package cream cheese, softened
- 1 cup (2 sticks) butter, softened
- 3 tablespoons fresh lemon juice
- 3 cups confectioners' sugar, sifted

Preheat the oven to 350°F. Spray two 9-inch round cake pans with cooking spray. Line the bottoms with waxed paper; spray the paper with cooking spray. Dust the pans with flour.

To make the cake: Sift together the flour, baking powder, baking soda, and salt; set aside. Beat the sugar, butter, and lemon juice in a large bowl with an electric mixer at high speed for about 5 minutes, until well blended. Add the eggs 1 at a time, beating well after each addition. Add the flour mixture alternately with the milk, beating at medium speed after each addition. Divide the batter evenly among the prepared pans.

Bake for 30 minutes or until a wooden pick inserted into the centers comes out clean. Cool in the pans for 10 minutes. Run a small knife between the cakes and the sides of the pans. Remove from the pans to wire racks. Remove the waxed paper, then invert the layers top sides up; cool completely. *(Cake can be made 1 day ahead. Cover tightly and store at room temperature.)*

To make the lemon curd: Melt the butter in a heavy, medium saucepan over medium-low heat. Remove from the heat; whisk in the sugar, lemon zest, and juice. Add the egg yolks and whisk until smooth. Cook over medium-low heat, stirring constantly, about 10 minutes, until the mixture thickens and coats the back of a wooden spoon. Do not bring to a boil or the eggs will cook. Pour through a fine strainer set over a bowl. Cool to room temperature, whisking occasionally. Refrigerate, covered, for at least 2 hours. *(Lemon curd can be made 5 days ahead. Store, covered, in the refrigerator.)*

To make the frosting: Beat the cream cheese, butter, and lemon juice in a large bowl with an electric mixer at high speed until smooth. Gradually add the confectioners' sugar at low speed until well blended. Beat at high speed until smooth.

To assemble: Place 1 cake layer, top side down, on a cake platter. Spread with 1 cup of the frosting, then the lemon curd. Top with the second layer, top side up; gently press together. Spread a thin layer of frosting over the top and side of the cake. Spread the remaining frosting over the entire cake. Refrigerate, loosely covered, until ready to serve. Let stand at room temperature for 30 minutes before serving.

Makes 12 servings

Delicious Fruit Desserts

Orange

Peak season: Oranges grown in the U.S. are available year-round. Navel oranges are available from November to May with peak supplies January through March. Valencia oranges, often called summer oranges, are available from February to October with peak supplies May through July. Other orange varieties are imported from Australia, Jamaica, Mexico, and Israel.

Florida ranks as the largest domestic orange grower in the U.S., producing about three times the amount as second-ranked California. The often green-tinged oranges from Florida produce the sweetest juice and are used mainly for this purpose while California yields a more attractive-looking fruit that is found mainly in supermarket produce bins.

Selection: When buying oranges, first decide how they are to be used and select suitable varieties. While all sweet varieties can be eaten out of hand, Valencia oranges are best used for juicing.

The juiciest oranges are firm, plump, and heavy for their size. Choose those with smooth skins that are free of blemishes, wrinkles, soft spots, and mold. Color does not indicate quality or freshness. Fully ripened oranges may have brown-speckled skins or turn green again. Select navel oranges with small-sized navels as larger navels indicate the fruit was overripe when picked.

Storage: For maximum freshness, refrigerate oranges, away from vegetables, for up to 2 weeks. Or leave them out at a cool room temperature for up to 1 week. If the zest has been removed from an orange, store the zested orange in the refrigerator and use it within a few days.

Preparation: Both the orange juice and zest play important roles in dessert making. Orange juice adds a sweet flavor while the aromatic zest adds flavor and fragrance. Scrub oranges thoroughly in warm, soapy water to remove surface wax and traces of insecticides. This is especially important if the zest is to be used. One medium orange yields about 3 tablespoons juice and 1 tablespoon grated zest.

(continued)

A Little History: Oranges are the most important citrus crop in the world, valued both for their juice and aromatic peel. Originally from Southeast Asia, the orange symbolized good fortune and prosperity. Arabs introduced bitter oranges to the Mediterranean and the Moors brought them to Spain where they flourished and became known as Seville oranges. By the fifteenth century, both sweet and bitter oranges made their way from Asia to the New World via Christopher Columbus. Spanish missionaries, finding the climate perfect in Florida, planted orange groves there in the sixteenth century. The first three navel orange trees were brought from Brazil and planted in Riverside, California in 1873. The quality of this new sweet orange was far superior to any other grown in California and it quickly became the most popular variety. Today, one of the three original trees is still alive and producing fruit.

More about Oranges

Zesting: The outermost, colored part of orange skin is called the zest. (The white part underneath the zest is the pith and has a bitter taste.) Cut orange zest into wide strips to use in poaching liquids and julienne strips for garnishing, or finely grate it for baking. Several types of kitchen tools are used to remove the zest. For grated zest, use the fine holes on a box-shaped grater or a rasp grater. Use a vegetable peeler or sharp paring knife to remove the zest in wide strips and a zester to create thin strips. Avoid removing the white pith to prevent a bitter taste. Since it's easier to remove zest from a whole orange, zest it before cutting.

Juicing: To extract the most juice from an orange, bring it to room temperature. Roll the orange on the counter a few times using firm pressure to release the juice inside. While electric juicers make extracting large quantities of juice easier, there are good low-tech juicing options. One is to simply squeeze the juice into an upturned palm with fingers split just enough to let the juice, but not the seeds, through. Another is to press and rotate the orange half over a hand-held reamer (a grooved, cone-shaped tool) or a citrus juicer with a bowl to catch the juices.

Sectioning: Citrus sections that have all the peel, pith, and membranes removed are known as "supremes." Preparing orange sections this way makes them more attractive and easier to eat in some dishes. Cut off and discard both ends of the orange and stand it upright on a cutting board. Cut downward in vertical strips following the curve of the orange to remove the peel and pith. Working over a bowl to catch the juice, cut down on either side of each membrane to release and lift out the individual orange sections.

Varieties: There are three main categories of oranges: bitter, sweet, and loose-skinned. The best-known bitter orange is the Seville from Spain. Sweet orange varieties include the navel, Valencia, and blood orange. Loose-skinned oranges are juicy with thin, easy-to-peel skins. Popular varieties include mandarin oranges, clementines, and tangerines.

Blood: These sweet oranges have a rich orange flavor with hints of strawberry and raspberry. They're ideal both for juicing and eating. Both the flesh and juice possess a deep-red pigment that gives these oranges a dramatic visual presentation.

Mandarin: Usually sold canned, loose-skinned mandarin oranges are sweet, juicy and easy to peel. They can be used for eating, juicing, and zesting.

Navel: These oranges are considered the best eating variety in the world. Sweet and seedless with thick, easy-to-peel skins and segments that separate cleanly, navels can be juiced but their juice must be used immediately or it turns bitter. The word "navel" comes from the belly-button look at one end of the orange caused by the growth of a secondary fruit. The navel is actually a smaller fruit attached to the main orange.

Seville: Too sour to be eaten raw, these bitter oranges are used in Mediterranean cooking, orange marmalades, candied peels, and liqueurs.

Valencia: This is the world's most important commercial variety and is used mainly for juice. Small to medium-sized Valencia oranges are thin-skinned, nearly seedless and have a high juice content that makes them refreshing, delicious, and sweet. Valencia oranges go through a natural process called "regreening" in the late spring and summer that produces a greenish tint on their skins. This color change has no effect on the sweetness of the fruit.

Candied Orange Zest

Garnish any fruit dessert with candied orange zest for an extra-special touch.

Ingredients

- 6 **large navel oranges**
- 2 **cups sugar**
- 2 **cups water**
- $^1/_2$ **cup light corn syrup**
- $^1/_4$ **cup fresh orange juice**
- $^1/_2$ **teaspoon vanilla extract**

In the Orient, oranges were regarded as a sacred fruit, representing everlasting life.

Wash the oranges thoroughly. Cut off and discard the ends. Cut each orange lengthwise into quarters. Remove the zest with a sharp knife, leaving the white pith on the orange. Cut each piece of zest lengthwise into $^1/_4$-inch-wide strips.

Fill a medium saucepan with water; bring to a boil. Add the orange zest; return the water to a boil. Cook for 5 minutes. Drain and rinse under cold water; set aside.

Bring the sugar, water, corn syrup, orange juice, and vanilla to a boil in the same saucepan over high heat, stirring until the sugar dissolves. Boil for 2 minutes; reduce the heat to medium-low. Add the orange zest. Simmer, covered, for 1 hour or until the zest is translucent.

Remove from the heat; cool the zest in the syrup for 1 hour at room temperature. Pour the syrup and candied zest into a glass jar. Refrigerate, tightly covered, for up to 1 month. Drain and discard the syrup from the zest before using.

Uses: Stir candied orange zest into quick bread, fruitcakes, and muffin batters. Or, cut into thin ribbons and use as a garnish for poached fruits, pies, tarts, and cakes. Dipped into melted chocolate, it makes a wonderful candy.

Crystallized Orange Zest:

To make crystallized orange zest, drain off the syrup and toss the candied zest in granulated sugar to coat. Place in a single layer on a wire rack and let stand 8 to 12 hours at room temperature, until completely dry. (Or place the wire rack on a baking sheet and dry in a 175°F oven.) Store the crystallized zest in an airtight container for up to 1 week. Dip into melted chocolate for the ultimate treat.

White Chocolate & Orange Cookies

Orange flavor complements the white chocolate, macadamia nuts, and coconut in these yummy cookies.

Ingredients

2 1/4 cups flour

1 teaspoon baking soda

1/2 teaspoon salt

1 cup (2 sticks) butter, softened

1/2 cup granulated sugar

1/2 cup packed light brown sugar

1 egg

1 tablespoon grated orange zest

1 teaspoon orange extract

1 (12-ounce) package white chocolate chips

1/2 cup macadamia nuts, chopped

1/2 cup flaked coconut

Preheat the oven to 350°F. Grease 2 cookie sheets.

Sift together the flour, baking soda, and salt; set aside. Beat the butter and sugars in a large bowl with an electric mixer at high speed until fluffy. Beat in the egg, orange zest, and orange extract. Gradually add the flour mixture, beating at low speed just until combined. Stir in the white chocolate chips, macadamia nuts, and coconut by hand.

Drop the dough by rounded teaspoonfuls 2 inches apart onto the prepared cookie sheets. Bake for about 12 minutes, until lightly browned. Cool on the pans for 10 minutes. Remove to wire racks; cool completely.

Makes 3 dozen cookies

One medium orange is 70 calories and provides over 100% of the recommended daily value of vitamin C.

Orange-Fig Bars

If you like chewy fig cookies, you'll love these delicious bars.

Crust

1 ³/₄ cups flour

1 teaspoon baking powder

¹/₄ teaspoon salt

6 tablespoons butter, softened

¹/₄ cup sugar

¹/₄ cup honey

1 teaspoon vanilla extract

1 egg

Filling

2 cups dried figs, coarsely chopped

2 tablespoons sugar

1 tablespoon grated orange zest

¹/₄ cup boiling water

3 tablespoons fresh orange juice

2 tablespoons honey

1 teaspoon vanilla extract

1 egg yolk

1 tablespoon milk

To make the crust: Sift together the flour, baking powder, and salt; set aside. Beat the butter and sugar in a large bowl with an electric mixer at high speed until well blended. Add the honey, vanilla, and egg; beat well. Gradually add the flour mixture, beating at low speed just until a soft dough forms. Divide the dough into halves. Shape each half into a small square. Wrap in plastic wrap; refrigerate for 1 hour.

Preheat the oven to 375°F. Spray a 9x9x2-inch baking dish with cooking spray.

To make the filling: Process the figs, sugar, and orange zest in a food processor until the figs are minced. Combine the boiling water, orange juice, honey, and vanilla in a small bowl until combined. With the processor on, add the juice mixture to the fig mixture, processing until well blended.

Roll out 1 dough half to a 9-inch square on a lightly floured surface. Press onto the bottom of the prepared dish. Spread the fig filling evenly over the dough. Roll out the remaining dough to a 9-inch square on a lightly floured surface. Place over the filling. Combine the egg yolk and milk in a small bowl. Brush over the top crust.

Bake for 30 minutes or until the crust is lightly browned. Cool completely on a wire rack. Cut into 20 squares.

Makes 20 bars

Early Spanish explorers, such as Ponce de León, are credited with planting the first orange trees around St. Augustine, Florida between 1513 and 1565.

Orange Cake

There's a burst of fresh orange flavor when you bite into this delicious cake.

Cake

- 3 navel oranges
- 2 cups flour
- 1 teaspoon baking soda
- ¼ teaspoon salt
- 10 tablespoons butter, softened
- ½ cup sugar
- 2 eggs
- ½ cup milk
- ½ cup raisins
- ½ cup walnuts, toasted and coarsely chopped

Icing

- 3 tablespoons butter, softened
- ¼ cup fresh orange juice
- ½ teaspoon vanilla extract
- 2 cups confectioners' sugar, sifted

Preheat the oven to 375°F. Grease and flour a 13x9x2-inch baking pan.

To make the cake: Cut off and discard both ends of each orange and stand it upright on a cutting board. Working with 1 orange at a time, cut downward in vertical strips following the curve of the orange to remove the peel and pith. Holding the orange over a bowl to catch the juice, cut down on either side of each membrane to release and lift out the individual orange sections. Cut the sections into small pieces; set aside.

Sift together the flour, baking soda, and salt; set aside. Beat the butter and sugar in a large bowl with an electric mixer at high speed until well blended. Add the eggs 1 at a time, beating well after each addition. Add the flour mixture alternately with the milk, beating at medium speed after each addition. Stir in the oranges, raisins, and walnuts by hand. Pour into the prepared pan, spreading evenly.

Bake for 35 to 40 minutes, until a wooden pick inserted into the center comes out clean. Cool completely in the pan on a wire rack.

To make the icing: Beat the butter, orange juice, and vanilla in a large bowl with an electric mixer at high speed until smooth. Gradually add the confectioners' sugar, beating at low speed until well blended. Beat at high speed until smooth. Spread the icing evenly over the cake.

Makes 12 servings

All oranges contain carotene—a pigment that gives them their bright orange color.

Orange Cheesecake Bars

These delicious bars will remind you of creamy orange ice cream bars.

Crust

- 2 cups vanilla wafer crumbs
- 1/3 cup butter, melted
- 2 tablespoons sugar

Filling

- 2 (8-ounce) packages cream cheese, softened
- 3/4 cup sugar
- 2 eggs
- 1/2 cup sour cream
- 1 teaspoon vanilla extract

Topping

- 4 ounces white baking chocolate, chopped
- 1/2 cup heavy cream
- 2 tablespoons butter
- 1/3 cup frozen orange juice concentrate, thawed
- 2 teaspoons grated orange zest

Preheat the oven to 350°F. Spray a 13x9x2-inch baking pan with cooking spray.

To make the crust: Combine the vanilla wafer crumbs, butter, and sugar in a small bowl. Toss with a fork until the crumbs are moistened. Press onto the bottom of the prepared pan. Bake for 15 minutes. Cool completely on a wire rack.

To make the filling: Beat the cream cheese and sugar in a large bowl with an electric mixer at high speed until blended. Add the eggs 1 at a time, beating well after each addition. Add the sour cream and vanilla; beat at medium speed until combined. Spread evenly over the crust. Bake for 30 to 35 minutes, until set. Cool completely in the pan on a wire rack.

To make the topping: Place the white chocolate in a large bowl. Bring the cream and butter to a simmer in a small saucepan over medium-high heat. Pour the cream mixture over the white chocolate. Whisk until the chocolate is melted and smooth. Place the pan over low heat. Add the orange juice concentrate and orange zest; stir until combined. Pour into a bowl. Refrigerate for 45 minutes or until slightly thickened but still spreadable, stirring occasionally. Spread the topping evenly over the bars. Refrigerate, covered, for at least 1 hour before serving. Cut into 36 squares.

Makes 3 dozen bars

*Fresh navel orange sections are a popular snack
with athletes because they can be easily eaten
for a burst of energy.*

Crêpes Suzette

In the 1930's, this dessert was the essence of sophistication.

Crêpes

- 3 eggs
- 4 teaspoons sugar
- ³/₄ cup flour
- ³/₄ cup milk
- 2 teaspoons butter, melted

Filling

- 3 large navel oranges
- 4 tablespoons (¹/₂ stick) butter, cold and cut into small pieces
- 6 tablespoons sugar
- 2 teaspoons grated orange zest
- 2 teaspoons grated lemon zest
- ¹/₃ cup Grand Marnier liqueur
- ¹/₃ cup brandy

Note: Since the alcohol is ignited in this recipe, *do not* use a nonstick skillet.

To make the crêpes: Beat the eggs and sugar in a large bowl with an electric mixer at high speed for 2 minutes, until the eggs are foamy. Add the flour alternately with the milk, beating at medium speed after each addition. Stir in the butter until blended. Let the batter stand for at least 1 hour at room temperature. *(Batter can be made 1 day in advance. Cover and store in the refrigerator.)*

Spray a crêpe pan or 6-inch nonstick skillet with cooking spray. Heat the pan over medium-high heat until drops of water sprinkled onto the surface sizzle. Pour 2 tablespoons of the batter into the hot pan while tilting it to spread the batter evenly over the bottom. Cook for 2 to 3 minutes, until the bottom of the crêpe is lightly browned and the edge pulls away from the side of the pan. Carefully flip the crêpe with a spatula and brown the other side for 1 minute. Remove the crêpe from the pan to a plate; cool. Repeat with the remaining batter to make 12 crêpes, stacking them on the plate. *(Crêpes can be made 1 month in advance. Wrap tightly in plastic wrap and refrigerate for 2 days or freeze for longer storage. Bring the crêpes to room temperature when ready to use.)*

To make the filling: Cut off and discard both ends of each orange and stand it upright on a cutting board. Working with 1 orange at a time, cut downward in vertical strips following the curve of the orange to remove the peel and pith. Holding the orange over a bowl to catch the juice, cut down on either side of each membrane to release and lift out the individual orange sections; set aside. Melt the butter in a medium skillet or flambé pan over medium heat. Add the sugar, orange zest, lemon zest, and 6 tablespoons of the reserved orange juice. Bring to a boil, stirring constantly. Reduce the heat to low. Place the crêpes 1 at a time into the orange sauce, heating them until warm. Remove the crêpe from the pan and fold it into quarters. Place 2 crêpes on each of 6 dessert plates.

Remove the pan from the heat. Add the liqueur and brandy. Return the pan to the heat and carefully ignite the alcohol using a long-stemmed match. As the flame dies down, remove the pan from the heat. Stir in the orange segments. Spoon the oranges and sauce over the crêpes. Serve immediately.

Makes 6 servings

Orange-Chocolate Cheesecake

Layers of orange and chocolate make this cheesecake a taste sensation.

Crust

- 1 cup chocolate graham cracker crumbs
- 3 tablespoons butter, melted
- 1 tablespoon sugar
- 1 tablespoon grated orange zest
- $^1/_4$ teaspoon cinnamon

Filling

- 4 (8-ounce) packages cream cheese, softened
- $^3/_4$ cup sugar
- 4 eggs
- $^1/_2$ cup sour cream
- 1 teaspoon vanilla extract
- 4 ounces semisweet baking chocolate, melted and cooled
- Boiling water
- 2 tablespoons frozen orange juice concentrate
- 2 teaspoons grated orange zest

Preheat the oven to 325°F. Spray a 9-inch springform pan with cooking spray. Wrap the outside of the pan with 2 layers of foil.

To make the crust: Combine the graham cracker crumbs, butter, sugar, orange zest, and cinnamon in a small bowl. Toss with a fork until the crumbs are moistened. Press onto the bottom of the prepared pan. Bake for 10 minutes; cool on a wire rack. *Increase the oven temperature to 350°F.*

To make the filling: Beat the cream cheese and sugar in a large bowl with an electric mixer at high speed until smooth. Add the eggs 1 at a time, beating well after each addition. Beat in the sour cream and vanilla. Pour 3 cups of the filling into another bowl; add the chocolate and stir until blended. Pour the chocolate batter evenly over the crust. Place the springform pan in a roasting pan. Pull out the oven rack and place the roasting pan on the rack. Pour enough boiling water into the pan to come halfway up the side of the springform pan. Bake for 30 minutes.

Meanwhile, add the frozen orange juice concentrate and orange zest into the remaining batter; stir until blended. Remove the cheesecake from the oven. Pour the orange batter over the top, spreading evenly.

Bake for about 30 minutes more, until the center barely moves when the pan is gently shaken. Turn the oven off and leave the cheesecake in the oven for 1 hour with the door ajar. Remove the foil from the pan. Cool completely in the pan on a wire rack. Run a knife between the cheesecake and the side of the pan. Release the side of the pan. Refrigerate, covered, for at least 8 hours before serving. Let stand at room temperature for 30 minutes before serving.

Makes 12 servings

Tip: For best results, do not remove the bottom of the springform pan once the cheesecake is chilled. To prevent it from sliding around, place a rubber jar gripper between the pan bottom and serving plate.

Bittersweet Chocolate & Orange Cake

There's chocolate in the cake and nestled between the layers of this decadent dessert.

Cake

3	cups cake flour
4 1/2	teaspoons baking powder
1/2	teaspoon salt
1 1/2	cups sugar
3/4	cup (1 1/2 sticks) butter, softened
2	teaspoons vanilla extract
6	large egg yolks
1	cup milk
2	ounces bittersweet baking chocolate, chopped
1	tablespoon grated orange zest

Frosting

10	ounces bittersweet baking chocolate, chopped
1	cup heavy cream
6	tablespoons butter, cut into small pieces
1	teaspoon vanilla extract
1/2	teaspoon orange extract

(continued)

Preheat the oven to 350°F. Grease and flour two 9-inch round cake pans.

To make the cake: Sift together the flour, baking powder, and salt; set aside. Beat the sugar, butter, and vanilla in a large bowl with an electric mixer at medium speed for about 5 minutes, until well blended. Add the egg yolks 1 at a time, beating well after each addition. Add the flour mixture alternately with the milk, beating at medium speed after each addition. Beat in the chocolate and orange zest until well blended. Divide the batter evenly between the prepared pans.

Bake for 33 to 40 minutes, until a wooden pick inserted into the centers comes out clean. Cool in the pans for 10 minutes. Run a small knife between the cakes and the sides of the pans. Remove from the pans to wire racks; cool completely. *(Cake can be made 1 day ahead. Cover tightly and store at room temperature.)*

To make the frosting: Place the chocolate in a large bowl. Bring the cream and butter to a simmer in a heavy, medium saucepan over medium-high heat. Pour the cream mixture over the chocolate. Whisk until the chocolate is melted and smooth. Blend in the vanilla and orange extract. Pour into a bowl. Refrigerate for 45 minutes or until slightly thickened but still spreadable, stirring occasionally. Meanwhile, make the filling.

Filling

1 1/2 **cups fresh orange juice**

3 **tablespoons sugar**

1 **tablespoon Grand Marnier liqueur (optional)**

1 **(18-ounce) jar sweet orange marmalade**

To make the filling: Bring the orange juice and sugar to a boil in a small saucepan over medium-high heat. Boil for 15 minutes until the mixture is reduced by half, watching carefully to prevent the syrup from boiling over. Stir in the liqueur, if desired. Cool slightly. Heat the orange marmalade in a small saucepan over low heat for 2 minutes, until melted. Cool slightly.

To assemble: Cut each cake layer horizontally into halves. Place a top layer, cut side up, on a cake platter. Brush generously with the orange syrup and spread with a thin layer of the frosting. Cover with a bottom layer, cut side down. Brush generously with the syrup and spread with the orange marmalade. Cover with the last bottom layer, cut side up. Brush generously with the syrup and spread with a thin layer of the frosting. Cover with the last top layer, cut side down. Spread the remaining frosting over the entire cake, making decorative swirls. Refrigerate, loosely covered, until ready to serve. Let stand at room temperature for 30 minutes before serving.

Makes 16 servings

Note: Orange marmalade is traditionally made with bitter Seville oranges. If it's too bitter for your tastes, a sweet version is now available at most supermarkets, labeled "sweet orange marmalade."

Tips: To easily cut a cake layer horizontally, wrap a long piece of unflavored dental floss tightly around the perimeter of the cake where it should be split. Cross the ends of the floss and slowly but firmly pull on each end. The floss will cut cleanly and evenly through the cake.

To avoid getting cake crumbs in the frosting bowl, use separate spatulas for removing the frosting from the bowl and spreading.

To easily cut 16 equal slices, first cut the cake in half, then cut each half into 8 slices.

Orange Cream Tart
with Mandarin Oranges

Crust

1 1/2 cups flour

1/4 cup sugar

1/2 cup (1 stick) butter, cold and cut into small pieces

3 tablespoons milk

1 egg yolk

Filling

4 tablespoons (1/2 stick) butter

3/4 cup sugar

1 tablespoon grated orange zest

6 tablespoons fresh orange juice

4 egg yolks

(continued)

For best results, prepare the crust, filling, cake, and topping a day ahead and assemble the tart the day it's served.

To make the crust: Process the flour and sugar in a food processor until blended. Add the butter. Pulse until the mixture resembles coarse crumbs. Whisk the milk and egg yolk in a small bowl. With the processor on, slowly add the egg mixture, processing just until moist clumps form. Gather the dough into a ball; flatten into a disk. Wrap in plastic wrap; refrigerate for 1 hour. *(Pastry dough can be refrigerated for up to 3 days. Let the dough stand at room temperature to soften slightly before rolling.)*

Spray a 9-inch tart pan with a removable bottom with cooking spray. Roll out the dough to an 11-inch round between 2 sheets of parchment paper. Remove the top paper and invert the pastry into the tart pan. Remove the second paper. Press the dough firmly onto the bottom and side of the pan. If there are places where the dough doesn't reach to the top of the pan, break off any excess dough and press it into place. Reinforce the seam where the bottom and side meet with excess dough. Pierce the bottom of the crust all over with a fork. Cover; freeze for 30 minutes.

Preheat the oven to 350°F. Place the crust on a baking sheet. Bake for 20 minutes or until lightly browned. Cool completely on a wire rack. Gently loosen and remove the edge and bottom of the pan.

To make the filling: Melt the butter in a heavy, medium saucepan over medium-low heat. Remove from the heat. Add the sugar, orange zest, and juice; whisk until blended. Add the egg yolks; whisk until smooth. Cook over medium-low heat, whisking constantly, for 10 minutes or until the mixture thickens enough to coat the back of a wooden spoon. Do not bring to a boil or the eggs will cook. Cool to room temperature, whisking occasionally. Refrigerate, covered, for at least 2 hours. *(Filling can be made 1 day ahead.)*

Preheat the oven to 450°F. Spray two 9-inch round cake pans with cooking spray. Line the bottoms with waxed paper; spray the paper with cooking spray. Dust the pans with flour.

Cake

- 1/3 cup cake flour, sifted
- 2 1/2 tablespoons cornstarch
- 2 eggs
- 3 egg yolks
- 1/2 cup sugar
- 3/4 teaspoon vanilla extract
- 2 egg whites
- 1/4 teaspoon cream of tartar
- 1 tablespoon sugar

Topping

- 2 (15-ounce) cans mandarin oranges, drained
- 1/4 cup Grand Marnier liqueur
- 1/2 cup heavy cream, whipped to soft peaks

To make the cake: Combine the cake flour and cornstarch in a small bowl; set aside. Beat the eggs, egg yolks, and 1/2 cup sugar in a large bowl with an electric mixer at high speed for 5 minutes, until the mixture thickens and turns pale yellow. Beat in the vanilla at low speed. Add the flour mixture and gently fold it in by hand. Beat the egg whites in a large bowl with an electric mixer at high speed until foamy. Add the cream of tartar and 1 tablespoon sugar; beat until stiff peaks form. Gently fold into the batter. Do not overmix or the batter will deflate. Divide the batter evenly between the prepared pans.

Bake for 10 minutes or until lightly browned and the surface springs back when lightly touched. Cool in the pans for 5 minutes. Run a small knife between the cakes and the sides of the pans. Remove from the pans to wire racks. Remove the waxed paper, then invert the layers top sides up; cool completely. *(Cake can be made 1 day ahead. Cover tightly and store at room temperature.)*

To make the topping: Place the oranges in a medium bowl and pour the liqueur over them. Let stand at room temperature for at least 1 hour. *(Topping can be made 1 day ahead.)*

To assemble: Whisk the chilled filling until smooth. Fold in the whipped cream just until combined. Spoon the filling into the crust, spreading evenly. Gently scrape the top of 1 cake layer with a serrated knife to remove the browned surface. Place the cake over the filling. Arrange the mandarin oranges in concentric circles over the cake. Pour the liqueur over the oranges so that it soaks into the cake. Serve immediately. Refrigerate any leftover tart.

Makes 8 servings

Note: Only one cake layer is used in this recipe. Freeze the extra layer for up to two months. Use it to prepare the Pineapple-Rum Tart (page 168), if desired.

Fresh Orange Tart

Fresh, sweet, juicy oranges take center stage in this tart.

Crust

1 1/2 **cups flour**

1/4 **cup sugar**

1/2 **cup (1 stick) butter, cold and cut into small pieces**

3 **tablespoons milk**

1 **egg yolk**

Filling

6 **large navel oranges**

1/4 **cup sugar**

1 1/2 **tablespoons cornstarch**

1/8 **teaspoon salt**

1/2 **teaspoon vanilla extract**

1/2 **cup sweet orange marmalade**

To make the crust: Process the flour and sugar in a food processor until blended. Add the butter. Pulse until mixture resembles coarse crumbs. Whisk the milk and egg yolk in a small bowl. With the processor on, slowly add the egg mixture, processing just until moist clumps form. Do not overprocess. Gather the dough into a ball; flatten into a disk. Wrap in plastic wrap; refrigerate for 1 hour. *(Pastry dough can be refrigerated for up to 3 days.)*

Spray a 9-inch tart pan with a removable bottom with cooking spray. Roll out the dough to an 11-inch round between 2 sheets of parchment paper. Remove the top paper and invert the pastry into the tart pan. Remove the second paper. Press the dough firmly onto the bottom and side of the pan. If there are places where the dough doesn't reach to the top of the pan, break off any excess dough and press it into place. Reinforce the seam where the bottom and side meet with excess dough. Pierce the bottom of the crust all over with a fork. Cover; freeze for 30 minutes.

Preheat the oven to 350°F. Place the crust on a baking sheet. Bake for 20 minutes or until lightly browned. Cool completely on a wire rack. Gently loosen and remove the edge and bottom of the pan.

To make the filling: Cut off and discard both ends of each orange and stand it upright on a cutting board. Cut downward in vertical strips following the curve of the orange to remove the peel and pith. Holding the orange over a bowl to catch the juice, cut down on either side of each membrane to release and lift out the individual orange sections; reserve. Squeeze the orange membranes over the juice bowl to release any residual juice; reserve the juice.

Combine the sugar, cornstarch, and salt in a small saucepan. Whisk in 1/2 cup of the reserved orange juice until blended. Bring to a boil over medium heat, stirring constantly. Reduce the heat to low; cook for 1 minute. Remove from the heat. Stir in the vanilla; cool completely. Place the marmalade in a small microwavable bowl. Microwave on High for 30 seconds or until the marmalade melts. Spread the marmalade over the bottom of the crust. Arrange half the orange sections in concentric circles over the marmalade. Spoon 1/3 cup of the filling over the oranges. Top with the remaining orange sections and filling. Refrigerate, covered, for at least 4 hours before serving.

Makes 8 servings

Delicious Fruit Desserts

Peach

Peak Season: Commercial peaches are grown in thirty U.S. states. California produces two-thirds of the crop with Georgia, South Carolina, Texas, and New Jersey being the other important growing areas. While domestically grown peaches are available from May to October, the peak season is in July and August. Peaches found in supermarkets outside of this season are usually imported from Chile.

Selection: The aroma of a peach is its best indicator of ripeness. In addition to a deep fruity fragrance, choose peaches that yield to gentle pressure along their seams and have yellow or cream background colors. A green undertone means the fruit was picked early and will not be as sweet. Avoid any that have bruises, cuts on the skin, or feel soft all over.

Storage: Ripen peaches in a paper bag at room temperature away from direct sunlight. When peaches yield to gentle pressure, they are ripe and can be refrigerated for up to 5 days. Once ripe, it is best to use them within a few days.

Preparation: Peaches can be eaten with or without the skin, although they are usually peeled when used in cooking and baking. To easily peel peaches, blanch them in boiling water for about 30 seconds. Remove them from the water with a slotted spoon and immediately plunge them into cold water to cool. Use a sharp paring knife to pull the loosened peels off the flesh.

To pit a freestone peach, cut it lengthwise into halves along the natural seam. Twist the halves in opposite directions to separate them. Remove the

(continued)

A Little History: Originating in China, peaches once possessed symbolic importance. Ornamental varieties were cultivated for their blossoms, which were considered an ancient fertility symbol, and eating a peach on New Year's Day was believed to bring good luck and immortality. Peaches traveled to Europe through Persia, where they became known as Persian apples. The Spanish brought this fuzzy fruit to the New World and it eventually arrived in America. Peach trees were planted on the east coast as early as the mid-1700's and were later introduced to California by Spanish missionaries. Only apple trees rival peach trees in importance.

More about Peaches

pit with the tip of a knife. To remove the pit while keeping the peach whole, cut an almond-shaped opening around the stem end through to the pit. At the opposite end, poke a skewer into the peach and push the pit out through the opening at the top.

Clingstone peaches cannot be pitted. To slice or quarter them, make cuts with a paring knife toward the center and then around the pit, lifting out each slice.

Once peaches are cut, prevent them from turning brown by immediately tossing them with lemon juice. Canned and frozen peaches can often be substituted for fresh peaches in recipes. One pound peaches (4 medium) yields $2^3/_4$ cups sliced or $2^1/_4$ cups chopped.

Varieties: There are hundreds of peach varieties and all fall in two main categories: freestone and clingstone. As their names imply, freestone peaches have pits that are easily removed and clingstone peaches have pits that adhere firmly to the flesh. The majority of fresh peaches sold in supermarkets are freestones. Clingstones are used primarily for canning. A new category, called semi-freestone, is a combination of the freestone and clingstone varieties. Depending on their variety, peaches range in skin color from red-blushed yellow to pink-blushed cream and in flesh color from yellow-gold to pinkish white. Most of the peaches sold are yellow, but white peaches are becoming more widely available.

Elegant Lady and **O'Henry** are the two most popular freestone peach varieties.

Red Haven is another freestone that is considered the best yellow-fleshed peach grown in the Midwest.

Elberta is the most widely planted of all peach varieties and is considered the best yellow-fleshed peach grown in California.

Flavorcrest and **Gold Dust** peaches are popular semi-freestone varieties.

Belle and **Babcock** are two of the most popular white peach varieties.

Baked Peaches

Baked peaches satisfy a sweet tooth quickly and easily.
Feel free to vary the filling ingredients to suit your tastes.

Ingredients

- ¹/₂ cup (1 stick) butter, melted
- ¹/₄ cup peach schnapps or dark rum
- ¹/₂ cup orange juice
- 4 large ripe peaches
- 1 tablespoon fresh lemon juice
- ¹/₃ cup flaked coconut
- ¹/₄ cup chopped dates
- ¹/₄ cup chopped walnuts

Preheat the oven to 350°F. Combine the butter, peach schnapps, and orange juice in an 8x8x2-inch baking dish; set aside.

Peel the top third of each peach. Using a paring knife, cut an almond-shaped opening around the stem end through to the pit. At the opposite end, poke a skewer into the peach and push the pit out through the opening at the top. Remove the pit gently with your fingers, keeping the peach totally intact. If necessary, cut a thin slice off the bottom of each peach so it stands upright. Brush the inside cavity and outside of each peach with lemon juice. Spoon the coconut into the cavities. Top with the dates and walnuts. Place the peaches upright in the prepared baking dish. Bake for 40 minutes or until the peaches are tender. Serve warm, spooning the juices from the baking dish over the peaches.

Makes 4 servings

In England during Queen Victoria's reign,
fashionable dinners were not considered a success
unless peaches were served.

Peach Melba

This classic dessert pairs fresh peaches with vanilla ice cream.

Ingredients

- 1 **cup sugar**
- 2 **cups water**
- 2 **tablespoons fresh lemon juice**
- 1 **teaspoon vanilla extract**
- 2 **large ripe peaches, peeled**
- 2 **cups fresh raspberries or frozen raspberries, thawed**
- 3 **tablespoons sugar**
- 1 **pint vanilla ice cream**

Combine the 1 cup sugar and water in a medium nonaluminum saucepan. Bring to a boil over medium-high heat. Boil for 5 minutes or until the sugar completely dissolves. Stir in the lemon juice and vanilla. Add the peaches; cook over low heat about 5 minutes, until tender. (Cooking time depends on fruit ripeness.) Let the peaches cool to room temperature in the syrup. Refrigerate, covered, until cold. *(Peaches can be made up to 2 days ahead.)*

Process the raspberries in a blender or food processor until puréed. Pour through a fine strainer set over a bowl to remove the seeds, pressing the purée through the strainer. Discard the seeds in the strainer. Add 3 tablespoons sugar to the purée; stir to dissolve the sugar.

To serve, cut the peaches into halves and remove the pits. Place a scoop of ice cream in each of 4 dessert dishes. Top each scoop with a peach half, rounded side up. Drizzle with raspberry sauce.

Makes 4 servings

The legendary French chef George-Auguste Escoffier created this dessert for the famous Australian opera singer, Dame Nellie Melba.

Peach Sorbet

This sweet ice is a refreshing end to a meal any time of the year.

Ingredients

- 1 (20-ounce) package frozen sliced peaches
- 1/2 cup sugar
- 1/8 teaspoon cinnamon
- Fresh mint leaves, as a garnish

Let the peaches stand at room temperature for 20 minutes or until slightly thawed. Pulse the peaches, sugar, and cinnamon in a food processor several times to break up the fruit. Process continuously until the sugar is dissolved and the peaches are puréed. Transfer to a covered container and freeze for at least 1 hour. *(Sorbet can be made up to 3 days ahead.)*

Before serving, let the sorbet stand at room temperature for 5 to 10 minutes, until slightly thawed. Spoon it into small dessert dishes. Garnish with mint leaves.

Makes 4 servings

Tip: Serve the sorbet in frozen whole peaches for a special presentation. Prepare 4 large peaches as follows: Using a paring knife, cut an almond-shaped opening around the stem end of each peach through to the pit. At the opposite end, poke a skewer into the peach and push the pit out through the opening at the top. Remove the pit gently with your fingers, keeping the peach totally intact. Scoop out the peach flesh, leaving a 1/4-inch-thick shell. Brush the inside of each peach with lemon juice. Wrap tightly in plastic wrap and freeze for at least 1 hour. *(Peaches can be prepared up to 3 days ahead.)*

At 40 calories, one medium peach is a good source of potassium and vitamins A and C.

Peach & Blueberry Ambrosia

This easy summer dessert marries fresh blueberries and peaches with sparkling wine.

Ingredients

- 3 tablespoons honey
- 1 1/2 tablespoons fresh lemon juice
- 1 teaspoon grated lemon zest
- 2 peaches, peeled, pitted, and diced
- 2 cups fresh blueberries
- 1 cup chilled sparkling wine

Heat the honey and lemon juice in a small saucepan over low heat until the honey melts. Remove from the heat; stir in the lemon zest. Cool for 10 minutes.

Combine the peaches, blueberries, and honey syrup in a small bowl, stirring gently. Spoon into 4 tall sundae dishes or wine glasses. Refrigerate for 2 hours. To serve, pour 1/4 cup sparkling wine into each dish.

Makes 4 servings

Compared to ancient times, peaches are now a real bargain. In first-century Rome, a single peach cost the equivalent of $4.50 today.

Peach-Raspberry Crisp

Peaches and raspberries are baked with a crisp topping
for a simply scrumptious dessert.

Topping

- ¹/₂ **cup flour**
- ¹/₂ **cup old-fashioned oats**
- ¹/₃ **cup packed brown sugar**
- ¹/₂ **teaspoon baking powder**
- ¹/₂ **teaspoon cinnamon**
- ¹/₄ **teaspoon nutmeg**
- 3 **tablespoons butter, cold and cut into small pieces**

Filling

- 2 **tablespoons sugar**
- 1 **tablespoon cornstarch**
- 12 **peaches, peeled, pitted and cut into ¹/₂-inch slices**
- 1 **cup fresh raspberries**

Preheat the oven to 375°F. Spray a 9x9x2-inch baking dish with cooking spray.

To make the topping: Combine the flour, oats, brown sugar, baking powder, cinnamon, and nutmeg in a medium bowl. Cut in the butter with a pastry blender or 2 knives until the mixture resembles coarse crumbs; set aside.

To make the filling: Combine the sugar and cornstarch in a medium bowl. Add the peaches and raspberries; toss to coat. Spoon into the prepared baking dish. Sprinkle the topping evenly over the fruit, lightly pressing it in place. Bake for 45 minutes, until the filling is bubbling. Serve warm or at room temperature.

Makes 8 servings

Tip: When you need a quick dessert for four, cut the ingredient amounts in half and divide the filling and topping among four 8-ounce ramekins. Reduce the baking time to 25 minutes.

Peach Shortcakes

Oatmeal shortcakes are the perfect backdrop for luscious fresh peaches.

Shortcakes

- 2 cups flour
- 1/2 cup old-fashioned oats
- 1/4 cup packed brown sugar
- 1 tablespoon baking powder
- 1/2 teaspoon salt
- 1/2 cup (1 stick) butter, cold and cut into small pieces
- 2/3 cup milk
- 2 teaspoons granulated sugar

Filling

- 1/3 cup sugar
- 1/2 teaspoon ground ginger
- 1/8 teaspoon cinnamon
- 4 large peaches, peeled, pitted and cut into 1/2-inch slices
- 1 tablespoon fresh lemon juice
- 1 (12-ounce) package frozen raspberries, thawed

Whipped cream, as a garnish

Preheat the oven to 425°F. Grease a baking sheet.

To make the shortcakes: Combine the flour, oats, brown sugar, baking powder, and salt in a large bowl. Cut in the butter with a pastry blender or 2 knives until the mixture resembles coarse crumbs. Add the milk; gently toss with a fork until a soft dough forms. Knead the dough in the bowl until all of the flour is incorporated. Shape by hand into six 2-inch rounds. Place the rounds 2 inches apart on the prepared pan. Sprinkle with the granulated sugar. Bake for 20 minutes or until browned. Cool on a wire rack. *(Shortcakes can be made 1 day ahead.)*

To make the filling: Combine the sugar, ginger, and cinnamon in a small bowl. Combine the peaches and lemon juice in a medium bowl. Add the sugar mixture and stir gently to combine; set aside.

Process the raspberries in a blender or food processor until puréed. Pour through a fine strainer set over a small bowl to remove the seeds, pressing the purée through the strainer.

Spread 2 tablespoons raspberry purée over each of 6 dessert plates. Cut the shortcakes horizontally into halves. Place the bottom halves on the purée. Spoon the peaches evenly over the shortcake bottoms; cover with the shortcake tops. Garnish each with a dollop of whipped cream.

Makes 6 servings

Peach Cobbler

Nothing says summer more than fresh peaches nestled under a cobbler topping.

Topping

- ³/₄ **cup flour**
- ¹/₃ **cup sugar**
- ¹/₄ **cup cornmeal**
- 1 ¹/₂ **teaspoons baking powder**
- ¹/₈ **teaspoon salt**
- 3 **tablespoons butter, cold and cut into small pieces**
- ¹/₃ **cup milk**

Filling

- 3 **pounds peaches, peeled, pitted and cut into ¹/₂-inch slices**
- 2 **tablespoons fresh lemon juice**
- ¹/₂ **teaspoon vanilla extract**
- 3 **tablespoons sugar**
- 2 **teaspoons cornstarch**
- ¹/₄ **teaspoon cinnamon**

Whipped cream, as a garnish

Preheat the oven to 375°F. Spray a 9x9x2-inch baking dish with cooking spray.

To make the topping: Whisk the flour, sugar, cornmeal, baking powder, and salt in a medium bowl. Cut in the butter with a pastry blender or 2 knives until the mixture resembles coarse crumbs. Stir in the milk just until a stiff dough forms; set aside.

To make the filling: Combine the peaches, lemon juice, and vanilla in a large bowl. Combine the sugar, cornstarch, and cinnamon in a small bowl. Add to the peaches and stir gently to combine. Spoon evenly into the prepared baking dish.

Drop the dough topping by heaping tablespoonfuls onto the filling, spacing evenly. Bake for about 45 minutes, until the filling is bubbling and a wooden pick inserted into the topping comes out clean. Serve warm garnished with whipped cream.

Makes 8 servings

Peach Upside-Down Cake

Apples are traditional in classic French tarte Tatin, but peaches are divine!

Ingredients

1 ¼ cups flour

1 ½ teaspoons baking powder

½ teaspoon salt

⅓ cup butter, softened

⅔ cup granulated sugar

¾ cup milk

1 egg

1 teaspoon vanilla extract

4 tablespoons (½ stick) butter

6 tablespoons brown sugar

⅓ cup walnuts, chopped

3 ripe peaches, peeled, pitted, and cut into ¼-inch slices

Preheat the oven to 350°F.

Sift together the flour, baking powder, and salt; set aside. Beat ⅓ cup butter and granulated sugar in a large bowl with an electric mixer at high speed until blended. Beat in the milk, egg, and vanilla. Add the flour mixture and beat at low speed until blended.

Melt 4 tablespoons butter in a small saucepan over low heat. Stir in the brown sugar. Cook over medium heat for 1 minute or until the sugar dissolves. Remove from the heat; stir in the walnuts. Pour the walnut mixture into a 9-inch round cake pan. Arrange the peaches in concentric circles over the walnut mixture. Pour the batter over the peaches.

Bake for 30 minutes or until a wooden pick inserted into the center comes out clean. Cool in the pan for 5 minutes. Run a small knife between the cake and side of the pan. Carefully invert the cake onto an ovenproof or microwavable platter. Cool for 15 minutes. Serve warm.

Makes 8 servings

Note: The cake can be baked up to 6 hours ahead. Reheat in a 350°F oven for 10 minutes or microwave on Medium for about 2 minutes before serving.

Peach-Ginger Cheesecake

A triple dose of ginger spices up this creamy peach cheesecake.

Crust

- 2 **cups gingersnap cookie crumbs**
- 6 **tablespoons butter, melted**

Filling

- 4 **(8-ounce) packages cream cheese, softened**
- ²/₃ **cup honey**
- 4 **eggs**
- 2 **teaspoons ground ginger**
- ¹/₄ **cup finely chopped crystallized ginger**
- 4 **peaches, peeled, pitted, and cut into ¹/₄-inch slices**

Topping

- ³/₄ **cup peach preserves**
- 1 **peach, peeled, pitted, and cut into ¹/₈-inch slices**

Preheat the oven to 350°F. Spray a 10-inch springform pan with cooking spray.

To make the crust: Combine the cookie crumbs and butter in a medium bowl. Toss with a fork until the crumbs are moistened. Press onto the bottom and three-fourths of the way up the side of the prepared pan. Bake for 8 minutes; cool on a wire rack. Maintain the oven temperature at 350°F.

To make the filling: Beat the cream cheese and honey in a large bowl with an electric mixer at high speed until smooth. Add the eggs 1 at a time, beating well after each addition. Stir in the ground ginger and crystallized ginger. Pour half the filling evenly over the crust. Arrange the peaches in concentric circles over the filling in the pan. Pour the remaining filling over the peaches.

Bake on the lower oven rack for 1 hour or until the center barely moves when the pan is gently shaken. Cool completely in the pan on a wire rack. Run a knife between the cheesecake and the side of the pan. Release the side of the pan. Refrigerate, covered, for at least 8 hours.

To make the topping: Heat the preserves in a small, heavy saucepan over medium heat until melted to a spreading consistency. Arrange the peach slices in concentric circles in the center of the cheese-cake. Spread the preserves over the peaches and entire top of the cheesecake. Refrigerate, covered, for at least 1 hour before serving. Let stand at room temperature for 30 minutes before serving.

Makes 12 servings

Note: Crystallized or candied ginger is fresh gingerroot that has been cooked in a sugar syrup and coated with coarse sugar. Look for it in the spice section of supermarkets or at specialty food stores.

Tip: For best results, do not remove the bottom of the springform pan once the cheesecake is chilled. To prevent it from sliding around, place a rubber jar gripper between the pan bottom and serving plate.

Peach-Berry Tart

Fresh berries and peaches are the centerpiece of this easy tart.

Crust

- ³/₄ **cup flour**
- ¹/₂ **cup yellow cornmeal**
- 3 **tablespoons sugar**
- ¹/₄ **teaspoon salt**
- 6 **tablespoons butter, cold and cut into small pieces**
- 1 **egg yolk**
- 1 **tablespoon milk**
- ¹/₂ **teaspoon vanilla extract**

Filling

- 5 **peaches, pitted and cut into quarters**
- 3 **cups assorted berries (raspberries, blueberries, and blackberries)**
- 5 **tablespoons sugar**

Whipped cream, as a garnish

Preheat the oven to 400°F. Spray a 9-inch tart pan with a removable bottom with cooking spray; place on a baking sheet.

To make the crust: Process the flour, cornmeal, sugar, and salt in a food processor until blended. Add the butter. Pulse until the mixture resembles coarse crumbs. Whisk the egg yolk, milk, and vanilla in a small bowl. With the processor on, slowly add the egg mixture, processing just until the dough begins to come together. Transfer the dough to the prepared pan. Press evenly onto the bottom and side of the pan. Bake for about 15 minutes, until lightly browned. (Gently press the bottom of the crust to flatten if it puffed up during baking.) Cool on a wire rack. *Reduce the oven temperature to 350°F.*

To make the filling: Gently toss the peaches and berries with the sugar in a medium bowl. Let stand at room temperature for 15 minutes.

Spoon the fruit into the prepared crust. Bake at 350°F for 40 to 45 minutes, until the peaches are juicy and tender. Cool completely on a wire rack. Gently loosen and remove the edge of the pan. Serve warm garnished with whipped cream.

Makes 8 servings

Peach Nutmeg-Custard Tart

Fresh peaches and creamy nutmeg custard are a wonderful combination.

Crust

- 1 1/2 **cups flour**
- 1/4 **cup sugar**
- 1/2 **cup (1 stick) butter, cold and cut into small pieces**
- 3 **tablespoons milk**
- 1 **egg yolk**

Custard

- 1 1/2 **cups whole milk**
- 6 **egg yolks**
- 1/3 **cup sugar**
- 2 **tablespoons cornstarch**
- 4 **tablespoons (1/2 stick) butter, softened**
- 1 **teaspoon freshly grated nutmeg**

OR 3/4 **teaspoon ground nutmeg**

- 1/2 **teaspoon vanilla extract**

- 2 **peaches, peeled, pitted, and cut into 1/4-inch slices**
- 3 **tablespoons apricot preserves, melted**

To make the crust: Process the flour and sugar in a food processor until blended. Add the butter. Pulse until the mixture resembles coarse crumbs. Whisk the milk and egg yolk in a small bowl. With the processor on, slowly add the egg mixture, processing until moist clumps form. Gather the dough into a ball; flatten into a disk. Wrap in plastic wrap; refrigerate for at least 1 hour. *(Pastry dough can be refrigerated for up to 3 days. Let the dough stand at room temperature to soften slightly before rolling.)*

Spray a 9-inch tart pan with a removable bottom with cooking spray. Roll out the dough to an 11-inch circle between 2 sheets of parchment paper. Remove the top paper and invert the pastry into the tart pan. Remove the second paper. Press the dough firmly onto the bottom and side of the pan. If there are places where the dough doesn't reach to the top of the pan, break off any excess dough and press it into place. Reinforce the seam where the bottom and side meet with excess dough. Pierce the bottom of the crust all over with a fork. Cover; freeze for 30 minutes.

Preheat the oven to 350°F. Place the crust on a baking sheet. Bake for 30 to 35 minutes, until lightly browned. Cool completely on a wire rack. Gently loosen and remove the edge and bottom of the pan.

To make the custard: Bring the milk to a simmer in a heavy, medium saucepan over medium heat. Meanwhile, whisk the egg yolks, sugar, and cornstarch in a large bowl about 3 minutes, until the mixture thickens and turns pale yellow. Pour the hot milk into the egg mixture, whisking to combine. Pour the mixture back into the saucepan. Cook, whisking constantly, over medium heat about 3 minutes, until the custard thickens and comes to a boil. Remove from the heat; stir in the butter, nutmeg, and vanilla. Cool slightly.

Spoon the custard into the crust, spreading evenly. Cover with plastic wrap, gently pressing it directly onto the surface of the custard. Refrigerate for 4 to 8 hours. *(Tart can be made 1 day ahead.)*

About 30 minutes before serving, arrange the peaches over the custard. Brush with the warm preserves. Refrigerate, covered, for 30 minutes.

Makes 8 servings

Peach-Custard & Meringue Torte

Fresh peaches are nestled in the custard and piled on top of this stunning torte.

Cake

  1 **cup flour**

  1 **teaspoon baking powder**

  ¹/₄ **teaspoon salt**

  ¹/₂ **cup shortening**

  ¹/₂ **cup sugar**

  1 **teaspoon vanilla extract**

  4 **egg yolks**

  5 **tablespoons milk**

Meringue

  4 **egg whites**

  1 **cup sugar**

  ¹/₂ **cup walnuts, chopped**

(continued)

Preheat the oven to 325°F. Grease and flour two 9-inch round cake pans with removable bottoms.

To make the cake: Sift together the flour, baking powder, and salt; set aside. Beat the shortening, sugar, and vanilla in a large bowl with an electric mixer at medium speed until well blended. Add the egg yolks 1 at a time, beating well after each addition. Beat in the milk. Gradually add the flour mixture, beating at medium speed until blended. Divide the batter evenly between the prepared pans; set aside.

To make the meringue: Beat the egg whites in a large bowl with an electric mixer at high speed until soft peaks form. Gradually add the sugar, beating constantly just until the meringue is stiff and shiny; do not overbeat. Spread evenly over the batter in the pans. Top with the walnuts.

Bake for 30 minutes or until the meringue is lightly browned and a wooden pick inserted into the centers of the cakes comes out clean. Cool in the pans for 10 minutes. Run a small knife between the cakes and the sides of the pans. Remove the edges of the pans. Slide a long sharp knife between the pan bottoms and the cakes to release them without inverting. Cool completely on wire racks. *(Cake can be made 1 day ahead. Cover tightly and store at room temperature.)*

Peach-Custard & Meringue Torte (cont.)

Custard

- 1 cup whole milk
- 2 egg yolks
- 1/2 cup sugar
- 2 tablespoons cornstarch
- 1/2 teaspoon vanilla extract

- 2 peaches, peeled, pitted, and chopped
- 4 peaches

To make the custard: Bring the milk to a simmer in a heavy, medium saucepan over medium heat. Meanwhile, whisk the egg yolks, sugar, and cornstarch in a medium bowl about 3 minutes, until the mixture thickens and turns pale yellow. Pour the hot milk into the egg mixture, whisking to combine. Pour the mixture back into the saucepan. Cook, whisking constantly, over medium heat about 3 minutes, until the custard thickens and comes to a boil. Remove from the heat; stir in the vanilla. Cool slightly. Pour the custard into a medium bowl and cover with plastic wrap, gently pressing it directly onto the surface of the custard. Refrigerate 4 hours or overnight.

To assemble: Whisk the chilled custard until smooth. Place 1 cake layer, meringue side up, on a cake platter. Spread evenly with the custard. Arrange the 2 chopped peaches over the custard. Top with the second layer, meringue side up; gently press together. Refrigerate, loosely covered, until ready to serve. Just before serving, peel, pit and cut the 4 peaches into 1/4-inch slices. Arrange in 3 concentric circles on the top of the cake.

Makes 12 servings

Tip: To easily cut 12 equal slices, first cut the cake in half, then cut each half into 6 slices.

Peach Pie

*When ripe peaches are in season, it's time to make peach pie—
the ultimate summer dessert!*

Crust

- 2 cups sifted flour
- 1 teaspoon salt
- 1/3 cup shortening, cold
- 1/3 cup butter, cold and cut into small pieces
- 5 to 7 tablespoons ice water, divided

Filling

- 4 pounds ripe peaches, peeled, pitted, and cut into 1/4-inch slices
- 1 tablespoon fresh lemon juice
- 2/3 cup sugar
- 1/4 cup quick-cooking tapioca
- 1 teaspoon freshly grated nutmeg
- OR 1/2 teaspoon ground nutmeg
- 2 tablespoons butter, cut into small pieces

- 1 egg white, lightly beaten
- 1 tablespoon sugar
- Vanilla ice cream (optional)

Makes 8 servings

To make the crust: Combine the flour and salt in a large bowl. Cut in the shortening with a pastry blender or 2 knives until the mixture resembles coarse crumbs. Cut in the butter until the pieces become the size of small peas. Sprinkle 4 tablespoons water over the flour mixture; gently toss with a fork. Add enough of the remaining water, 1 tablespoon at a time, tossing until all the flour is moistened. Gather the dough into 2 balls, one slightly smaller than the other; flatten each into a disk. Wrap in plastic wrap; refrigerate for at least 1 hour. *(Pastry dough can be refrigerated for up to 3 days. Let the dough stand at room temperature to soften slightly before rolling.)*

Roll out the larger dough disk to a 12-inch round on a lightly floured surface. (The dough should be about 1/8 inch thick.) Transfer to a 9-inch pie plate. If the dough does not uniformly cover the side of the pan, cut off some excess dough and press it over the bare spots. Trim any excess dough to within 1/2 inch from the edge of the pan. Cover the pastry crust loosely with plastic wrap. Refrigerate for at least 1 hour or up to 24 hours.

Preheat the oven to 375°F.

To make the filling: Combine the peaches and lemon juice in a large bowl. Combine the 2/3 cup sugar, tapioca, and nutmeg in a small bowl. Add to the peaches and toss to coat. Spoon evenly into the prepared pastry crust, mounding the peaches slightly in the center. Dot with the butter.

Roll out the second dough disk to a 10-inch round on a lightly floured surface. Place over the peaches. Trim any excess dough to within 1 inch from the edge of the pan. Fold the top crust edge under the bottom edge, pressing together to seal. Flute the edge by crimping it between your fingers or with the round end of a knife. Cut several slits in the top crust to allow steam to escape. Brush the top with the egg white; sprinkle with 1 tablespoon sugar.

Place the pie on a baking sheet. Bake on the lower oven rack for 1 hour or until the crust is lightly browned and the juices are bubbling. (If the crust browns too quickly, cover the edge with foil.) Cool on a wire rack for at least 2 hours. Serve warm or at room temperature with ice cream, if desired.

Delicious Fruit Desserts

Pear

Peak Season: All pears are picked unripe to produce the best texture and flavor. U.S. pears are grown primarily in California, Washington, and Oregon, where harvesting begins in late summer and peaks during the winter. The pears are stored and sold through the following spring. Bartletts are the first variety to appear in late August while Anjou pears are available through June.

Selection: Even unripe pears are fragile, so handle them carefully. Select pears that are smooth, firm, and well shaped with no bruises or spots. It is best to buy them unripe and ripen them at home, so avoid any that are very yellow or have a soft stem end. Since pears ripen from the inside out, don't let them get too soft or they will be overripe. To check ripeness, press gently near the stem end. When it yields to gentle pressure, it's ready to use.

Storage: Store unripe pears at room temperature in an open container. Avoid stacking too many on top of one another. To speed up ripening, place them in a brown paper bag. Refrigerate ripe pears for 3 to 5 days. Once ripe, pears spoil quickly even when refrigerated.

Preparation: Just before using, rinse pears under cold water and pat dry. Peel them with a vegetable peeler or paring knife. To core a whole pear for poaching or baking, insert a melon baller into the bottom and twist several times to remove the seeds and core. Pears turn brown once they are peeled or cut, so use them right away. Toss them with a little lemon juice while preparing them to prevent discoloration. One pound pears (3 to 4 medium) yields 2 cups sliced.

(continued)

A Little History: Pears have been cultivated for over four thousand years in Europe and Asia. In ancient Greece, this botanical cousin of apples was called "the fruit of the gods," and Romans ended lavish meals with bowls of grapes, apples, and pears. France has been known throughout history for growing superior-quality pears. During the Middle Ages, a large orchard with exotic fruits was a symbol of power for French and Italian noblemen, and pear trees were a favorite indulgence. Although pears were brought from Europe to the American colonies, a good pear was a luxury until pear orchards were established in the milder climate of the west coast. Pears have another history out west as they traveled from Spain to South America and up the coast to California via missionaries. Today, there are three main commercially grown pear varieties in the U.S. that still retain at least part of their original French names: Beurré d'Anjou, Beurré Bosc, and Doyenné du Comice.

Pear Varieties

Most pears are suitable for eating, baking, and cooking. Firmer varieties, such as Bosc, are better suited for poaching and baking whole. Many of the recipes in this chapter use Bartlett pears, but feel free to experiment with your favorite varieties.

Anjou: These short-necked, almost cone-shaped pears have a firm, buttery texture, making them a good choice for cooking and baking. Sweet and juicy with a mild flavor, Anjous are available with both green and red skins. Since they don't change color as they ripen, test often for ripeness at home.

Asian pears: Also called Chinese or apple pears, these range from huge and golden brown to tiny and yellowish green. They have a lightly sweet taste and crunchy, very juicy texture even when ripe. Best suited for eating, Asian pears are not readily available in the U.S., although some varieties are grown in California. The most popular variety is the Twentieth Century, or Nijisseiki.

Bartlett: With their sweet, buttery flavor, juicy texture, and classic pear shape, green- and red-skinned Bartletts are the most widely grown pears worldwide. The more common green Bartletts have a slight blush and turn yellow as they ripen. While they are good all-purpose pears, most of the crop is used for canning.

Bosc: Bosc pears are distinguished by their long, tapering necks and russet-colored skins. With their firm flesh and rich, nutty flavor, they are good for cooking and eating, and are especially suited for poaching and baking whole. These pears take a bit longer to ripen and their skins don't change color.

Comice: With their large, portly shape and sweet, succulent flesh, Comice pears are the best eating pears in the world. Because they are so fragile to ship, they are relatively expensive and are used exclusively for eating.

Seckel: A hybrid of European and Asian pears, the Seckel pear is the smallest variety with dark green, red-blushed skins. Almost heart-shaped with a very sweet flavor and slightly grainy texture, these bite-size pears are great for eating, cooking, and canning.

Baked Pears
with Bourbon Sauce

Enjoy the full flavor of the pears, complemented by this sinfully delicious sauce.

Sauce

- ¹/₃ **cup apricot preserves**
- ¹/₃ **cup plus 2 tablespoons bourbon**
- 3 **tablespoons fresh orange juice**
- 2 **teaspoons fresh lemon juice**
- ¹/₄ **teaspoon cinnamon**
- ¹/₈ **teaspoon ground cloves**
- ¹/₈ **teaspoon ginger**
- 1 **tablespoon butter**

- 3 **large ripe, firm Bartlett or Anjou pears, peeled, cored, and cut into halves**

Topping

- ¹/₃ **cup pecans, coarsely chopped and toasted**
- ¹/₄ **cup packed brown sugar**
- 2 **tablespoons butter, cold**

- 2 **tablespoons heavy cream**
- **Vanilla ice cream (optional)**

Preheat the oven to 350°F.

To make the sauce: Combine the apricot preserves, bourbon, orange juice, lemon juice, cinnamon, cloves, and ginger in a small saucepan. Bring to a simmer over medium heat. Cook for 2 to 3 minutes, until the preserves are melted, stirring frequently. Add the butter and stir until melted. Remove from the heat.

Place the pear halves, cut sides up, in a 9x9x2-inch baking dish. Pour the bourbon sauce over the pears; set aside.

To make the topping: Combine the pecans and brown sugar in a small bowl. Cut in the butter with a pastry blender or 2 knives until the mixture resembles coarse crumbs. Spoon the topping into the pears' cavities, mounding it on top and pressing to compact.

Bake for 15 minutes. Baste the pears with the sauce. Bake for about 15 minutes more, until the pears are tender and the sauce is caramelized. Divide the pears among 6 dessert plates. Stir the cream into the sauce in the baking dish; spoon the sauce over the pears. Serve warm with ice cream, if desired.

Makes 6 servings

At one time, today's ubiquitous Bartlett pears were rare. In the 1800's, one Bartlett pear cost the equivalent to today's $20.00!

Poached Pears

Poached pears served with sauce make a simple yet elegant dessert.

Poaching is a simple way to enjoy pears. Because poached pears can be refrigerated for several days, they are an elegant dessert with make-ahead convenience. Experiment with the following poaching liquids, garnishes, and sauces to create your own favorite flavor combinations.

Here are several poaching liquid options. Each recipe makes enough liquid to poach six pears.

Pears Poached in Wine

- 2 cups fruity white or red wine
- 1 cup water
- 1 cup sugar
- 1 cinnamon stick
- Zest of 1 lemon, cut into 3x1-inch strips

Pears Poached in Honey Syrup

- 4 cups water
- 1 cup honey
- 2 cinnamon sticks
- 10 whole cloves
- Zest of 1 lemon, cut into 3x1-inch strips

Pears Poached in Juice

- 2 cups cran-raspberry or white grape juice
- 1 cup water
- 1 cup packed brown sugar
- 1 cinnamon stick

Selecting Pears: Firm, ripe Bosc pears are best for poaching. It's best to buy them several days in advance to let them ripen properly. When the stem ends yield to gentle pressure, they are ready for poaching.

Pear Preparation: Peel the pears just before submerging them in the poaching liquid to prevent them from turning brown. Keeping the stem intact, insert a melon baller into the bottom of each pear and twist several times to remove the seeds and core. Cut a thin slice off the bottom of each pear so it stands upright.

Poaching Liquids: Pears are poached whole, completely submerged in a sugar syrup. The syrup can be flavored with juices (white grape juice, apple cider, cranberry juice), red or white wine, and spices.

To make Poached Pears: Combine the poaching liquid ingredients in a nonaluminum stockpot. Bring to a boil, stirring to dissolve the sugar or honey. Meanwhile, peel and core the pears. Add them, stem sides up, to the poaching liquid. (To keep the pears submerged in the liquid, cover them with a piece of parchment paper and a plate.) Return to a boil; reduce the heat to low. Simmer, covered, for 45 minutes or until the pears are tender. (A paring knife should pierce the center of the pear without resistance.) Remove the pears with a slotted spoon to a dish. Refrigerate for 2 to 24 hours. Strain the liquid, discarding the solids. To make a sauce, continue cooking the poaching liquid over medium heat until thickened. (*The poaching liquid can be refrigerated for up to 1 week and used again for poaching.*) Serve the pears and sauce cold or gently reheat the pears in the sauce until warm.

Poached Pears (cont.)

Drizzle one of these sauces over poached pears for an extra-special touch. Each recipe makes enough sauce for six pears.

Caramel Sauce

- ¹/₂ **cup light corn syrup**
- ¹/₂ **cup packed brown sugar**
- 1 **teaspoon vanilla extract**
- ¹/₂ **cup heavy cream**

Chocolate Sauce

- ¹/₃ **cup heavy cream**
- ¹/₃ **cup Frangelico liqueur**
- ¹/₄ **cup sugar**
- 8 **ounces semisweet or bittersweet baking chocolate, chopped**

To make the Caramel Sauce: Combine the syrup and brown sugar in a medium saucepan. Bring to a boil over medium heat. Cook for 5 minutes, until the sugar dissolves and the sauce thickens. Remove from the heat; stir in the vanilla and cream. Serve warm or at room temperature.

To make the Chocolate Sauce: Combine the cream, liqueur, and sugar in a small, heavy saucepan. Bring to a boil. Remove from the heat. Add the chocolate and stir until melted and the sauce is smooth. *(Sauce can be made 3 days ahead and refrigerated. Reheat in a saucepan over low heat before serving. If the sauce becomes too thick while reheating, thin it with a few drops of cream.)*

Garnishes: Stuff the poached pears' cavities with chopped dried fruits and nuts, or mascarpone cheese. Serve with the thickened poaching liquid or another sauce.

*"On the first day of Christmas my true love gave to me,
a partridge in a pear tree."*

Pears Hélène

Impress your guests with this classic French dessert—
originally named Belle Hélène for beautiful Helen of Troy.

Poached Pears

4 **cups sweet white wine or white grape juice**

2 **cups water**

1 **cup sugar**

Zest of 1 orange, cut into 3x1-inch strips

1 **cinnamon stick**

8 **whole cloves**

6 **slightly underripe Bosc pears**

Chocolate Sauce

$^1/_3$ **cup heavy cream**

$^1/_3$ **cup Frangelico liqueur**

$^1/_4$ **cup sugar**

8 **ounces semisweet or bittersweet baking chocolate, chopped**

6 **scoops vanilla ice cream**

To make the poached pears: Combine the wine, water, sugar, orange zest, cinnamon stick, and cloves in a nonaluminum stockpot. Bring to a boil, stirring to dissolve the sugar. Meanwhile, peel the pears. Keeping the stem intact, insert a melon baller into the bottom of each pear and twist several times to remove the seeds and core. Cut a thin slice off the bottom of each pear so it stands upright. Add the pears, stem sides up, to the poaching liquid. (To keep the pears submerged in the liquid, cover them with a piece of parchment paper and a plate.) Return to a boil; reduce the heat to low. Simmer, covered, for 45 minutes or until the pears are tender. (A paring knife should pierce the center of the pear without resistance.) Remove the pears with a slotted spoon to a dish. Refrigerate for 2 to 24 hours. *(The poaching liquid can be refrigerated for up to 1 week and used again for poaching. Strain the liquid before storing, discarding the solids.)*

To make the chocolate sauce: Combine the cream, liqueur, and sugar in a small, heavy saucepan. Bring to a boil. Remove from the heat. Add the chocolate and stir until melted and the sauce is smooth. *(Sauce can be made 3 days ahead and refrigerated. Reheat in a saucepan over low heat before serving. If the sauce becomes too thick while reheating, thin it with a few drops of cream.)*

Stand a chilled pear on each of 6 dessert plates. Place a scoop of ice cream next to each pear. Spoon the warm chocolate sauce over the pears and ice cream. Serve immediately.

Makes 6 servings

Delicious Fruit Desserts

Pear Squares

These easy-to-make bars make a delectable snack or dessert.

Ingredients

- 1 ½ cups flour
- 1 cup old-fashioned oats
- 1 cup packed light brown sugar
- 1 teaspoon baking powder
- ½ teaspoon salt
- ½ teaspoon cinnamon
- ¼ teaspoon nutmeg
- ¼ cup milk
- 3 tablespoons vegetable oil
- 3 Bartlett pears, peeled, cored, and diced
- ½ cup walnuts, chopped

Preheat the oven to 350°F. Spray a 9x9x2-inch baking pan with cooking spray.

Combine the flour, oats, brown sugar, baking powder, salt, cinnamon, and nutmeg in a large bowl. Add the milk and oil; stir with a fork until coarse crumbs form. Firmly press 2 cups of the oat mixture onto the bottom of the prepared pan. Top with the pears. Stir the walnuts into the remaining oat mixture; sprinkle evenly over the pears.

Bake for 30 minutes or until lightly browned. Cool completely in the pan on a wire rack. Cut into 16 squares.

Makes 16 squares

*A medium pear has about 100 calories and is
a good source of dietary fiber and vitamin C.
It also contains no saturated fat and is low in sodium.*

Mini Pear-Spice Cakes

These individual cakes are so easy to make and so delicious!

Ingredients

- 3 tablespoons butter, softened and cut into 6 pieces
- 12 teaspoons packed brown sugar
- 6 tablespoons golden raisins
- 6 tablespoons chopped walnuts, toasted
- 1 Bartlett pear, peeled and cored
- 2 cups flour
- 1 teaspoon baking powder
- 1/2 teaspoon baking soda
- 1 teaspoon cinnamon
- 1/2 teaspoon nutmeg
- 1/4 teaspoon salt
- 1/4 teaspoon ginger
- 1/4 teaspoon ground allspice
- 2/3 cup granulated sugar
- 1/4 cup (1/2 stick) butter, softened
- 1 egg
- 1 egg yolk
- 1/2 teaspoon vanilla extract
- 3/4 cup milk
- Whipped cream, as a garnish

Preheat the oven to 350°F. Generously butter 6 jumbo muffin cups.

Divide the 6 butter pieces evenly among the prepared muffin cups. Top with the brown sugar, raisins, and walnuts, dividing them evenly. Cut the pear into thin slices to fit the muffin cups. Place 3 or 4 slices over the raisins and nuts; set aside.

Sift together the flour, baking powder, baking soda, cinnamon, nutmeg, salt, ginger, and allspice; set aside. Beat the granulated sugar and 1/4 cup butter in a large bowl with an electric mixer at high speed until fluffy. Add the egg, egg yolk and vanilla; beat until smooth. Add the flour mixture alternately with the milk, beating at low speed after each addition. Divide the batter evenly among the prepared muffin cups. Gently tap the bottom of the pan against the counter several times to evenly distribute the batter.

Bake for 25 minutes or until a wooden pick inserted into the centers comes out clean. Cool on a wire rack for 5 minutes. Slice the rounded tops off the cakes to make them flat. Run a small knife between the cakes and the sides of the cups. Carefully invert the cakes onto a wire rack. Serve warm with whipped cream, if desired.

Makes 6 servings

Note: Six mini Bundt cake pans, each with a 1-cup capacity, can be substituted for the jumbo muffin cups.

Pear Clafouti

This classic country French dessert is simply divine!

Ingredients

4 eggs

$1/2$ cup granulated sugar

$3/4$ cup flour

1 cup whole milk

$1/4$ cup ($1/2$ stick) butter, melted

$1/2$ teaspoon vanilla extract

$1/8$ teaspoon salt

$1/8$ teaspoon nutmeg

3 large Bartlett or Anjou pears, peeled, cored, and cut into $1/2$-inch slices

Confectioners' sugar

Preheat the oven to 325°F. Butter a 10-inch pie plate.

Beat the eggs and granulated sugar in a large bowl with an electric mixer at high speed until well blended. Beat in the flour. Add the milk, butter, vanilla, salt, and nutmeg; beat until smooth. Arrange the pears in concentric circles over the bottom of the prepared pie plate with the stem ends toward the center. Pour the batter over the pears.

Bake for 55 minutes or until lightly browned and a wooden pick inserted into the center comes out clean. Sprinkle with confectioners' sugar and serve warm.

Makes 6 servings

Birth trees are a European custom in which apple trees are planted for the birth of boys and pear trees for girls.

Pear Upside-Down Gingerbread Cake

The inviting aroma of gingerbread will have everyone clamoring for this pear delight.

Ingredients

- 1 **cup flour**
- 1/4 **cup packed brown sugar**
- 1 **teaspoon baking powder**
- 1 **teaspoon ginger**
- 1 **teaspoon cinnamon**
- 1/2 **teaspoon baking soda**
- 1/4 **teaspoon salt**
- 1/4 **teaspoon ground cloves**
- 1/2 **cup milk**
- 1/4 **cup molasses**
- 5 **tablespoons butter, melted and divided**
- 6 **tablespoons brown sugar**
- 1/4 **cup walnuts, chopped**
- 2 **Bartlett pears, peeled, cored, and cut into 1/4-inch slices**

Preheat the oven to 375°F.

Combine the flour, 1/4 cup brown sugar, baking powder, ginger, cinnamon, baking soda, salt, and cloves in a large bowl with an electric mixer at high speed until well blended. Combine the milk, molasses and 2 tablespoons of the butter in a small bowl. Add to the flour mixture and beat until blended. Combine the remaining 3 tablespoons butter and 6 tablespoons brown sugar in a small saucepan. Cook over medium heat for 1 minute. Remove from the heat; stir in the walnuts. Pour the walnut mixture into a 9-inch round cake pan. Arrange the pears in concentric circles over the walnut mixture with the stem ends toward the center. Pour the batter over the pears.

Bake for 30 minutes or until a wooden pick inserted in the center comes out clean. Cool in the pan for 5 minutes. Run a small knife between the cake and side of the pan. Carefully invert cake onto an ovenproof or microwavable platter. Cool for 15 minutes. Serve warm.

Makes 8 servings

Note: The cake can be baked up to 6 hours ahead. Reheat in a 350°F oven for 10 minutes or microwave on Medium for about 2 minutes before serving.

Pear Cake
with Pine Nuts

The combination of pine nuts and pears in this simple cake is sublime.

Ingredients

- 1 1/4 cups flour
- 3/4 cup sugar
- 1/8 teaspoon salt
- 1/4 cup (1/2 stick) butter, cold and cut into small pieces
- 2 tablespoons pine nuts, toasted
- 1/4 teaspoon cinnamon
- 1/3 cup sour cream
- 1/4 cup milk
- 1 egg
- 1 teaspoon vanilla extract
- 1/2 teaspoon baking powder
- 1/4 teaspoon baking soda
- 2 Bartlett pears, peeled, cored, and cut into 1/4-inch slices

Preheat the oven to 350°F. Spray a 9-inch round cake pan with cooking spray.

Combine the flour, sugar, and salt in a large bowl. Cut in the butter with a pastry blender or 2 knives until the mixture resembles coarse crumbs. Remove 1/3 cup of the flour mixture to a small bowl; stir in the pine nuts and cinnamon and set aside.

Add the sour cream, milk, egg, vanilla, baking powder, and baking soda to the remaining flour mixture. Beat with an electric mixer at high speed until well blended. Pour into the prepared pan. Arrange the pears evenly over the batter. Sprinkle with the pine nut mixture.

Bake for 45 minutes or until a wooden pick inserted into the center comes out clean. Cool completely in the pan on a wire rack.

Makes 8 servings

Pear & Dried Cranberry Crisp

Almonds and coconut create a delicious topping for sweet, juicy pears.

Topping

- ³/₄ **cup flour**
- ¹/₄ **cup packed light brown sugar**
- ¹/₄ **teaspoon cinnamon**
- ¹/₈ **teaspoon nutmeg**
- 6 **tablespoons butter, cold and cut into small pieces**
- ³/₄ **cup flaked coconut**
- ²/₃ **cup sliced almonds**

Filling

- 1 **cup dried cranberries**
- 3 **tablespoons orange marmalade**
- 2 **tablespoons sugar**
- 2 **tablespoons amaretto liqueur**
- ¹/₂ **teaspoon ground allspice**
- ¹/₂ **teaspoon almond extract**
- 5 **Anjou or Bosc pears, peeled, cored, and cut into ³/₄-inch cubes**

Preheat the oven to 350°F. Spray a 9x9x2-inch baking dish with cooking spray.

To make the topping: Combine the flour, brown sugar, cinnamon, and nutmeg in a medium bowl. Cut in the butter with a pastry blender or 2 knives until the mixture resembles coarse crumbs. Stir in the coconut and almonds; set aside.

To make the filling: Combine the dried cranberries, orange marmalade, sugar, liqueur, allspice, and almond extract in a large bowl. Add the pears; toss gently to coat. Spoon into the prepared baking dish. Sprinkle the topping evenly over the fruit, lightly pressing in place.

Bake for 35 to 40 minutes, until the filling is bubbling. Serve warm or at room temperature.

Makes 8 servings

Pear-Cranberry Shortcakes

*These cornmeal shortcakes with pears and cranberries
nestled in a brandy cream sauce are simply exquisite!*

Shortcakes

1 1/4 **cups flour**

1/2 **cup yellow cornmeal**

3 **tablespoons sugar**

1 1/4 **teaspoons baking powder**

1/2 **teaspoon salt**

1/4 **teaspoon baking soda**

6 **tablespoons butter, cold and
cut into small pieces**

6 **tablespoons milk**

1 **egg, beaten**

Filling

6 **tablespoons dark brown sugar**

2 **tablespoons water**

4 **ripe, firm Anjou or Bosc pears,
peeled, cored, and cut into
1/4-inch slices**

1 **cup fresh cranberries**

1/2 **teaspoon cinnamon**

1/2 **cup heavy cream**

2 **tablespoons brandy**

Whipped cream, as a garnish

Preheat the oven to 400°F. Grease a baking sheet.

To make the shortcakes: Process the flour, cornmeal, sugar, baking powder, salt, and baking soda in a food processor until blended. Add the butter. Pulse until the mixture resembles coarse crumbs. Add the milk and pulse just until moist clumps form. Do not overprocess.

Turn the dough out onto a lightly floured surface. Gently pat the dough to a 1/2-inch thickness. Cut out with a 3-inch round biscuit cutter. Repeat with the scraps to make a total of 6 shortcakes. Place 1 inch apart on the prepared pan. Brush the egg over the tops. Bake for about 15 minutes, until a wooden pick inserted into the centers comes out clean. Cool on a wire rack. *(Shortcakes can be made 1 day ahead.)*

To prepare the filling: Heat the brown sugar and water in a large skillet over medium heat until the sugar dissolves. Add the pears, cranberries, and cinnamon. Cook and stir for about 10 minutes, until the pears are crisp-tender. Remove from the heat. Stir in the cream and brandy. Bring to a boil over medium heat. Cook for about 5 minutes, until the sauce thickens.

Cut the shortcakes horizontally into halves. Place the bottom halves on 6 individual plates. Spoon the pears and some sauce over and around the shortcake bottoms. Cover with the shortcake tops; spoon more sauce over the shortcakes. Garnish each with a dollop of whipped cream.

Makes 6 servings

Pear-Walnut Layer Cake
with Dried Fruits

This luscious spice cake makes a beautiful presentation for a sophisticated birthday party.

Cake

- 5 Bosc pears, peeled, cored, and coarsely grated
- 2 cups flour
- 1 1/2 cups sugar
- 2 teaspoons baking soda
- 2 teaspoons cinnamon
- 1 teaspoon salt
- 1 teaspoon nutmeg
- 3/4 cup vegetable oil
- 2 eggs
- 1/3 cup milk
- 1 teaspoon vanilla extract
- 1/2 cup walnuts, toasted and chopped

Topping

- 1/2 cup dried pears, chopped
- 1/2 cup dried apricots, chopped
- 1/2 cup rum
- 1/4 cup water

Frosting

- 2 (8-ounce) packages cream cheese, softened
- 1/2 cup (1 stick) butter, softened
- 2 teaspoons vanilla extract
- 1 1/2 cups confectioners' sugar, sifted
- 1 cup walnuts, toasted and chopped

Preheat the oven to 325°F. Spray two 9-inch round cake pans with cooking spray. Line the bottoms with waxed paper; spray the paper with cooking spray. Dust the pans with flour.

To make the cake: Drain the grated pears in a strainer, pressing with the back of a spoon to extract as much juice as possible. Discard the juice; set aside the pears. Whisk the flour, sugar, baking soda, cinnamon, salt, and nutmeg in a large bowl. Combine the oil, eggs, milk, and vanilla in a small bowl. Add to the flour mixture and stir just until combined. Fold in the pears and walnuts. Divide the batter evenly between the prepared pans.

Bake for 40 minutes or until a wooden pick inserted into the centers comes out clean. Cool in the pans for 10 minutes. Run a small knife between the cakes and sides of the pans. Remove from the pans to wire racks. Remove the waxed paper, then invert the layers top sides up; cool completely.

To make the topping: Combine the dried pears, apricots, rum, and water in a small saucepan. Bring to a simmer over medium heat. Remove from the heat. Let stand for 30 minutes. Drain; set aside.

To make the frosting: Beat the cream cheese, butter, and vanilla in a large bowl with an electric mixer at high speed until smooth. Gradually add the confectioners' sugar, beating at low speed until well blended. Beat at high speed until smooth.

To assemble: Place 1 cake layer, top side down, on a cake platter. Spread with a thin layer of frosting. Top with 1/3 cup of the walnuts and 1/2 cup of the fruit mixture, leaving a 1/2-inch border around the edge. Top with the second layer, top side up; gently press together. Spread a thin layer of frosting over the top and side of the cake. Spread the remaining frosting over the entire cake. Sprinkle the remaining 2/3 cup walnuts over the top edge of the cake, creating a 1 1/2-inch border. Spoon the remaining fruit mixture inside the nut border. Refrigerate, loosely covered, until ready to serve.

Makes 12 servings

Pear, Fig & Hazelnut Crumb Pie

Take a break from the ordinary and try this unique fruit and nut pie.

Crust

- 1 1/2 cups sifted flour
- 1/2 teaspoon salt
- 1/4 cup shortening, cold
- 1/4 cup (1/2 stick) butter, cold and cut into small pieces
- 4 to 5 tablespoons ice water, divided

Topping

- 1/2 cup sugar
- 1/2 cup flour
- 1 teaspoon cinnamon
- 1/4 cup (1/2 stick) butter, cold and cut into small pieces
- 3/4 cup hazelnuts, toasted, skins removed, and coarsely chopped

Filling

- 1/2 cup packed brown sugar
- 3 1/2 tablespoons cornstarch
- Finely grated zest of 1 lemon
- Juice of 1 lemon
- 1 teaspoon cinnamon
- 1/2 teaspoon ginger
- 8 ripe Anjou pears, peeled, cored, and cut into 1/2-inch slices
- 1 cup dried calimyrna figs, stemmed and quartered

Vanilla ice cream (optional)

To make the crust: Combine the flour and salt in a large bowl. Cut in the shortening with a pastry blender or 2 knives until the mixture resembles coarse crumbs. Cut in the butter until the pieces become the size of small peas. Sprinkle 3 tablespoons water over the flour mixture; gently toss with a fork. Add enough of the remaining water, 1 tablespoon at a time, tossing until all the flour is moistened. Gather the dough into a ball; flatten into a disk. Wrap in plastic wrap; refrigerate for at least 1 hour. *(Pastry dough can be refrigerated for up to 3 days. Let the dough stand at room temperature to soften slightly before rolling.)*

Roll out the dough to a 12-inch round on a lightly floured surface (The dough should be about 1/8 inch thick.) Transfer to a 9-inch pie plate. If the dough does not uniformly cover the side of the pan, cut off some excess dough and press it over the bare spots. Trim any excess dough to within 1 inch from the edge of the pan. Fold the dough under to form a smooth, even edge. Flute the edge by crimping it between your fingers or with the round end of a knife. Cover the pastry crust loosely with plastic wrap. Refrigerate for at least 1 hour or up to 24 hours.

Preheat the oven to 375°F.

To make the topping: Combine the sugar, flour, and cinnamon in a medium bowl. Cut in the butter with a pastry blender or 2 knives until the mixture resembles coarse crumbs. Stir in the hazelnuts; set aside.

To make the filling: Combine the brown sugar, cornstarch, lemon zest, lemon juice, cinnamon, and ginger in a large bowl. Add the pears and figs; toss gently to coat. Spoon the fruit into the prepared crust, spreading it out evenly and mounding slightly in the center. Sprinkle the topping evenly over the fruit, lightly pressing it in place.

Place the pie on a baking sheet. Bake on the lower oven rack for 15 minutes. *Reduce the oven temperature to 350°F.* Bake for 45 to 50 minutes more, until the crust is browned and the filling is bubbling. Serve warm or at room temperature with ice cream, if desired.

Makes 8 servings

Pear-Almond Custard Tart

Not only will your guests enjoy the flavors in this simple dessert,
they will admire the beautiful presentation.

Poached Pears

1 1/2 **quarts water**

3/4 **cup sugar**

Zest of 1 lemon, cut into 3x1-inch strips

1 **cinnamon stick**

8 **whole cloves**

2 **teaspoons vanilla extract**

4 **ripe Anjou pears**

Almond Cream

2/3 **cup whole unblanched almonds**

2 **tablespoons flour**

1/2 **cup (1 stick) butter, softened**

1/2 **cup sugar**

2 **eggs**

Custard

1 1/2 **cups heavy cream**

3 **eggs**

6 **tablespoons sugar**

1 **teaspoon vanilla extract**

1/4 **cup sliced almonds**

To make the poached pears: Combine the water, sugar, lemon zest, cinnamon stick, cloves, and vanilla in a nonaluminum stockpot. Bring to a boil, stirring to dissolve the sugar. Meanwhile, peel, core, and cut the pears lengthwise into halves. Place them in the liquid. (To keep the pears submerged in the liquid, cover them with a piece of parchment paper and a plate.) Return to a boil; reduce the heat to low. Simmer, covered, for 25 minutes or until the pears are just tender. Remove the pears with a slotted spoon to a cutting board. Pat dry with paper towels. Slice each pear half lengthwise into quarters; set aside. *(The poaching liquid can be refrigerated for up to 1 week and used again for poaching. Strain the liquid before storing, discarding the solids.)*

Preheat the oven to 350°F. Butter a 10x1 1/2-inch fluted quiche dish.

To make the almond cream: Pulse the almonds and flour in a food processor until the almonds are finely ground; do not overprocess. Transfer to a large bowl. Add the butter and sugar. Beat with an electric mixer at medium speed until creamy. Add the eggs 1 at a time, beating well after each addition. Continue beating for 1 to 2 minutes, until fluffy. Spread evenly over the bottom of the prepared dish.

Bake for 18 to 20 minutes, until lightly browned. Remove from the oven. Cool on a wire rack for 15 minutes. Arrange the pear quarters over the almond cream with cut sides down and stem ends toward the center. Place the dish on a baking sheet; set aside. *Reduce the oven temperature to 325°F.*

To make the custard: Beat the cream, eggs, sugar, and vanilla in a large bowl with an electric mixer at high speed until smooth. Pour over the pears; sprinkle with the almonds. Bake at 325°F for 1 hour to 1 hour and 20 minutes, until the custard is set. Cool completely on a wire rack. Serve at room temperature.

Makes 12 servings

Pineapple

Peak Season: Pineapples are available year-round, but March to July is their peak season. Most of those sold in U.S. markets come from Hawaii, Puerto Rico, Costa Rica, and Mexico. Since pineapples are harvested when fully ripe, they are shipped by air and reach most major markets within thirty-six hours after harvesting.

There are three major pineapple varieties: Cayenne (the prevalent golden-skinned variety from Hawaii), Red Spanish (from Puerto Rico and Florida), and Sugar Loaf (from Mexico).

Selection: While pineapples do not become sweeter after harvesting, they do become juicier and less acidic. Choose a fresh-looking pineapple that seems heavy for its size. It should have a sweet, tropical fragrance and deep green leaves. The bottom should yield to medium pressure and have no sign of mold. Avoid any with a dull yellow color, dry brown leaves, bruises, soft spots, or a fermented aroma. Many grocery stores will peel and core fresh pineapples on demand using a simple machine, or sell them peeled and cored in packages.

Storage: Fresh pineapple is quite perishable and bruises easily despite its seemingly tough exterior. If it has a weak aroma, let stand at room temperature for two to three days until it softens slightly and becomes more aromatic. Then refrigerate it in a perforated plastic bag for up to five days. Do not let a pineapple stand too long at room temperature or it will ferment. Once peeled and cored, store the pineapple with its juice in a nonmetallic airtight container for up to 3 days. Or, freeze it for use in blender drinks.

A Little History: A native Brazilian fruit, pineapple was first grown in South and Central America. Columbus discovered pineapple on his second voyage to the New World and introduced it to Spain. Pineapple cultivation in Europe spurred the development of the greenhouse and growing the fruit became a symbol of wealth. Also considered a sign of friendship and hospitality, the pineapple was a popular motif used by architects and artisans over the front doors and on gateposts of houses to welcome visitors.

Named after the piña, or pine cone it resembles, pineapple was carried on long voyages of Portuguese ships to prevent scurvy. The sailors unwittingly spread its growth by discarding pineapple crowns around the tropics. Today, Central America, Malaysia, Brazil, and Hawaii are the world's biggest pineapple producers. Pineapples are grown from the crowns or tops of other pineapples. When the plants are one year old, a pink flower appears and about six months later it develops into a single pineapple.

More about Pineapple

Preparation: The skin and core of a pineapple are not suitable for eating. While the core is edible, it's too tough for most uses. The skin can, however, be left on as a decorative element. Hollowed-out pineapple halves are often used as decorative containers for serving salads or cut-up fresh fruit.

There are several simple techniques for cutting pineapples. While there are specialized kitchen tools to remove pineapple cores, a large sharp knife and cutting board are the only equipment needed.

Throughout colonial times in America, the pineapple shape was commonly used in food creations and table decorations. Pineapple-shaped cakes, pineapple-shaped gelatin molds, candies pressed out like small pineapples, pineapples molded of gum and sugar, and cookies cut like pineapples were popular.

❧

Ceramic bowls were formed like pineapples, fruit and sweet trays incorporated pineapple designs, and pineapple pitchers, cups and even candelabras were made.

❧

The pineapple became a symbol of our founding society's commitment to hospitality as well as its fondest memories of families, friends and good times.

For spears with skin: Cut off the crown and bottom. Lay the pineapple on its side and cut it lengthwise into quarters. Trim away and discard the core from the segments, then cut them lengthwise into spears of desired thickness.

For rings: Cut off the crown and bottom to form two flat bases. Stand the pineapple upright and cut downward in vertical strips to remove the skin. Remove the brown pineapple "eyes" with the tip of a knife. (Remove the core at this point if you have a pineapple corer, otherwise wait until after cutting into rings.) Lay the pineapple on its side and cut it crosswise into rounds of desired thickness. Cut out the core with an apple corer, a small round cookie cutter, or a knife.

For chunks: Cut off the crown and bottom to form two flat bases. Stand the pineapple upright and cut downward in vertical strips to remove the skin. Remove the brown pineapple "eyes" with the tip of a knife. Lay the pineapple on its side and cut it lengthwise into quarters. Trim away and discard the core from the segments, then cut them into chunks of desired size.

Though canned or cooked pineapple can be added to gelatin mixtures, fresh pineapple cannot. The enzyme brom-elin is found in fresh pineapple and counteracts the solidifying effects of gelatin. For the same reason, fresh pineapple should not be mixed with dairy products, such as cottage cheese and sour cream, until just before the dish is served. The acid in pineapple juice prevents other cut fruits, such as apples and pears, from turning brown. One medium pineapple yields about 3 cups cubed.

Pineapple & Macadamia Nut Cookies

These cookies are packed with tropical treats.

Ingredients

- 1 (20-ounce) can crushed pineapple
- 2 cups flour
- 1 teaspoon baking soda
- 1/2 teaspoon baking powder
- 1/2 cup (1 stick) butter, softened
- 1 cup packed brown sugar
- 1 egg
- 2 cups old-fashioned oats
- 1/2 cup flaked coconut
- 1/2 cup macadamia nuts, chopped
- 1/2 cup white chocolate chips

Preheat the oven to 350°F. Grease 2 cookie sheets.

Drain the pineapple, reserving 2 tablespoons of the juice; set aside. Sift together the flour, baking soda, and baking powder; set aside. Beat the butter and brown sugar in a large bowl with an electric mixer at high speed until well blended. Add the reserved pineapple juice and egg; beat well. Gradually add the flour mixture and oats, beating at low speed until well blended. Stir in the pineapple, coconut, macadamia nuts and white chocolate chips by hand.

Drop the dough by rounded teaspoonfuls 2 inches apart onto the prepared cookie sheets. Bake for 13 minutes or until lightly browned. Cool on a wire rack.

Makes 3 dozen cookies

Spanish explorers named the pineapple piña *since it resembled a pine cone. The English added* apple *to associate it with a juicy, delicious fruit.*

Pineapple-Coconut Bars

*This is a favorite bar cookie that my mother made for our family.
They're easy to make and so scrumptious!*

Crust

- ¹/₂ cup (1 stick) butter, softened
- ¹/₄ cup sugar
- 1 ¹/₄ cups flour, sifted

Filling

- 1 (20-ounce) can crushed pineapple, well drained
- ¹/₂ cup sugar
- 1 egg
- 1 tablespoon butter, melted
- 1 ¹/₂ cups flaked coconut

Preheat the oven to 350°F. Spray an 8x8x2-inch baking pan with cooking spray.

To make the crust: Beat the butter and sugar in a large bowl with an electric mixer at high speed until well blended. Add the flour; beat at low speed until crumbly. Press evenly onto the bottom and ¹/₂ inch up the sides of the prepared pan. Bake for 20 minutes or until lightly browned.

To make the filling: Spread the pineapple evenly over the hot crust. Beat the sugar and egg in a large bowl with an electric mixer at high speed until well blended. Fold in the butter and coconut. Spread evenly over the pineapple. Bake for 25 to 30 minutes, until the coconut is lightly browned. Cool completely on a wire rack. Cut into 16 squares.

Makes 16 bars

*When King Louis XIV of France first tried pineapple,
he bit into the strange fruit without peeling it first
and cut his mouth on the scaly skin.
Pineapple was banned from France after that.*

Caramelized Pineapple Parfaits

*A touch of coconut in the chocolate sauce
complements the pineapple in these delectable parfaits.*

Sauce

- 1 (15-ounce) can sweetened cream of coconut
- 6 tablespoons unsweetened cocoa
- 1/2 teaspoon vanilla extract
- 1/2 teaspoon coconut extract

Fruit

- 4 tablespoons (1/2 stick) butter
- 1 ripe pineapple, peeled, cored, and cut into 1/4-inch chunks
- 1/2 cup packed brown sugar
- 1/2 cup dark rum

- 1 1/2 pints vanilla ice cream
- 6 maraschino cherries, drained

To make the sauce: Combine the cream of coconut and cocoa in a heavy, medium saucepan. Heat to a simmer over medium-low heat, whisking until smooth. Remove from the heat. Stir in the vanilla and coconut extract. Cool to room temperature.

To prepare the fruit: Melt the butter in a large skillet over medium-high heat. Add the pineapple. Cook for 8 to 10 minutes, until well browned on both sides. Add the brown sugar. Cook until the sugar dissolves. Remove the pan from the heat and add the rum. Simmer for 3 minutes or until the sauce thickens, scraping any caramelized pineapple from the bottom of the pan.

Divide the pineapple among 6 sundae dishes. Pour the rum sauce over the pineapple. Top each serving with a scoop of ice cream, chocolate sauce, and a maraschino cherry.

Makes 6 servings

*One serving of fresh pineapple (2 thin slices)
contains about 60 calories and over 50%
of the recommended daily value of vitamin C.*

Pineapple-Mango Bars

The flavors in the fruit filling of these bars are out of this world!

Filling

- 2 cups chopped fresh pineapple
- 2 cups chopped fresh mango
- 3/4 cup packed brown sugar
- 1/2 cup fresh orange juice
- 1 teaspoon grated orange zest
- 1 teaspoon grated lemon zest
- 1/2 teaspoon ground allspice

Crust

- 1 cup (2 sticks) butter, softened
- 1/2 cup sugar
- 1 teaspoon coconut extract
- 1/8 teaspoon salt
- 2 cups flour

To make the filling: Combine the pineapple, mango, brown sugar, orange juice, orange zest, lemon zest, and allspice in a heavy, medium saucepan. Bring to a boil over medium heat. Reduce the heat to low; simmer for 1 hour and 30 minutes or until the fruit is tender and the liquid thickens, stirring frequently. Cool slightly.

To make the crust: Beat the butter, sugar, coconut extract, and salt in a large bowl with an electric mixer at high speed until blended. Gradually add the flour, beating at low speed just until a soft dough forms. Divide the dough into 2 pieces, one slightly larger than the other. Shape each dough piece into a square. Wrap in plastic wrap; refrigerate for 1 hour.

Preheat the oven to 375°F. Spray a 9x9x2-inch baking dish with cooking spray.

Roll out the larger dough square to a 10-inch square on a lightly floured surface. Press onto the bottom and 1/2 inch up the sides of the prepared dish. Spoon the filling into the crust, spreading evenly. Roll out the remaining dough to a 9-inch square on a lightly floured surface. Cut into nine 1-inch-wide strips. Place 4 strips over the filling, spacing evenly. Place the remaining 5 strips diagonally over the top, forming a lattice. Trim any excess dough even with the edges of the pan.

Bake for 50 minutes or until the crust is lightly browned and the filling is bubbling. Cool completely in the pan on a wire rack. Cut into 16 squares.

Tip: A fresh mango has a long, flat seed that runs down the center. Here's one easy method for cutting a mango into cubes:
1. Cut both ends off the mango to determine the seed location.
2. Hold the mango upright on a cutting board. Cut down about 1/2 inch to the right of the seed. Repeat on the opposite side of the fruit, forming 2 oval-shaped halves.
3. Score the flesh in a crisscross pattern, cutting up to but not through the skin.
4. Holding 1 mango half in both hands, use your thumbs to press against the skin, popping up the mango cubes. Cut across the bottom of the cubes to separate them from the skin.

Makes 16 bars

Delicious Fruit Desserts

Pineapple-Macadamia Crisp

Fresh pineapple, coconut, and macadamia nuts
give a tropical twist to a classic dessert.

Topping

- ¹/₂ cup flour, sifted
- ¹/₃ cup vanilla wafer crumbs
- ¹/₄ cup packed brown sugar
- 3 tablespoons granulated sugar
- ³/₄ teaspoon cinnamon
- ¹/₄ teaspoon nutmeg
- 6 tablespoons butter, cold and cut into small pieces
- ¹/₂ cup chopped macadamia nuts
- ¹/₂ cup flaked coconut

Filling

- 1 ripe pineapple, peeled, cored, and cut into ¹/₂-inch chunks
- ¹/₄ cup fresh orange juice
- 3 tablespoons granulated sugar
- 1 tablespoon dark rum

Preheat the oven to 375°F. Spray a 9x9x2-inch baking dish with cooking spray.

To make the topping: Combine the flour, vanilla wafer crumbs, sugars, cinnamon, and nutmeg in a medium bowl. Cut in the butter with a pastry blender or 2 knives until the mixture resembles coarse crumbs. Stir in the macadamia nuts and coconut; set aside.

To make the filling: Combine the pineapple, orange juice, sugar, and rum in a medium bowl. Spoon into the prepared baking dish. Sprinkle the topping evenly over the fruit, lightly pressing it in place. Bake for 35 minutes, until the filling is bubbling. Serve warm or at room temperature.

Makes 8 servings

Throughout history, the pineapple has been a symbol
of friendship and hospitality.

Pineapple Upside-Down Cake

This easy cake is still an all-time favorite.

Ingredients

- 1 (20-ounce) can pineapple slices
- 1 1/4 cups flour
- 1 1/2 teaspoons baking powder
- 1/2 teaspoon salt
- 1/2 cup granulated sugar
- 1/3 cup shortening
- 1 egg
- 1 teaspoon vanilla extract
- 4 tablespoons (1/2 stick) butter
- 2/3 cup packed brown sugar
- 7 maraschino cherries, drained

Preheat the oven to 350°F.

Drain the pineapple, reserving the juice; set aside. Sift together the flour, baking powder, and salt; set aside. Beat the granulated sugar and shortening in a large bowl with an electric mixer at high speed until well blended. Add the egg, vanilla, and 1/2 cup of the reserved pineapple juice; beat at low speed until combined. Gradually add the flour mixture, beating at low speed until blended.

Melt the butter in a small saucepan over low heat. Stir in the brown sugar and 2 tablespoons of the reserved pineapple juice. Cook over medium heat for 1 minute or until the sugar dissolves and the mixture thickens. Remove from the heat; pour into a 9-inch round cake pan. Place 1 pineapple slice in the center of the pan and surround it with 6 more slices. Place 1 maraschino cherry in the center of each pineapple slice. Pour the batter over the pineapple, spreading evenly.

Bake for 40 to 45 minutes, until a wooden pick inserted into the center comes out clean. Cool in the pan for 5 minutes. Run a small knife between the cake and side of the pan. Carefully invert the cake onto an ovenproof or microwavable platter. Cool for 15 minutes. Serve warm.

Makes 8 servings

Note: The cake can be baked up to 6 hours ahead. Reheat in a 350°F oven for 10 minutes or microwave on Medium for about 2 minutes before serving.

Pineapple-Carrot Cake

Pineapple adds new flavor to traditional carrot cake.

Cake

- 2 **cups flour**
- 2 **teaspoons baking soda**
- 2 **teaspoons cinnamon**
- 1/4 **teaspoon salt**
- 4 **eggs**
- 1 1/2 **cups sugar**
- 1 1/2 **cups vegetable oil**
- 2 **cups grated carrots**
- 1 **(20-ounce) can crushed pineapple, well drained**

Frosting

- 11 **ounces cream cheese, softened**
- 12 **tablespoons (1 1/2 sticks) butter, softened**
- 1/2 **teaspoon vanilla extract**
- 2 **cups confectioners' sugar, sifted**
- 1 **(8-ounce) can crushed pineapple, well drained**

Preheat the oven to 350°F. Grease and flour a 13x9x2-inch baking pan.

To make the cake: Sift together the flour, baking soda, cinnamon, and salt; set aside. Beat the eggs and sugar in a large bowl with an electric mixer at high speed for 3 minutes or until the mixture thickens and turns pale yellow. Gradually add the oil, beating at low speed until blended. Add the flour mixture half at a time, beating at medium speed after each addition. Add the carrots and pineapple; beat at low speed until blended. Pour into the prepared pan, spreading evenly.

Bake for 45 minutes or until a wooden pick inserted into the center comes out clean. Cool completely in the pan on a wire rack.

To make the frosting: Beat the cream cheese, butter, and vanilla in a large bowl with an electric mixer at high speed until smooth. Gradually add the confectioners' sugar, beating at low speed until well blended. Beat at high speed until smooth. Stir in the pineapple by hand. Spread the frosting evenly over the cake. Refrigerate, covered, until ready to serve. Refrigerate any leftover cake.

Makes 12 servings

Tip: To neatly cut the cake, thoroughly wipe off the knife blade between each cut.

Pineapple Surprise Cake

My mother and her friends made this cake for my birthday one year—
it's an unusual cake packed with lots of yummy ingredients.

Ingredients

- ¹/₂ **cup flour**
- 1 **teaspoon baking powder**
- ¹/₄ **teaspoon salt**
- 4 **eggs, separated**
- 1 **cup sugar**
- 2 **teaspoons vanilla extract**
- 1 **cup chopped dates**
- 1 **cup walnuts, chopped**
- 1 **(20-ounce) can crushed pineapple**
- 2 **oranges, peeled and chopped**
- 2 **bananas, sliced**
- 1 **cup heavy cream**
- 2 **tablespoons sugar**
- 1 **teaspoon vanilla extract**
- 2 **strawberries, stems intact, as a garnish**
- 1 **kiwifruit, peeled and cut into ¹/₈-inch slices, as a garnish**

Preheat the oven to 350°F. Spray a 13x9x2-inch baking pan with cooking spray.

Sift together the flour, baking powder, and salt; set aside. Beat the egg yolks and 1 cup sugar in a large bowl with an electric mixer at high speed for 3 minutes or until the mixture thickens and turns pale yellow. Beat in 2 teaspoons vanilla. Gradually add the flour mixture at low speed, beating until blended. Stir in the dates and walnuts. Beat the egg whites in a large bowl with an electric mixer at high speed until stiff peaks form. Gently fold into the batter just until combined; do not overmix. Pour into the prepared pan, spreading evenly.

Bake for 30 to 40 minutes, until a wooden pick inserted into the center comes out clean. Cool completely in the pan on a wire rack. *(Cake can be made 1 day ahead. Cover tightly and store at room temperature.)*

Drain the pineapple, reserving the juice; set aside. Cut the cake into 1-inch cubes. Arrange half the cake cubes in a 9-inch round on a large cake platter. Top with the oranges and bananas. Cover the fruit with the remaining cake cubes, mounding them into a half-dome shape. Spread the pineapple over the entire dome, pouring the reserved pineapple juice over the top.

Beat the cream in a large bowl with an electric mixer until soft peaks form. Add 2 tablespoons sugar and 1 teaspoon vanilla. Beat until stiff peaks form; do not overbeat. Spread over the entire cake, making decorative peaks. Make several lengthwise cuts from the pointed end of each strawberry, not quite cutting to the stem end. Spread the slices apart slightly, forming a fan. Garnish the cake with kiwifruit slices, arranging them in a row following the curve of the dome in the center of the cake. Place the strawberry fans on top of the dome, on either side of the kiwifruit. Refrigerate for 2 hours before serving. Use a large spoon to serve the cake.

Makes 10 servings

Delicious Fruit Desserts

Pineapple Cheesecake

This luscious cheesecake is laced and crowned with fresh pineapple.

Crust

1 **cup vanilla wafer crumbs**

¹/₂ **cup toasted whole blanched almonds**

3 **tablespoons sugar**

3 **tablespoons butter, melted**

Filling

1 **fresh pineapple, peeled and cored**

3 **(8-ounce) packages cream cheese, softened**

1 **cup sugar**

3 **eggs**

1 **cup sour cream**

1 **tablespoon grated orange zest**

1 **teaspoon orange extract**

Topping

¹/₂ **cup orange marmalade**

1 **tablespoon dark rum**

Preheat the oven to 400°F. Spray a 9-inch springform pan with cooking spray.

To make the crust: Place the vanilla wafer crumbs in a medium bowl. Process the almonds in a food processor until finely ground; do not overprocess. Stir the ground almonds and sugar into the wafer crumbs. Add the butter and toss with a fork until the crumbs are moistened. Press onto the bottom and three-fourths of the way up the side of the prepared pan. Bake for 10 minutes; cool on a wire rack. *Reduce the oven temperature to 325°F.*

To make the filling: Finely dice enough pineapple to measure 1 cup; set aside. Beat the cream cheese and sugar in a large bowl with an electric mixer at high speed until smooth. Add the eggs 1 at a time, beating well after each addition. Beat in the sour cream, orange zest, and orange extract. Stir in the 1 cup diced pineapple by hand. Pour the filling evenly over the crust. Bake at 325°F on the lower oven rack for about 1 hour and 50 minutes, until the center barely moves when the pan is gently shaken. Cool completely in the pan on a wire rack. Run a knife between the cheesecake and the side of the pan. Release the side of the pan. Refrigerate, covered, for at least 8 hours before serving.

To make the topping: Cut the remaining pineapple into ¹/₄-inch pieces (there should be 2 cups). Place the pineapple in a colander and press gently to remove any excess juice; set aside. Heat the orange marmalade in a small saucepan over low heat for 3 minutes or until melted, stirring frequently. Remove the pan from the heat. Stir in the rum; cool slightly. Stir in the pineapple. Spread the pineapple mixture evenly over the top of the cheesecake. Refrigerate, covered, for at least 1 hour before serving. Let stand at room temperature for 30 minutes before serving.

Makes 12 servings

Note: Orange marmalade is traditionally made with bitter Seville oranges. If it's too bitter for your tastes, a sweet version is now available at most supermarkets, labeled "sweet orange marmalade."

Pineapple-Rum Tart

*Rum-soaked cake, rum custard, and pineapple are layered
in a macadamia crust for a tempting tropical tart.*

Crust

- 1 **cup roasted and salted
  macadamia nuts**
- 2 **tablespoons sugar**
- 1¼ **cups all-purpose flour**
- ½ **cup (1 stick) butter, cold and
  cut into small pieces**
- 3 **to 4 teaspoons water, divided**

Custard

- 1½ **cups whole milk**
- 6 **egg yolks**
- ⅓ **cup sugar**
- 2 **tablespoons cornstarch**
- 4 **tablespoons (½ stick) butter,
  softened and cut into pieces**
- 2 **teaspoons dark rum**

(continued)

*For best results, prepare the crust, custard, and cake a day ahead
and assemble the tart the day it's served.*

To make the crust: Process the macadamia nuts and sugar in a
food processor until the nuts are finely ground. Add the flour and
pulse until blended. Add the butter. Pulse until the mixture resembles coarse crumbs. Add 2 teaspoons water and pulse 6 times.
Pinch a small amount of the dough between your fingers. If it
does not hold together, add 1 teaspoon water and pulse 3 times.
Repeat this procedure until the dough is the proper consistency.
Gather the dough into a ball; flatten into a disk. Wrap in plastic
wrap; refrigerate for at least 1 hour. *(Pastry dough can be refrigerated for up to 3 days. Let the dough stand at room temperature to
soften slightly before rolling.)*

Spray a 9-inch tart pan with a removable bottom with cooking
spray. Roll out the dough to an 11-inch circle on a lightly floured
surface. Gently lift the dough just enough to move the prepared
pan underneath it. Press the dough firmly onto the bottom and
side of the pan. If there are places where the dough doesn't reach
to the top of the pan, break off any excess dough and press it into
place. Reinforce the seam where the bottom and side meet with
excess dough. Pierce the bottom of the crust all over with a fork.
Cover; freeze for 30 minutes.

Preheat the oven to 350°F. Place the crust on a baking sheet. Bake
for 20 minutes or until lightly browned. Cool completely on a wire
rack. Gently loosen and remove the edge and bottom of the pan.
*(Crust can be made 1 day ahead. Cover tightly and store at room
temperature.)*

To make the custard: Bring the milk to a simmer in a heavy,
medium saucepan over medium heat. Meanwhile, whisk the egg
yolks, sugar, and cornstarch in a large bowl about 3 minutes, until
the mixture thickens and turns pale yellow. Pour the hot milk into
the egg mixture, whisking to combine. Pour the mixture back into
the saucepan. Cook, whisking constantly, over medium heat about
3 minutes, until the custard thickens and comes to a boil. Remove
from the heat; stir in the butter and rum. Cool slightly.

Makes 8 servings

Delicious Fruit Desserts

Pineapple-Rum Tart (cont.)

Cake

1/3 cup cake flour, sifted

2 1/2 tablespoons cornstarch

2 eggs

3 egg yolks

1/2 cup sugar

3/4 teaspoon vanilla extract

2 egg whites

1/4 teaspoon cream of tartar

1 tablespoon sugar

Topping

3 tablespoons butter

3 cups sliced fresh pineapple (1/4 inch thick)

1/3 cup packed brown sugar

1/4 cup dark rum

Note: Only one cake layer is used in this recipe. Freeze the extra layer for up to two months. Use it to prepare the Orange Cream Tart with Mandarin Oranges (page 122), if desired.

Spoon the custard into the crust, spreading evenly. Cover with plastic wrap, gently pressing it directly onto the surface of the custard. Refrigerate for 4 to 8 hours.

Preheat the oven to 450°F. Spray two 9-inch round cake pans with cooking spray. Line the bottoms with waxed paper; spray the paper with cooking spray. Dust the pans with flour.

To make the cake: Combine the cake flour and cornstarch in a small bowl; set aside. Beat the eggs, egg yolks, and 1/2 cup sugar in a large bowl with an electric mixer at high speed for 5 minutes, until the mixture thickens and turns pale yellow. Beat in the vanilla at low speed. Add the flour mixture and gently fold it in by hand. Beat the egg whites in a large bowl with an electric mixer at high speed until foamy. Add the cream of tartar and 1 tablespoon sugar; beat until stiff peaks form. Gently fold into the batter. Do not overmix or the batter will deflate. Divide the batter evenly between the prepared pans.

Bake for 10 minutes or until lightly browned and the surface springs back lightly when lightly touched. Cool in the pans for 5 minutes. Run a small knife between the cakes and the sides of the pans. Remove from the pans to wire racks. Remove the waxed paper, then invert the layers top sides up; cool completely. *(Cake can be made 1 day ahead. Cover tightly and store at room temperature.)*

To make the topping: Melt the butter in a large skillet over medium-high heat. Add the pineapple. Cook for 8 to 10 minutes, until lightly browned on both sides. Add the brown sugar. Cook until the sugar dissolves. Remove the pan from the heat and add the rum. Simmer for 3 minutes or until the sauce thickens, scraping any caramelized pineapple from the bottom of the pan. Cool slightly.

To assemble: Whisk the chilled custard until smooth. Spoon it into the crust, spreading evenly. Gently scrape the top of 1 cake layer with a serrated knife to remove the browned surface. Place the cake over the custard. Using a slotted spoon, spread the cooked pineapple evenly over the cake. Pour the rum sauce over the pineapple so that it soaks into the cake. Serve immediately while the pineapple is warm. Refrigerate any leftover tart.

Pineapple-Coconut Cream Pie

Flavored with pineapple and macadamia nuts,
this is no ordinary coconut cream pie.

Crust

1 ½ cups crushed vanilla wafers
⅓ cup macadamia nuts
3 tablespoons sugar
3 tablespoons butter, melted

Custard

1 ½ cups whole milk
6 egg yolks
⅓ cup sugar
2 tablespoons cornstarch
1 teaspoon coconut extract
1 (8-ounce) can crushed pineapple, well drained
¼ cup flaked coconut

Topping

1 cup heavy cream
¼ teaspoon coconut extract
2 tablespoons flaked coconut, toasted

Preheat the oven to 350°F. Spray a 9-inch pie plate with cooking spray.

To make the crust: Place the vanilla wafer crumbs in a medium bowl. Process the macadamia nuts in a food processor until finely ground; do not overprocess. Stir the ground nuts and sugar into the wafer crumbs. Add the butter and toss with a fork until the crumbs are moistened. Press onto the bottom and side of the prepared pie plate. Bake for 10 minutes; cool on a wire rack.

To make the custard: Bring the milk to a simmer in a heavy, medium saucepan over medium heat. Meanwhile, whisk the egg yolks, sugar, and cornstarch in a large bowl about 3 minutes, until the mixture thickens and turns pale yellow. Pour the hot milk into the egg mixture, whisking to combine. Pour the mixture back into the saucepan. Cook, whisking constantly, over medium heat about 3 minutes, until the custard thickens and comes to a boil. Remove from the heat; stir in the coconut extract, pineapple, and coconut. Cool slightly. Spoon the custard into the crust, spreading evenly. Cover with plastic wrap, gently pressing it directly onto the surface of the custard. Refrigerate for 4 to 8 hours.

To make the topping: Beat the cream in a large bowl with an electric mixer until soft peaks form. Add the coconut extract and beat until stiff peaks form; do not overbeat. Spread evenly over the custard, making decorative peaks. Sprinkle with the toasted coconut. Refrigerate, covered, until ready to serve. *(Can be made up to 8 hours ahead.)*

Makes 8 servings

Strawberry

Peak Season: The peak season for most locally grown strawberries is short—mid-June to early July. Commercial strawberries are imported year-round from New Zealand, Argentina, Chile, and Mexico. In the U.S., winter and spring crops are shipped from Florida and other southeastern states. California produces 83% of the nation's strawberries, providing an almost year-round supply. The California coast is considered the best place in the world to grow strawberries because the fields are protected from extreme temperatures by the ocean.

Selection: Strawberries don't ripen after picking, so select plump, fragrant, bright-red berries with fresh green caps. Avoid any that are tinged with white or pale green and never buy strawberries that are sprayed with water, as they will become moldy faster. If packaged in a container, check the bottom for bruised, moldy or shriveled berries, avoiding any that leak juice.

Storage: Remove strawberries from their basket, discarding any that are moldy or bruised. Don't wash or hull until just before using; washing removes their natural protective coating and the caps help lock in flavor, texture, and nutrients. Arrange the berries in a single layer on a paper-towel-lined tray and refrigerate for 2 to 3 days. Freeze washed and hulled strawberries on a baking sheet for 1 hour or until hard, then transfer to airtight freezer containers or bags. Frozen berries may not be pristine enough for a tart, but work well in shortcakes, smoothies, and sauces.

Preparation: Handle strawberries gently because they are delicate and easily crushed. Just before using, place the unhulled berries in a colander and rinse quickly with cool water. Gently pat dry with paper towels. Never soak strawberries in water or they will become waterlogged. To hull, gently twist off the caps and use the point of a sharp paring knife to cut out the soft white cores.

To quickly and uniformly slice strawberries, use an egg slicer. One pint strawberries yields about 2 cups sliced.

A Little History: The romantic history of strawberries dates back to the Greeks and Romans. Ancient Greeks had a taboo against eating any red foods, including wild strawberries. This added mystery to the fruit, leading many to believe it possessed great powers. As time passed, the strawberry's reputation changed. Medieval stonemasons began carving strawberry designs on altars and the tops of pillars in churches and cathedrals, symbolizing perfection and righteousness. During the same time period, strawberries were served at important state occasions and festivals to ensure peace and prosperity.

For centuries, the only strawberries available were tiny, ultrasweet, and wild. When North America was first settled, wild strawberries were abundant and the colonists soon invented the now-classic American dessert, strawberry shortcake. Cultivated strawberries were created in the late 1700's when the wild beach strawberry from Chile was crossbred with American plants. This new variety produced a much larger red-hearted, gold-seeded berry from which all other varieties have been developed. By 1800, commercial strawberry growing began in America.

Simple Strawberries

Try these easy ideas when you want to quickly enhance fresh strawberries.

If you look closely at a strawberry, you will see that the outside flesh is covered with tiny seeds. Can you guess how many seeds are in just one strawberry?

There are 200 tiny seeds in every strawberry!

One of the best qualities of strawberries is that they're naturally delicious and taste great when simply prepared with only a few extra ingredients.

Balsamic Berries: Toss sliced strawberries with enough melted butter to lightly coat. Stir in a splash of balsamic vinegar and a pinch of coarsely ground black pepper for a sweet and tangy flavor. Enjoy them as is or spoon over ice cream or angel food cake.

Chocolate Dipped: Dip large berries (with or without stems) partway into melted semisweet chocolate. Place on a waxed-paper-lined cookie sheet and refrigerate to set the chocolate.

Parfait: Alternate layers of sliced strawberries with purchased vanilla pudding or rice pudding in parfait glasses.

Super Shake: Combine strawberries with vanilla ice cream or frozen yogurt in a blender, adding a bit of milk to thin if necessary.

Strawberry Sauce: Combine 1 pint hulled strawberries, 2 tablespoons sugar and 2 teaspoons fresh lemon juice in a medium saucepan. Cook over medium-high heat for 5 to 7 minutes, until the berries are soft, stirring occasionally. Serve warm or at room temperature over ice cream, pound cake, or cheesecake.

Potent Strawberries: Spoon sliced strawberries over vanilla ice cream. Drizzle a tablespoon of Scotch whisky or orange-flavored liqueur, such as Grand Marnier, over the top.

Strawberry Truffle Brownies

Laced with strawberry preserves and berry liqueur,
these rich chocolate brownies are truly decadent.

Ingredients

- 3/4 cup (1 1/2 sticks) **unsalted butter**
- 4 ounces **semisweet baking chocolate, chopped**
- 3 **eggs**
- 1 **cup sugar**
- 1/2 **cup strawberry preserves**
- 3 **tablespoons crème de cassis or other berry-flavored liqueur**
- 1 **cup flour**
- 1/4 **teaspoon salt**
- 1 **cup semisweet chocolate chips**
- **Confectioners' sugar, for dusting**

Preheat the oven to 350°F. Spray a 9x9x2-inch baking pan with cooking spray.

Melt the butter and baking chocolate in a large saucepan over low heat, stirring constantly. Remove from the heat; set aside to cool slightly.

Whisk the eggs in a medium bowl. Add the sugar, preserves, and liqueur; mix well. Pour into the chocolate mixture and blend well. Add the flour and salt; mix well. Stir in the chocolate chips. Pour into the prepared pan.

Bake for about 45 minutes, until a wooden pick inserted in the center comes out with moist crumbs. Cool completely in the pan on a wire rack. Run a small knife between the brownies and the sides of the pan. Cut into 16 squares. Just before serving, dust the tops with confectioners' sugar.

Makes 16 brownies

If all the strawberries produced in California in a year
were laid out end to end, they'd wrap around
the world 15 times. That's enough strawberries to
provide every U.S. household with 12 pints.

Strawberry-Lemon Bars

Strawberries nestled in lemon custard make a delicious treat!

Crust

- 1 **cup flour**
- 1/4 **cup confectioners' sugar**
- 1/2 **cup (1 stick) butter, softened**

Filling

- 1/2 **cup milk**
- 3 **egg yolks**
- **Grated zest of 1 lemon**
- 1/4 **cup fresh lemon juice**
- 1/2 **cup sugar**
- 3 **tablespoons flour**
- 1/4 **teaspoon salt**
- 3/4 **cup sliced strawberries**

Confectioners' sugar, for dusting

Preheat the oven to 350°F.

To make the crust: Combine the flour and confectioners' sugar in a medium bowl. Add the butter. Beat with an electric mixer at low speed until blended. Press the dough firmly onto the bottom and 1/2 inch up the sides of an 8x8x2-inch baking pan. Bake for 20 minutes; set aside.

To make the filling: Whisk the milk, egg yolks, lemon zest, and lemon juice in a medium bowl. Combine the sugar, flour, and salt in a small bowl. Whisk into the lemon mixture. Pour into a small saucepan. Cook over medium heat for about 5 minutes, until thickened, stirring constantly. Remove from the heat; stir in the strawberries. Place the pan in a large bowl of ice water; stir occasionally until the custard is cooled.

Spread the cooled custard over the crust. Bake for about 30 minutes, until the custard is set. Cool completely in the pan on a wire rack. Cut into 16 squares. Just before serving, dust the tops with confectioners' sugar.

Makes 16 bars

Note: Don't add more strawberries than the amount specified in the recipe or the custard will become runny after baking.

A handful of fresh strawberries provides an adult's daily requirement of vitamin C.

Strawberry Shortbread Tarts

*These easy yet heavenly tarts feature strawberries sitting atop
a bed of lemon curd on buttery shortbread cookies.*

Ingredients

- 2/3 **cup flour**
- 2 **tablespoons cornstarch**
- 1/4 **teaspoon baking powder**
- 1/4 **teaspoon salt**
- 10 **tablespoons butter, softened**
- 1/3 **cup confectioners' sugar**
- 1 **teaspoon vanilla extract**
- 1/2 **cup (4 ounces) cream cheese, softened**
- 3/4 **cup Lemon Curd (page 107), chilled**
- 1 **pint strawberries, sliced**

Lemon zest or fresh mint sprigs, as a garnish

Sift together the flour, cornstarch, baking powder, and salt; set aside. Beat the butter, confectioners' sugar, and vanilla in a large bowl with an electric mixer at high speed until fluffy. Add the flour mixture. Beat at low speed just until moist clumps form. Gather the dough into a ball; flatten into a disk. Wrap in plastic wrap; refrigerate for at least 1 hour.

Preheat the oven to 325°F. Grease a large cookie sheet.

Roll out the dough 1/4 inch thick on a lightly floured surface. Cut out with a 3-inch round cookie cutter. Reroll and cut the dough scraps to make a total of 8 cookies. Place 2 inches apart on prepared pan. Bake for about 15 minutes, until lightly browned at the edges. Cool completely on the cookie sheet set on a wire rack.

Beat the cream cheese in a medium bowl with an electric mixer at high speed until smooth. Stir the lemon curd until smooth; fold into the cream cheese. Place the cookies on serving plates. Spread the lemon mixture evenly over the cookies. Arrange the strawberries on top. Garnish with lemon zest or mint sprigs, if desired.

Makes 8 servings

Note: Lemon curd may also be purchased at gourmet and specialty food stores.

Strawberries Romanoff

Remember this popular and glamorous dessert from the 1950's?
Your family and friends are sure to love it.

Ingredients

- 1 (10-ounce) package frozen raspberries in syrup, thawed and undrained
- 2 pints strawberries, cut into quarters
- 1/4 cup Grand Marnier liqueur
- 3 tablespoons sugar
- 1 tablespoon fresh lemon juice
- 1 teaspoon vanilla extract
- 1 quart vanilla ice cream, softened

Whipped cream, as a garnish

Process the raspberries with their syrup and 1 cup strawberries in a blender or food processor until puréed. Pour through a fine strainer set over a medium bowl to remove the seeds, pressing the purée through the strainer. Discard the seeds in the strainer. Add the liqueur, sugar, lemon juice, and vanilla to the purée; stir to dissolve the sugar. Blend 1/2 cup of the raspberry mixture with the softened ice cream in a large bowl; freeze, covered, for 1 to 4 hours. Combine the remaining strawberries and raspberry mixture in a medium bowl; refrigerate until ready to serve.

To serve, divide the strawberry sauce among 6 dessert dishes. Top each with a scoop of strawberry ice cream. Garnish with whipped cream, if desired.

Makes 6 servings

Invented by the renowned French pastry chef
Marie-Antoine Carême (1784-1833) for
the Russian Tsar Nicholas I, a member of the
Romanoff dynasty, the original version of this dessert
was simply whipped cream and strawberries
soaked in orange-flavored liqueur.

Strawberry-Rhubarb Cobbler

*Sweet strawberries and tart rhubarb are a
favorite flavor combination for cobblers and pies.*

Topping

- 1 **cup flour**
- 1 **teaspoon baking powder**
- 1/2 **teaspoon cinnamon**
- 1/8 **teaspoon nutmeg**
- 4 **tablespoons (1/2 stick) butter, softened**
- 1/2 **cup sugar**
- 1 **egg**
- 1/2 **teaspoon vanilla extract**

Filling

- 1 **pound fresh rhubarb, cut into 1/2-inch slices**
- 1 **pint strawberries, cut into halves if very large**
- 1/3 **cup sugar**
- 1 **tablespoon cornstarch**

Vanilla ice cream (optional)

Preheat the oven to 375°F. Spray an 8x8x2-inch baking dish with cooking spray.

To make the topping: Whisk the flour, baking powder, cinnamon, and nutmeg in a small bowl; set aside. Beat the butter and sugar in a large bowl with an electric mixer at high speed until smooth. Beat in the egg and vanilla. Stir in the flour mixture by hand just until a moist dough forms; set aside.

To make the filling: Combine the rhubarb, strawberries, sugar, and cornstarch in a large bowl. Let stand for about 5 minutes, until the sugar dissolves, stirring occasionally. Pour into the prepared dish.

Drop the dough topping by tablespoonfuls onto the filling, spacing evenly. Bake for about 55 minutes, until the filling is bubbling and a wooden pick inserted into the topping comes out clean. Serve warm with ice cream, if desired.

Makes 6 servings

Strawberry-Chocolate Shortcakes

These chocolate shortcakes are the perfect backdrops for fresh strawberries.

Filling

2 pints strawberries, sliced

1/4 cup sugar

Shortcakes

1 1/2 cups flour

3 tablespoons sugar

2 teaspoons baking powder

1/2 teaspoon baking soda

1/4 teaspoon salt

6 tablespoons butter, cold and cut into small pieces

1/2 cup buttermilk

3 ounces bittersweet or semi-sweet baking chocolate, chopped

1 teaspoon sugar

Whipped cream, as a garnish

To prepare the filling: Combine the strawberries and sugar in a large bowl. Let stand at room temperature for about 1 hour, until juices form, stirring occasionally.

Preheat the oven to 425°F. Grease a baking sheet.

To make the shortcakes: Process the flour, 3 tablespoons sugar, baking powder, baking soda, and salt in a food processor until blended. Add the butter. Pulse until the mixture resembles coarse crumbs. Add the buttermilk and chocolate; pulse just until moist clumps form. Do not overprocess.

Turn the dough out onto a lightly floured surface. Gently pat the dough to a 1/2-inch thickness. Cut out with a 3-inch round biscuit cutter. Repeat with the scraps to make a total of 6 shortcakes. Place 1 inch apart on the prepared pan. Sprinkle with 1 teaspoon sugar. Bake for about 15 minutes, until a wooden pick inserted into the center comes out clean. Cool on a wire rack. *(Shortcakes can be made 1 day ahead.)*

Cut the shortcakes horizontally into halves. Place the bottom halves on 6 individual plates. Spoon the strawberries evenly over the shortcake bottoms; cover with the shortcake tops. Garnish each with a dollop of whipped cream.

Makes 6 servings

American Indians crushed strawberries in a mortar and mixed them with cornmeal to make strawberry bread. From this bread, the colonists developed strawberry shortcake.

Strawberry-Peach Tart

This easy tart requires no baking!

Crust

1 ¹/₂ cups vanilla wafer crumbs

¹/₂ cup finely ground almonds

6 tablespoons butter, melted

Filling

1 (8-ounce) package cream cheese, softened

¹/₂ cup sugar

1 (6-ounce) container peach yogurt

2 pints strawberries, sliced

Spray a 9-inch tart pan with a removable bottom with cooking spray.

To make the crust: Combine the vanilla wafer crumbs and almonds in a large bowl. Add the butter and toss with a fork until the crumbs are moistened. Press onto the bottom and side of the prepared pan; set aside.

To make the filling: Beat the cream cheese and sugar in a medium bowl with an electric mixer at high speed until smooth. Add the yogurt and beat at low speed until well blended. Pour into the crust, spreading evenly. Refrigerate, loosely covered, for 4 hours or until set. To serve, gently loosen and remove the edge of the pan. Arrange the strawberry slices in concentric circles over the filling, pointed ends facing outward.

Makes 8 servings

Tips: Substitute a 9-inch pie plate for the tart pan, if desired.

To speed-set the tart so it's ready to serve in less time, freeze it for about 1 hour. Refrigerate any leftover tart.

Breton Butter Cake
with Strawberry Compote

This easy cake topped with strawberries is perfect any time of day.

Compote

- 4 **cups strawberries, sliced**
- ¼ **cup sugar**
- 2 **tablespoons Grand Marnier liqueur**
- 1 **tablespoon grated orange zest**

Cake

- 1 **cup (2 sticks) butter, softened**
- 1 **cup sugar**
- 1 **tablespoon vanilla**
- 6 **egg yolks**
- 2¾ **cups flour**
- ¼ **teaspoon salt**
- 1 **egg, lightly beaten**

Preheat the oven to 350°F. Spray a 9-inch tart pan with a removable bottom with cooking spray.

To make the compote: Combine the strawberries, sugar, liqueur, and orange zest in a large bowl. Let stand at room temperature for at least 30 minutes or up to 1 hour, stirring occasionally.

To make the cake: Beat the butter in a large bowl with an electric mixer at high speed until well blended. Add the sugar and vanilla; beat until fluffy. Add the egg yolks 1 at a time, beating well after each addition. Beat in the flour and salt at low speed just until combined. Do not overmix. Pour into the prepared pan, spreading evenly. Refrigerate for 15 minutes.

Brush beaten egg over the chilled cake batter. Make a decorative pattern on top by dragging a fork lightly through the batter 5 times vertically and 5 times diagonally, creating a crisscross pattern. Bake for 50 minutes or until deeply browned and the edge pulls away from the side of the pan. Cool on a wire rack for 10 minutes. Gently loosen and remove the edge of the pan.

Cut the warm cake into 10 pieces. Serve warm or at room temperature with the strawberry compote.

Makes 10 servings

This famous cake originates in Brittany, France, where the Bretons are renowned for their formidable butter consumption. For centuries, butter has not only been used in cooking, but even for slicking back women's hair under their starched Breton headdresses.

Strawberry-Chocolate Tart

Fluffy chocolate mousse topped with strawberries is the perfect way to end a meal!

Crust

- 1 cup flour
- 3 tablespoons sugar
- 1/4 teaspoon salt
- 1/3 cup walnuts
- 1/2 cup (1 stick) butter, cold and cut into 1/2-inch pieces
- 2 egg yolks

Mousse

- 6 ounces bittersweet or semi-sweet baking chocolate, chopped
- 1 cup heavy cream, whipped to soft peaks
- 1/3 cup seedless strawberry jam
- 2 pints strawberries, sliced

To make the crust: Process the flour, sugar, and salt in a food processor until blended. Add the walnuts; process until chopped. Add the butter. Pulse until the mixture resembles coarse crumbs. Add the egg yolks; pulse just until moist clumps form. Gather the dough into a ball; flatten into a disk. Wrap in waxed paper; refrigerate for 30 minutes. *(Pastry dough can be refrigerated for up to 1 day. Let the dough stand at room temperature to soften slightly before rolling.)*

Spray a 9-inch tart pan with a removable bottom with cooking spray. Unwrap the dough, keeping the waxed paper over the top. Roll out to an 11-inch circle on a lightly floured surface. Remove the waxed paper. (If the waxed paper sticks to the dough, chill it in the refrigerator for a few minutes.)

Gently lift the dough just enough to move the prepared pan underneath it. Press the dough firmly onto the bottom and side of the pan. If there are places where the dough doesn't reach to the top of the pan, break off any excess dough and press it into place. Reinforce the seam where the bottom and side meet with excess dough. Pierce the bottom of the crust all over with a fork. Cover; freeze for 30 minutes.

Preheat the oven to 375°F. Place the crust on a baking sheet. Bake for 20 to 25 minutes, until lightly browned on the bottom. (The side browns first so wait for the bottom to be lightly browned before removing from the oven.) Cool completely on a wire rack. Gently loosen and remove the edge of the pan.

To make the mousse: Melt the chocolate in a medium heatproof bowl set over a saucepan of simmering water, stirring constantly until smooth. Remove the bowl from the pan; cool slightly. Gently fold the whipped cream into the chocolate just until combined. Do not overmix; a few white streaks of cream may be visible.

To assemble: Spread the strawberry jam on the bottom of the crust. Spread the mousse evenly over the jam. Refrigerate, covered, for at least 2 hours. *(Tart can be made 1 day ahead.)*

Just before serving, arrange the strawberry slices over the mousse in concentric circles with the pointed ends facing outward.

Makes 8 servings

Honey Cheesecake
with Strawberry Compote

Try this cheesecake for a change from the ordinary.

Crust

- 35 vanilla wafers
- 3/4 cup whole unblanched almonds
- 3/4 cup walnuts
- 1/2 cup sugar
- 1/4 cup (1/2 stick) butter, melted

Filling

- 2 (8-ounce) packages cream cheese, softened
- 1 (15-ounce) container ricotta cheese
- 2/3 cup honey
- 4 eggs
- 2 teaspoons vanilla extract

Compote

- 2 pints strawberries, cut into quarters
- 1/4 cup honey

Preheat the oven to 350°F. Spray a 10-inch springform pan with cooking spray. Wrap the outside of the pan with 2 layers of foil; place on a baking sheet.

To make the crust: Process the vanilla wafers in a food processor to form fine crumbs; transfer to a large bowl. Process the almonds and walnuts until finely ground; do not overprocess. Stir the ground nuts and sugar into the cookie crumbs. Add the butter and toss with a fork until the crumbs are moistened. Press onto the bottom and three-fourths of the way up the side of the prepared pan. Bake for 12 minutes; cool on a wire rack. Maintain the oven temperature at 350°F.

To make the filling: Beat the cream cheese and ricotta cheese in a large bowl with an electric mixer at high speed until smooth. Add the honey and beat well. Add the eggs 1 at a time, beating well after each addition. Beat in the vanilla. Pour into the prepared crust. Bake at 350°F for about 1 hour and 40 minutes, until the center barely moves when the pan is gently shaken. (If the top starts to brown during baking, cover it with foil.) Remove the foil from the pan. Cool completely in the pan on a wire rack. (The cake will rise up to the top of the pan during baking but then sinks down as it cools.) Run a knife between the cheesecake and side of the pan. Release the side of the pan. Refrigerate, covered, for at least 6 hours. *(Cheesecake can be made 1 day ahead.)*

To make the compote: Combine the strawberries and honey in a medium bowl. Refrigerate, covered, for up to 4 hours.

To serve, place the cheesecake on a platter. Using a slotted spoon, place one-third of the strawberry compote in the center of the cheesecake. Spoon the remaining compote over individual pieces.

Makes 12 servings

Strawberry Layer Cake

Your family or guests will think you bought this luscious cake from a bakery!

Cake

- 2 1/4 cups flour
- 2 1/4 teaspoons baking powder
- 1/2 teaspoon salt
- 1 2/3 cups granulated sugar
- 1/2 cup butter (1 stick), softened
- 1 tablespoon vanilla extract
- 3 eggs
- 1 1/4 cups milk

Filling

- 1/2 cup sugar
- 2 tablespoons cornstarch
- 3/4 cup fresh orange juice
- 1/2 teaspoon red food coloring
- 1 pint strawberries, cut into quarters

Frosting

- 1/2 cup (4 ounces) cream cheese, softened
- 1/4 cup (1/2 stick) butter, softened
- 2 teaspoons vanilla extract
- 3 1/2 cups confectioners' sugar, sifted

Preheat the oven to 350°F. Spray two 9-inch round cake pans with cooking spray. Line the bottoms with waxed paper; spray the paper with cooking spray. Dust the pans with flour.

To make the cake: Sift together the flour, baking powder, and salt; set aside. Beat the sugar, butter, and vanilla in a large bowl with an electric mixer at medium speed for about 5 minutes, until well blended. Add the eggs 1 at a time, beating well after each addition. Add the flour mixture alternately with the milk, beating at medium speed after each addition. Divide the batter evenly between the prepared pans.

Bake for 30 minutes or until a wooden pick inserted into the centers comes out clean. Cool in the pans for 10 minutes. Run a small knife between the cakes and sides of the pans. Remove from the pans to wire racks. Remove the waxed paper, then invert the layers top sides up; cool completely. *(Can be made 1 day ahead. Cover tightly and store at room temperature.)*

To make the filling: Combine the sugar and cornstarch in a medium saucepan. Gradually add the orange juice, stirring until smooth. Bring to a boil over medium heat, stirring constantly. Boil for 1 minute; remove from the heat. Stir in the red food coloring; cool completely. Stir in the strawberries; set aside.

To make the frosting: Beat the cream cheese, butter, and vanilla in a large bowl with an electric mixer at high speed until smooth. Gradually add the confectioners' sugar, beating at low speed until well blended. Beat at high speed until smooth.

To assemble: Place 1 cake layer, top side down, on a cake platter. Spread with the strawberry filling. Top with the second layer, top side up; gently press together. Spread a thin layer of frosting over the top and side of the cake. Spread the remaining frosting over the entire cake. Refrigerate, loosely covered, until ready to serve.

Makes 12 servings

Tip: To easily cut 12 equal slices, first cut the cake in half, then cut each half into 6 slices.

Strawberry Pie

Fresh, luscious strawberry pie is hard to beat!

Crust

1 1/2 cups sifted flour

1/2 teaspoon salt

1/4 cup shortening, cold

1/4 cup (1/2 stick) butter, cold and cut into small pieces

4 to 5 tablespoons ice water, divided

Filling

2 pints strawberries, hulled

1/2 cup sugar

1/2 cup water

1/4 cup cornstarch

2 tablespoons butter

Red food coloring (optional)

1/2 cup confectioners' sugar

Whipped cream, as a garnish

To make the crust: Combine the flour and salt in a large bowl. Cut in the shortening with a pastry blender or 2 knives until the mixture resembles coarse crumbs. Cut in the butter until the pieces become the size of small peas. Sprinkle 3 tablespoons water over the flour mixture; gently toss with a fork. Add enough of the remaining water, 1 tablespoon at a time, tossing until all the flour is moistened. Gather the dough into a ball; flatten into a disk. Wrap in plastic wrap; refrigerate for at least 1 hour. *(Pastry dough can be refrigerated for up to 3 days. Let the dough stand at room temperature to soften slightly before rolling.)*

Roll out the dough to a 12-inch round on a lightly floured surface (The dough should be about 1/8 inch thick.) Transfer to a 9-inch pie plate. If the dough does not uniformly cover the side of the pan, cut off some excess dough and press it over the bare spots. Trim any excess dough to within 1 inch from the edge of the pan. Fold the dough under to form a smooth, even edge. Flute the edge by crimping it between your fingers or with the round end of a knife. Cover the pastry crust loosely with plastic wrap. Refrigerate for at least 1 hour or up to 24 hours.

Preheat the oven to 450°F.

Pierce the bottom of the crust all over with a fork. Bake for 15 to 18 minutes, until lightly browned. Cool completely on a wire rack.

To make the filling: Process 1 pint of the strawberries in a blender or food processor until puréed. Pour into a medium saucepan. Stir in the sugar, water, and cornstarch. Cook over medium-high heat until the mixture is thick and mounds when dropped from a spoon. Add the butter, stirring constantly, until melted. Remove from the heat; cool slightly. Stir in a few drops of red food coloring to deepen the red color, if desired. Cool completely.

Pour the filling into the prepared crust. Roll the remaining 1 pint strawberries in the confectioners' sugar to coat. Arrange over the filling, pointed ends up. Refrigerate, covered, at least 2 hours. *(Pie can be made up to 1 day ahead.)* Serve garnished with whipped cream.

Makes 8 servings

150